WISDOM OF THOTH

———∞———

authorHOUSE

AuthorHouse™ UK
1663 Liberty Drive
Bloomington, IN 47403 USA
www.authorhouse.co.uk
Phone: 0800.197.4150

© 2019 Pantheon of Aeternam. All rights reserved.

No part of this book may be reproduced, stored in a retrieval system, or transmitted by any means without the written permission of the author.

Published by AuthorHouse 02/19/2019

ISBN: 978-1-7283-8474-0 (sc)
ISBN: 978-1-7283-8475-7 (e)

Print information available on the last page.

Any people depicted in stock imagery provided by Getty Images are models, and such images are being used for illustrative purposes only.
Certain stock imagery © Getty Images.

This book is printed on acid-free paper.

Because of the dynamic nature of the Internet, any web addresses or links contained in this book may have changed since publication and may no longer be valid. The views expressed in this work are solely those of the author and do not necessarily reflect the views of the publisher, and the publisher hereby disclaims any responsibility for them.

CONTENTS

Acknowledgement xv
Preface xvii
Book Introduction by Thoth xxv

Chapter I

Wisdom of Thoth: Why does Illusion Exist in the Cosmos? 2
Wisdom of Thoth: The Importance of Connecting
    to the Cosmic Light 3
Wisdom of Thoth: Earth's Receivers and Transmitters 5
Wisdom of Thoth: Knowing your Purpose 6
Wisdom of Thoth: Can you Walk the Path of Truth? 8
Wisdom of Thoth: Suffering 9
Wisdom of Astaroth: Healing Yourself and Others 10
Wisdom of Astaroth: You cannot Control the
    Cosmic Light, Let it Heal you 11
Wisdom of Thoth: Disconnect from Distortion and
    Connect to Growth 13
Wisdom of Thoth: Are you creating a space of peace? 14
Wisdom of Thoth: Creating Communities of Truth
    and Growth 15
Wisdom of Thoth: Near Death Experience 16
Wisdom of Thoth: Unity and Healing on Earth 18
Wisdom of Thoth: The Illusion of the Mind 19
Wisdom of Thoth: Become the Womb for the
    Cosmic Light to Create 21

Chapter II

Wisdom of Thoth: Return to the Astral Plane 24
Wisdom of Thoth: The Purpose of Humanity 25
Wisdom of Thoth: The Golden Age exists in the
    Inner Earth 27
Wisdom of Thoth: Earth's Position in the Galaxy 29
Wisdom of Thoth: The Path of Perfection 31
Wisdom of Thoth: Addictions 32
Wisdom of Thoth: The Light of the Cosmos is a
    Great Guide and Healer 34
Wisdom of Thoth: Creating strong bonds with your family ... 36
Wisdom of Astaroth: Your True-Self will Become
    Known to you 37
Wisdom of Thoth: Receivers and Transmitters of
    the Cosmic Creation Force 39
Wisdom of Thoth: Effective Communication 41
Wisdom of Thoth: On your Path of Growth 43
Wisdom of Thoth: An Act of Life and Creation 44
Wisdom of Thoth: Ignoring your Life and Purpose 46
Wisdom of Thoth: Accept Truth 48
Wisdom of Astaroth: A Pure State of Existence 49
Wisdom of Thoth: Your True-Self is Part of your
    Divine Plan 51
Wisdom of Thoth: Allow Earth's Healing to Reach You 52
Wisdom of Thoth: Our Source's Intention 54
Wisdom of Thoth: How Can You Win the Battle
    against Illusion and the Control Mechanisms 55

Chapter III

Wisdom of Thoth: Earth's Creation and Position in
    the Galaxy 58
Wisdom of Astaroth: Earth's Growth 59
Wisdom of Astaroth: Cosmic Laws 61
Wisdom of Thoth: The Difference Between the
    Cosmic Laws and the Natural Laws 62
Wisdom of Thoth: The astral plane 63

Wisdom of Thoth: The Use of Ancient Psychedelic Herbs 65
Wisdom of Astaroth: Animals and their process of
 growth and evolution 66
Wisdom of Thoth: The toxic invasion 67
Wisdom of Thoth: Experience Growth and Unity
 with the Cosmos 69
Wisdom of Thoth: The Existence of the Sun in
 Earth's Galaxy 70
Wisdom of Thoth: Connecting to the Cosmic Light 72
Wisdom of Thoth: Spirit Guides 74
Wisdom of Thoth: Energy Centres 75
Wisdom of Thoth: Prayer 76
Wisdom of Thoth: Fighting for Injustice 78
Wisdom of Thoth: Understanding the Connection
 between the Physical and the Astral Body 80
Wisdom of Thoth: Understanding the connection
 between the physical and the astral body. Part 2 81
Wisdom of Thoth: The Enormous Potential of Self 83
Wisdom of Thoth: Earth's Purification 85
Wisdom of Thoth: A Faithful Representation of a
 Human Being 88
Wisdom of Thoth: Healing in Ancient Times 90
Wisdom of Thoth: What is distortion? 92
Wisdom of Thoth: Becoming Superhuman 93
Wisdom of Thoth: Observing Limitation 94
Wisdom of Thoth: Observe Yourself, Connect to
 your True-Self 97
Wisdom of Thoth: Telepathy 98
Wisdom of Thoth: Planetary Phenomena 99
Wisdom of Thoth: Strengthening your Aura 100
Wisdom of Thoth: Sacred Places on Earth 102
Wisdom of Thoth: Transformations on Earth 103
Wisdom of Thoth: The Darkness of Confusion 104
Wisdom of Thoth: High Creation 106
Wisdom of Thoth: Symptoms of Imbalance 108
Wisdom of Thoth: Sacred Temples 110

Wisdom of Thoth: Mind Manipulation..................................111
Wisdom of Thoth: The Movement of the Body....................115
Wisdom of Thoth: Galaxies..116
Wisdom of Thoth: Strengthen your Bonds..........................117
Wisdom of Thoth: The Anatomy of the Physical Body..........118
Wisdom of Thoth: Space of Growth.....................................119
Wisdom of Thoth: Returning to the Astral Plane 120
Wisdom of Thoth: Connecting to your Essence 121
Wisdom of Thoth: The Hierarchy of the Gods..................... 122
Wisdom of Thoth: Fighting Illusion 124
Wisdom of Astaroth: Coming Back to Life.......................... 125
Wisdom of Thoth: How Can you heal Yourself? 126
Wisdom of Astaroth: Enter a Space of Peace and
   Truth will be Restored.. 127

Chapter IV

Wisdom of Astaroth: Transforming Planet Earth 130
Wisdom of Thoth: The Path of Truth or the Path of
   Chaos 131
Wisdom of Thoth: Destructive Food and Lifestyle
   Patterns 133
Wisdom of Thoth: A State of Well-Being 135
Wisdom of Thoth: Staying Grounded 137
Wisdom of Thoth: Astral Beings Reincarnating on Earth 138
Wisdom of Thoth: Purification is a Process of
   Knowing Yourself... 140
Wisdom of Thoth: How Can we Support Earth and
   her Creation and How can we Escape Illusion
   and Return to Nature?.. 142
Wisdom of Thoth: Reincarnation of Human
   Beings, Animals and Other Species 143
Wisdom of Thoth: The Aura 145
Wisdom of Thoth: Standing at the Crossroads
   During a Transformation 147
Wisdom of Thoth: Your Intention and your Guide
   in this Reincarnation.. 148

Wisdom of Astaroth: Separation and Polarity 150
Wisdom of Thoth: Limitation 151
Wisdom of Astaroth: If you Wish to Experience a
    Cosmic State 153
Wisdom of Thoth: Your own Existence 154
Wisdom of Thoth: Staying on the Path of Truth is
    the Highest Reward 156
Wisdom of Thoth: A Diversion from your Path of Truth 158
Wisdom of Thoth: Fighting and Surrendering to the
    Manipulation of the Mind 160
Wisdom of Thoth: Achieving Unity 162
Wisdom of Thoth: Earth's Life Cycle 163
Wisdom of Thoth: Purifying Layers of Distortion 165
Wisdom of Thoth: The Cosmic Light unites all
    Creation with the Source 166
Wisdom of Thoth: Celebrate Unity 167
Wisdom of Thoth: Fear of Losing the Persona 169

Chapter V

Wisdom of Thoth: Connecting to your Astral Body
    and Experience Growth on Earth 172
Wisdom of Thoth: Energy Systems 174
Wisdom of Astaroth: The Dogma of Science 176
Wisdom of Thoth: The First Step towards Purification 177
Wisdom of Thoth: Experiencing Life beyond the
    Physical Body 179
Wisdom of Thoth: Your Body is a Unique Tool 180
Wisdom of Thoth: Are you Walking the Path of
    Truth or the Path of Illusion? 182
Wisdom of Thoth: How was Illusion Created on Earth 184
Wisdom of Thoth: Planetary Races 186
Wisdom of Thoth: Understanding Illusion 187
Wisdom of Thoth: Understanding Earth 189
Wisdom of Thoth: Higher Beings and the
    Guardians of Earth 191

Wisdom of Thoth: The Existence of Low Spirits
and Beings without Physicality?......................................193
Wisdom of Thoth: The Architects of Illusion 194
Wisdom of Thoth: The Coming of the Golden Era..............196
Wisdom of Thoth: How to Create your True Life 197
Wisdom of Thoth: The Cosmic Light is the
Extension of our Source..199
Wisdom of Thoth: Becoming the Seeds of Earth's
Transformation.. 201
Wisdom of Thoth: Waiting for a Change, a Shift
and a New Consciousness... 202
Wisdom of Thoth: To Be in Constant Growth and
Evolution.. 204
Wisdom of Thoth: Enlightenment is Closer than
you Think 205
Wisdom of Thoth: About Indigo Children........................... 207
Wisdom of Thoth: Why is it important to connect
to Earth.. 209
Wisdom of Thoth: A Space of Restriction 210
Wisdom of Thoth: Discovering Ancient Civilization.............211

Chapter VI

Wisdom of Astaroth: The History of Alchemy 215
Wisdom of Thoth: Help Each Other Grow 217
Wisdom of Thoth: The Gift of Freedom 219
Wisdom of Thoth: Within the Mind...................................... 220
Wisdom of Thoth: A Carrier of Cosmic Light...................... 222
Wisdom of Astaroth: The Mystery of Birth 224
Wisdom of Thoth: The Process of Earth's Creation.............. 226
Wisdom of Thoth: Tribes of Earth 227
Wisdom of Thoth: Ancient Communities 228
Wisdom of Thoth: Connecting to Earth for Nourishment ... 229
Wisdom of Thoth: The Subconscious Mind.......................... 230
Wisdom of Thoth: How can you Purify from Low
Energies? 231
Wisdom of Thoth: The Light of the Cosmos........................ 232

Wisdom of Thoth: Goddess Earth 234
Wisdom of Thoth: The Path of Self Discovery 235
Wisdom of Thoth: The Cycles of Growth in Lower Planes... 237
Wisdom of Thoth: Knowing your True-Self is
   Knowing Cosmic Wisdom 239
Wisdom of Thoth: Experience the Transformation............... 240
Wisdom of Astaroth: Life in the Cosmos............................. 242
Wisdom of Thoth: To Win or Lose and to Be in
   Light or Darkness... 244
Wisdom of Thoth: The Misunderstanding of the
   Great Potential of Being Young and Old 245
Wisdom of Thoth: Cosmic Movement 248
Wisdom of Thoth: Your Body Exists in Constant Motion.... 249
Wisdom of Thoth: Universal Path of Gnosis,
   Becoming Self-Conscious 251

Chapter VII

Wisdom of Thoth: Cosmic Healing....................................... 254
Wisdom of Thoth: The Path of Unity 255
Wisdom of Thoth: Low Spirits 257
Wisdom of Thoth: Trying to Understand the
   Planets, Galaxies and Universes...................................... 258
Wisdom of Thoth: How was Illusion Created on Earth.........259
Wisdom of Thoth: A Space of Truth 261
Wisdom of Thoth: Earth's Divine Plan 262
Wisdom of Thoth: Connect and Observe your Body............ 263
Wisdom of Thoth: Focus on Growth.................................... 264
Wisdom of Astaroth: Earth's Healing................................... 265
Wisdom of Thoth: Psychosis, Hypnotic State, Illusion 267
Wisdom of Thoth: What is your Intention?......................... 268
Wisdom of Thoth: A Unity of Multiple Reflections.............. 270
Wisdom of Thoth: The Unity of your Physical body
   and your Energy.. 271
Wisdom of Thoth: The Process of Becoming a God............. 272
Wisdom of Thoth: The Seeds of Purification 273
Wisdom of Thoth: Practising Purification............................274

Wisdom of Thoth: How can You Experience Life on
  Earth 275
Wisdom of Thoth: Imagination 276
Wisdom of Thoth: Earth's Light 277
Wisdom of Thoth: A Definition of Illusion and
  Distortion on Earth 279
Wisdom of Thoth: Cosmic Happiness 280
Wisdom of Thoth: About Climate Change 281
Wisdom of Thoth: Arch Angels 282
Wisdom of Thoth: Winter Solstice 282
Wisdom of Thoth: What is God? 284
Wisdom of Thoth: Your Purpose is to Exist in
  Unity with the Cosmos 284
Wisdom of Thoth: Start Creating your own Life
  according to the Divine Plan 286
Wisdom of Thoth: Stay in a Pure State 287
Wisdom of Thoth: Suffering from Limitation 288
Wisdom of Thoth: Confronting or Running Away
  from your Fears? 290
Wisdom of Astaroth: What is your Reality? 291
Wisdom of Thoth: The Creation of Earth 293
Wisdom of Thoth: Stay Alive, Connect to Truth 294

Chapter VIII
  Wisdom of Thoth: Purification 296
  Wisdom of Thoth: About Angels and Demons 297
  Wisdom of Thoth: The Process of Transformation 299
  Wisdom of Thoth: Allow the Cosmic Light to
    Transform You 300
  Wisdom of Thoth: Your own Energetic Flow is
    Creating the Path that will Lead you to your Purpose 302
  Wisdom of Thoth: Transformation and Growth 303
  Wisdom of Thoth: A Cosmic Being 304
  Wisdom of Thoth: Perfect Partners or win Flames 305
  Wisdom of Thoth: Earth's Gifts to Humanity 307
  Wisdom of Thoth: The Sun 308

- Wisdom of Thoth: The Path to Growth is an Effortless Path 309
- Wisdom of Astaroth: The Ego 311
- Wisdom of Thoth: The Downfall of Earth 312
- Wisdom of Thoth: The Land of Opportunity is the Kingdom of Illusion 315
- Wisdom of Thoth: Life is Effortless 316
- Wisdom of Thoth: The Sleep of Ignorance 318
- Wisdom of Astaroth: A House of Millions Rooms of Great Beauty and Splendour 320
- Wisdom of Thoth: The Eyes of Illusion 321
- Wisdom of Thoth: Earth's Essence 322
- Wisdom of Astaroth: High Beings 324
- Wisdom of Thoth: Pure Life is Effortless 325
- Wisdom of Thoth: Knowing the Divine Plan is only the Beginning of your Path 326
- Wisdom of Thoth: The Gift of Unity 328
- Wisdom of Thoth: The Light of the Cosmos 330
- Wisdom of Thoth: The Light of the Gods 332
- Wisdom of Thoth: The Cause of Imbalance in Humanity ... 334
- Wisdom of Thoth: Our Growth is our Unity with our Source 335
- Wisdom of Thoth: Colours 336
- Wisdom of Thoth: Communication 337
- Wisdom of Thoth: Beings with a Mental Disability 338
- Wisdom of Thoth: Life Patterns, Imbalances and Growth ... 340

Dialogue with Thoth 343
Vocabulary 375

ACKNOWLEDGEMENT

We would like to express the deepest gratitude to all our order members and supporters of our work who have helped us spreading the teachings of the gods. We express our warm thanks to Vera Dukic, Mary Milne, Hank Geda, Kjlland Waine and Farah Farola who helped with proofreading. Furthermore we would like to thank the readers of this book and all of you who continue to support our work. We are confident that the book of Thoth will open the way to all of you who seek truth to connect to your purpose and your light.

PREFACE

This book includes a series of teachings communicated to the messengers of Pantheon of Aeternam, Barbara and Robbert-jan. They have been instructed by the gods to receive their teachings and spread them to everybody who can connect to truth and cosmic wisdom. There is no secret knowledge to be kept for the selected few. All wisdom is revealed to all who are interested in becoming truth. We do not teach dogma, philosophy or other man- made theory. We teach ageless wisdom and cosmic truth given to us by the High Gods of the Pleroma. We want to inform people about the existence of gods, the different realms, the cosmic laws and all activity that is going on for the benefit of Earth and her inhabitants. We want to inform people about the creation of planet Earth and her full story of her creation and growth which was hidden for thousands of years. The teachings of gods will help humanity to connect to the Earth's energies, be part of the planet and live in harmony with all species. We all have to support Earth and restore her to the most graceful expression of herself, her golden age.

The process of communication between the gods and the messengers cannot be explained or described; it is a natural process. The messengers do not channel information they never did. They received this gift in order to assist the gods communicate and awake humanity during this crucial time on Earth's history. The messengers don't try to explain the communication process; they are very grateful that they were chosen and have made this work the focus of their lives.

The teachings presented in this book, have not been altered or edited. They are faithful accounts of the wisdom of the gods.

For more information about the Pantheon of Aeternam you can visit our website.

http://pantheonofaeternam.com
pantheonofaeternam@gmail.com

BOOK INTRODUCTION BY THOTH

I am Thoth, I am the creator of Earth and I am here to explain the golden era. It was the highest moment of Earth's existence. Earth was a high creator, the Pleroma of the gods. She was the sacred space, our temple, our creation.

I am spreading my light to connect to Earth; the time has come to support the planet that has been suffering from distortion and low vibration. We are here to make a connection with Earth and humanity. We have an offer for you: the only freedom that you can experience is truth. If you know your true-self you are free. If you are experiencing life as your true-self you are creating freedom. For some of you this first encounter with your true-self is going to be a shocking experience. Others will feel threatened and run away. They will be some who will open up to connect and receive healing and clarity. Whatever your reaction, we will connect you to your true-self. We are going to build bridges between the Pleroma and Earth. We are going to take our messengers around the world and have them talk about this connection. Everything we do is a connection and we can lead everybody to grow in a higher place. This is what we are offering you and I hope that you are there to receive it.

You all have to accept the path that leads to your purpose. This is a hard task for humans because they have no clarity. Now we are here with you to clear the fog of uncertainty and self-doubt. We are bringing light; we put all the pieces together and make you whole. Our next step is to make Earth whole. Earth requires purification. Earth requires a new life, a new cycle of growth; and she will receive it. It is part of her divine plan to connect and grow.

I know that many of you find it hard to experience truth and growth. You have only experienced fragmentation and many layers of distortion. This affects your thinking and the way you act in the society where you live. I want to bring truth and spread it to the planet. I hope you are open to receive it. I know that people on Earth try to cure themselves. You have many ways to cure yourself but you do not succeed.

There is no balance on Earth. I want to bring balance on Earth and heal your schisms. For this to happen you have to accept yourself. You have to see yourself. Observe yourself become a spectator of your own actions. You will soon realise that your thoughts and your actions are not really yours. You are playing a copy game. You mechanically copy the patterns that you see around you. You do that because you desperately need balance and because there is no truth in your existence. You think that the patterns you see are the balance you are looking for. This is your conditioning; this is the disease you are suffering from. You can observe your disease; the way it transforms in you and grow; the way it affects your ability to know yourself, connect to the cosmos and Earth and receive the light. You can win with truth, you can win with acceptance. You can win with freedom. We can build these bridges together. When we build the bridges and you are able to receive the light, the fear will disappear; negativity will evaporate. Strength, passion and love for life will take over. Balance that you are so desperately looking for, it is returning to you; you will become whole again.

All of you who are listening to me, you better do it with your ears open. I have been trying to communicate with the people of Earth but they could not understand how important it is to connect to Earth. They do not want to know their true purpose. They ignore all communications and they carry on living the illusion. For some, illusion is comfortable and convenient. Some of you have to wake up and fight for the others who are still sleeping. Some of you have to make plans to save the Earth. Some of you are going to ignore society restrictions and connect to your true-self. Some of you are going to have balanced and fulfilled lives on Earth, building strong bridges between the planet and the Pleroma. I want people on Earth to find ways to express their greatness. Your connection to Earth and the cosmos will show you the way. You are strong when you become a creator. Using your strength to support others and share with them the most precious gift, truth. Many of you are getting to receive this because I am here now.

I exist in a space of creation where there is constant transformation. I want you to go through a process of transformation and this can happen if we connect and exchange light. We are here to support all beings in all planes. We want to surround you with our light; it will come to you and will clearly communicate about your growth and purpose. I have to come with the gifts of truth, freedom and expression; expression of clarity. You are free when you know where your path is leading too. Most people are blind, they follow others to nowhere. Eventually you are going to discover that this is not your divine plan. You are your true-self. You are here to grow and learn, follow your path and fulfil your purpose. You can be free from fear and limitation; they are artificial products of illusion. You are free to know truth. If you can see your path, everything that you seek will coming to you. Freedom will be your guide and truth should be your purpose. You will find your voice and will start speaking to others about truth. This will be your gift to humanity. The golden era will come back again.

We all exist in the cosmos that has many ropes and all these beings in all different planes are tied up and connected to it. There is a high light that comes from the source and flows through us, reaching all beings and all points of life in the cosmos. We are sending light to all beings in all planes. It is important that all beings are in a process of growth.

Do not allow your physicality to restrict your understanding of cosmos. There are many different forms of life and they all exist in unity. They all receive and transmit light to each other. If you are not aware of these other planes, the other beings and their growth, you are not able to understand the cosmic laws. I want you to understand that your life is a point of balance. Your growth is a point of balance in this limitless creation of our source. All of you who are listening to my word should stand up and cross the bridges that connect Earth and the cosmos. They were built for you to help you connect to the light.

I am here to guide you and help you escape illusion. You will have to face yourself: what are you doing in this life time; have you experienced growth; do you know your tools to help you grow? Perhaps you have given all your powers to others: have you allowed other forces to manipulate your mind?

Are you on your path? Do you have enough power to move on and fulfil your purpose?

Some of you are seeking enlightenment but you are not moving forward on your path. You are not moving; stagnation is your life experience. What do you have to do to get out of this state? You need to show bravery and then clarity will return to you. First step is to accept that you are sleeping in a non-growth state. But this is not going to bring you clarity. Yes you have to act, you have to take decisions, and you have to change your life. Everybody can grow because this is a natural law for all beings. Connecting to your true-self, you are connecting to your astral body experiencing the growth that takes place in the astral body. You can exchange energy, receive high light and connect to the creation of our source. You can do all that when you turn your back to illusion. Human beings are always guided, they are always supported but you prefer to close your eyes and detach yourself from the astral plane. You have the power to create your own life and you can also help others receive the light.

I want to share our light with humanity. The light is coming to you through our messengers. If you have doubts about this connection, you should know that I have created Earth. I am the father of this planet and you are here to connect to the planet. Now you know my duty and yours. We are connecting to Earth through you. We are spreading the light and you are becoming the transmitters and receivers. When you are able to disconnect from all artificiality and balance your being then you will be able to become a clear channel of our light. You are listening to our teachings, you are connecting to our energy but you have to contribute too. You have to make the teachings your own tool. When you have clarity, you will be positive, you will accept your duty and you will be able to succeed.

We are not here to show you every step; we are not here to make your life easier or different; you are the creators of your lives. It is as important that you look after your body. When you pollute yourself is your responsibility to find your way back to growth. You may say that you follow others' advice or you follow the authority and the specialists. Nobody knows more than yourself your own body. Take responsibility and power; know yourself, bring clarity and truth into your being. This is the only way to find your path, fulfil your purpose and have a successful life on Earth.

There is not better success than fulfilling your purpose and duty but most of you do not know what your purpose is. You are convinced that your purpose is an extension of the social ideals, expectations and restrictions. Why you cannot create your life in truth and freedom? When you are able to exist in a space of truth, you are able to see imbalances, distortion and negativity trying to affect your mind and you will be able to connect to the light and heal yourself. Stand on your two feet and walk the path of truth. You exist to grow, you exist to follow your path of truth and if you do not follow it you do not exist.

Becoming one with the cosmic light, it is a great proposition. Becoming one with the cosmic light; what does it mean? How can you connect to the cosmic light and how can affect your life and grow. The only way to grow and fulfil your purpose is by connecting to the cosmic light. We are all united. We are all connected and the cosmic light is the greatest tool for unity and growth. If you are suffering from fragmentation, the ego disease, or the separation disease. You were not created to be fearful, negative and limited. You have created to experience growth on Earth. In this third dimensional reality with the body, mind and senses; you are on Earth right now to bring light to this planet. Connecting to the light you will heal fragmentation and experience unity; you will discover your true-self. The more you observe yourself, the more you are able to connect to what you truly are

The gods are here to give you light. They can receive your light; they connect to your intention. If your intention is wisdom and enlightenment, the gods will guide you to achieve that. Everything is connected; all blockages, all limitations, all fragmentation affects your whole being. You can become a pure channel when you find ways to heal yourself. Some of you may ask: what is healing? How can I heal myself from fragmentation and distortion if the planet is already suffering from this? You came down to Earth to heal her and by being a healer for Earth you can heal yourselves too. This is an important duty so you should make it your intention and plan. I see that most humans' plan is to survive and go through the social hoops in order to get to the top of the social pyramid. This top is illusionary. You cannot receive clarity and growth if you continue keeping your eyes closed and accept illusion as truth. Now you have the opportunity to open your eyes. You have the chance to create your own lives and you can exist, be happy, have a balanced life and fulfil your purpose. Being in this illusionary state, you harm yourself. You are here for a great duty to be a healer of Earth to connect to your true-self and grow. Connecting to the light, you have to place yourself in a space of truth and growth.

Purifying yourself is an easy process. You just have to observe yourself, your thoughts, actions and intention. You can observe yourself regularly: observe old patterns that are repeated frequently. You should this when you meditate. Do not allow artificiality and negativity to distract you. When you observe yourself with your essence, you heal yourself. During a purification process, old trauma may come to the surface and this can make you feel weak, confused or vulnerable. Your ego may try to defend the distortion and disconnect from truth. Purification can be a slow process. Especially when you are suffering from trauma and schisms.

Purification is an exercise of knowing, healing and empowerment and you should follow it. Look at your imbalances with acceptance. This way you disconnect from them. Look at the root of your imbalance and the cause of it. Learn to be an observer of your own actions and be aware of their impact. I will now guide you to a place of peace. Connect to your being, quieten your mind, disconnect from the persona. Connect to your essence and allow it to create in you. Truth is your only tool to high wisdom and this is what you seek. You are in a state of peace and you can listen to my word. Your essence is energy and will follow me to a space of truth. You can now visualise yourself, disconnecting from your body and being lifted up by a high energy. I am here to welcome you to a space of re-birth. Open to the light of the cosmos that can heal you and nourish you. In this space of truth, you are called to purify yourself and allow healing to reach your imbalances. Your connection to the light will purify and bring balance in you. Allow it to happen. Time on Earth is given to you to perform this act of truth. By connecting with the cosmic light, knowing yourself and have pure intention you are transforming and moving closer to your higher self.

You are created to grow. The light of the cosmos, the energies of Earth is here to nourish you and help you grow. Some people are attracted to the idea but they continue living their life according to illusion. Other people are digging in the dark, trying to discover a treasure. Others are thinking with their mind, trying to solve the problem. So what is your true-self and what is the path to take you there to the space of purity that is in you? I can only say to you that you do not have to look, you do not have to think and you do not have to plan because your true-self is you. True-self is your light, the way you grow, receive and transmit the light, the way you connect to other beings and the way you affect their lives.

Your mind cannot help you because it is designed to support the ego and your survival, your everyday survival. When you perform unconditional acts; when you do what you truly love and you see the fruit of it; when you create life structures that work in your life, you achieve all these by connecting to your true-self. The more you connect to your true-self the more you grow. Your true-self reminds you that you are always connected to the source. We are all supporting, sharing our light, teaching, connecting and healing. You can help the planet grow, you can transmit light to her because you are using her resources, and her energy and you are part of her growth. Connecting to your true-self is what keeps you alive.

We all want to connect to the light of the cosmos and the light of our source. This is our purpose, to connect to this high light and transform. This is a very important cosmic law and affects every single being in all planes. You should be able to understand and recognise that your purpose is to connect to the cosmic light. You should live your life to fulfil this purpose. You should connect to others to help them fulfil their purpose. A cosmic truth; it is perfect without limitation, fragmentation and distortion. Observe your physicality, observe yourselves in the space where you are right now. Connect to your body. Explore your physicality, every single sound, every single movement in your body.

Now connect to your aura; your aura is an extension of your physical body. It is the energy that helps you connect to your astral body. Connect to the energies of your aura; they are ropes, connecting you with the cosmos. Can you see these ropes? Can you understand the connection between the physical body and the cosmos? When you connect to the cosmos and the source; when you know that eternity and constant growth is reality then you have nothing to be afraid of. You have nothing to fight for because growth is a gift given to you. I want to see you connecting to the cosmos and the light of our source to support your growth.

I am here to connect to humanity and pass my light to all who open themselves to receive it. My light is healing and transformative that can help you purify yourself and go through a process of rebirth into a new being. Your journey of growth cannot be altered by me. You are the creator of your life. You are the ones who walk the path and accept existence, truth, creation being in unity. All human beings are suffering from imbalances and there is one imbalance that is shared by all. This is fragmentation. Your existence is divided into many different compartments of understanding, knowing and experiencing.

Many of you focus on different centres such as your mind, heart, your physical bodies, your energies, your ambition, creation and relationships; all these are the different expressions of you. Many of you exist separately in a distorted area of non-growth. Many of you cannot connect to your being because you see yourself as separation, duality and fragmentation. I want to introduce you to your physical body. This is the gift Earth gave you when you reincarnated in order to experience growth on Earth. With your body, you can connect to Earth's energies and you can also receive the cosmic light and become a perfect receiver and transmitter of cosmic light. Your body can guide you to truth when you do not ignore the different signals.

Negativity and distortion can also be absorbed by your body. In this case you will experience tiredness, inability to function, confusion, and disconnection from everything around you and general weakness. These symptoms can go away; there is an easy way to achieve that. When you stop experiencing your life with your mind, be in a state of peace and connect to your physical body, connect to your imbalances, observe them in an honest and truthful way. When you experience your special abilities and unique tools, you can use them to create your life. Connecting to your truth, you support your body; it becomes strong and healthy. When you are in this state of clarity, your body will transform, opening up to the cosmic light and becoming a cosmic tool, to help you and the cosmos go through a new cycle of evolution. When you are able to heal yourself by opening up to the cosmic light, you are healing others and you are transmitting high energies.

I am Thoth and I want to connect to humanity and Earth.

I am here to help you create a space of peace, so you can focus on finding your true-self and learn to connect to others with purity and unconditional love.

I am here to show you that your body is not a waste land but it is Earth's gift to help you fulfil your purpose in this lifetime. It is your responsibility to maintain and nourish your physical body and the best source for this is Earth herself. You can nourish your body when you connect to Earth. If you are wondering about your purpose, you should connect to Earth; her energies will reveal to you that your special abilities and unique gifts that exist in your physical body can help you fulfil your purpose. The truth that you carry can connect you to Earth and your purpose in this reincarnation but it can also connect you to the high light of the cosmos and the cosmic growth. The truth in you is not a belief or an idea; it is a living being that can connect you with Earth and her high light that is her golden era as well as the infinite cosmic growth.

When human beings understand and experience these connections, every moment of their lives without interruptions then all the obstacles, limitation, negativity and fear will stop to exist. These limitations affect the mind and the physical body when a being is confused, disconnected from truth and unaware of their purpose in this life time. When human beings are in this state they are powerless against distortion and the patterns that a restricting the ability to connect to truth and purpose. Life on Earth becomes a painful experience and the mind focuses on the pain. Human beings have the ability to share, to connect, to grow with others and if your mind is affected by distortion you can only spread distortion. Human beings should experience freedom. You are free to love yourself and connect to the sources of nourishment, healing and growth. Some of these sources are in you: your light, truth, pure intention can help you experience freedom. I want you to be creators of your own life. Why are you ignoring your unique abilities? Why are you turning your back to the path that is leading you to your purpose? There is a divine plan created just before you reincarnated on Earth and includes your unique abilities, your purpose and the way you are going to co-create your life according to the divine plan. You were reincarnated on Earth in order to connect to humanity and Earth and support their connection with the cosmos. This is the only truth that you should follow. It is the only truth that can help you fulfil your purpose on Earth.

CHAPTER I

Illusion can take many forms and can capture the people that are looking for truth. To avoid this and truly disconnect from all artificiality you have to look in you, your connection with your astral body and the Earth energies.

Connecting to truth will help you understand of your true purpose and how to connect to cosmic growth and high light. When you achieve clarity, you will connect to your true-self and you will follow a process of transformation, growth and well-being.

Introduction

Everything on Earth is distorted. There is no truth in people's actions, beliefs and motivation. Truth is an unpleasant companion for most Earthlings because it reminds them of their inability to walk their path and fulfil their purpose. People are kept prisoners of a man-made illusion. Most of them are isolated from Earth and the natural laws and have a false impression that they are superior. In reality they are prisoners and are kept away from the beauty, harmony and wisdom of the divine creation that exists on Earth.

Truth can transform you, empower you, guide you and give you enormous strength. When you accept truth, you are able to connect to your higher-self and then everything becomes clear. When you accept truth as your only companion, all doors open and you are suddenly in front of the grace of the gods.

Wisdom of Thoth: Why does Illusion Exist in the Cosmos?

Illusion is a fruit and the tree that is hanging from is distortion. The seed of this tree is the low vibrational state of Earth and her existence in a space that is not the golden era. The form of illusion that you are experiencing right now is part of Earth's transformation from the higher to the lower spheres.

The colonization of Earth and the great upheavals that took place, limited Earth's ability to follow the path of truth and fulfil her own purpose as a high creator God. The state of Earth is reflected to her creation and all beings that reincarnate on the planet are facing the same challenge. Earth as a creative force and all her creation have free will and this means that even though they exist in a lower vibration, they can always grow and connect to their purpose.

Free will is an opportunity for growth for all creation that exists in the lower spheres. Some of you may think that free will can trick you to pick illusion instead of truth. In reality you already exist in illusion and you are given the opportunity to transform, escape the maze of distortion and finally find your path of truth.

Your society and organizations of control do not help you to find your path so most of you do not have free will. If there was truth in your society, illusion will not have a strong hold on you. You are responsible for your own growth and if you have a pure intention to connect to truth then you will find the way to fulfil your divine plan of your reincarnation.

Questions

1. What is distortion?
2. Is Earth suffering from distortion? What has caused this?
3. What is free will?
4. How can you create a society of truth?

Introduction

Your purpose is a life of truth, higher consciousness and supporting others to rediscover their true-self. If you wish to be a creator that is the path you have to take.

All beings that reincarnate on Earth are responsible for connecting to the cosmic light; help their vibration to rise and the trauma to be healed.

Human beings have many opportunities in their lifetime to grow and connect to the cosmic light. When you understand the importance of becoming a receiver of light and experience it, you will allow it to transform you.

When you receive the cosmic light, you reach to your true-self. This discovery will lead you to a transformation and then your path is open and your purpose will be clear to you. The vision of the high creator gods is that the people wake up to their true potential and assist Earth with her own awakening.

Wisdom of Thoth: The Importance of Connecting to the Cosmic Light

The cosmic light brings life to the whole cosmic creation. When you connect to the cosmic light, you connect to everything that exists. You are in a communication with our Source and this communication can transform you, heal you and support your growth. The cosmic light enters your being and reaches all parts of your physical body as well as your aura and energies.

It brings balance and unity to your whole being and it also brings clarity, knowing and connection to your true-self, the Earth and the cosmos. Human beings are created to be Earth's receivers and transmitters of light. This way the cosmic light will enter Earth and offer her healing. When human beings are suffering from imbalances, they are still able to connect to the cosmic light but imbalances act as a blockage to balance and growth.

Human beings have to purify themselves. This means that they have to face the imbalance and observe the way it was created and all its different forms. Having a pure intention to connect to your true-self, the cosmic light will guide you and help you to purify your whole being. This experience will bring transformation to your being because you are opening up to the light and you are co-creating a new balanced existence of you. If you do not have a pure intention and you are not focusing on truth then imbalance will remain and in most cases they will expand and grow.

Questions

1. Why is important to connect to the cosmic light?
2. How can you transform when you connect to the cosmic light?
3. How can you heal Earth, connecting to the cosmic light?
4. What stops you from receiving the light of the cosmos?

Introduction

The cosmic light is the intention of our source to create life. When we receive the light, we are supported in our purification process; we experience growth and develop our ability to create. When you connect to the high light, creation will happen naturally and you will see yourself and others being transformed because of it. When people create, it affects their light and understanding of the cosmos. It also affects all people who are connected to them. One of the qualities of the cosmic light is to be able to spread, purify and transform all beings. All creation should be in a process of constant purification and transformation but this is not always possible because the light is not allowed to enter fragmented and distorted areas of growth. This is why Earth and all her creation are suffering right now. We were given the task to bring the light to all of you who want to be creators on Earth.

Wisdom of Thoth: Earth's Receivers and Transmitters

The cosmic light brings life to the whole cosmic creation. When you connect to it, you connect to everything that exists. You are in a communication with our Source and this communication can transform you, heal you and support your rebirth. The cosmic light enters your being and reaches all parts of your physical body as well as your aura and energies. It brings balance and unity to your whole being; it brings clarity, to help you connect to your true-self, the Earth and the cosmos. Human beings are created to be Earth's receivers and transmitters of light. This way the cosmic light will enter Earth and offer her healing.

When human beings are suffering from imbalances, they are still able to connect to the cosmic light but imbalances act as a blockage to balance and growth. Human beings have to purify themselves. This means that they have to face the imbalance and observe the way it was created and all its different forms.

Having a pure intention to connect to your true-self, the cosmic light will guide you and help you to purify yourself. This experience will bring transformation to your being because you are opening up to the light and you are co-creating a new balanced existence of you. If you do not have a pure intention and you are not focusing on connecting to truth then the imbalances will remain and in most cases they will expand and grow.

Questions

1. Are you a receiver and transmitter of light?
2. How can the cosmic light transform you?
3. Can the cosmic light help you purify?
4. What is your pure intention?

Introduction

People find it hard to understand that their artificial life style goes against their own growth and creates imbalances to their whole being. You have to see the truth in you and understand that you have not been created to follow social patterns but you are here to bring light to others and the planet and also receive light and grow to a being that is whole.

Illusion can take many forms and can capture the people that are looking for truth. To avoid this and truly disconnect from all artificiality you have to look in you, your connection with your astral body and the Earth energies.

Connecting to truth will help you understand of your true purpose and how to connect to cosmic growth and high light. When you achieve clarity, you will connect to your true-self and you will follow a process of transformation, growth and well-being.

Wisdom of Thoth: Knowing your Purpose

There are many ways to prevent the diseases that can affect your physicality. Most of you know that eating certain artificial substances, living a life of artificiality and not being able to connect to your true-self and purpose, can cause diseases that can affect your body at any age. So instead of talking and fantasizing about it you should take action to purify and nourish yourself and also connect to your being and receive cosmic light.

There are some people that even though they pollute themselves, they are not suffering from any diseases. This may mean that the disease is not yet formed into your body. In this case, you are able to stay healthy, if you decide to purify yourself right now. There are also people who are already suffering from diseases. If you are suffering from a chronic disease you also have to focus on your well-being but the result will be different for you.

You should crave live nutrients and focus on exploring different types of purification that can help your body if not fight, live with the disease. You should spend your life exploring the ability of different nutrients to heal you and rejuvenate you. You should live in peace, experiencing a life of growth and transformation. You should not be fooled that you have no purpose because of your disease; instead you should dedicate your life knowing and fulfilling your purpose.

The cosmic light connects to all human beings and offers them healing and growth. There is a divine plan and a purpose for all of you who have reincarnated on Earth. If you exist in fragmentation then the imbalances that cause the disease will grow even more. You are always responsible for your path and looking for truth you experience purity.

Questions

1. How can you prevent disease?
2. How can you nourish yourself?
3. Can you explain the following phrase: "You should not be fooled that you have no purpose because of your disease; instead you should dedicate your life knowing and fulfilling your purpose."
4. Are you responsible for your own growth?

Introduction

Thoth teaches us freedom and truth. When human beings connect to their true-self they will be able to follow their purpose and have a life full of remarkable and liberating experiences. Human beings should take a step out from their current spot of confusion and start to see life in its true authentic state. We can acquire awareness when we acknowledge the light in us and use it as a guide.

If you follow your true purpose, you follow truth and freedom and this is not promoted by your society. Your society teaches you a life of restriction where the individual has to restrict others too. A life of truth and freedom can only be a wild dream for most people on Earth and this is why they do not accept the true purpose. This happens to most people, even the ones who claim to be awake or aware or even enlightened.

Your life needs to be meaningful, full of interesting and liberating experiences in order to understand your purpose which is linked to the higher-self. Why do people move in circles activating multiple layers of negativity, fear and destruction? Is this related to their purpose?

Wisdom of Thoth: Can you Walk the Path of Truth?

Human beings need guidance in order to find the path of truth. They have given their power away including their ability to see and act with clarity, connecting to their true-self and be the creators of their own lives.

Human beings, from young age, are following instructions which force them to disconnect from their purpose, trying to achieve the ultimate goal which is an illusionary social reward. What will happen if all beings on Earth who are not connected to the planet's energies and the cosmos, stop following their everyday routine, disconnect from illusion and connect to their true-self?

If your rulers want to celebrate humanity, they should allow and encourage human beings to disconnect from artificiality and connect to their own growth. A great gift to all beings is the opportunity to experience growth and become creators of their own lives. When you make this connection with your true-self, you are able to bring balance into your being and follow the path of truth that will lead you to your purpose.

A river can clean your impurities. But will you stand in the middle of it without fear or negativity? While you are standing in the middle of the river, can you create the bridge that will take you to the river bank? This is your challenge; it can also be seen as an opportunity for growth and a high reward for all people that reincarnate on Earth.

Questions

1. How can you connect to your purpose?
2. What social rewards are coming your way?
3. What will happen to you when you focus on purifying from illusion?
4. Can you explain the following phrase "A river can clean your impurities. But will you stand in the middle of it without fear or negativity?"

Introduction

There is a fight, a war, between the Earth of the golden era and the Earth of distortion.

They are many beings who are going through the same suffering as Earth, either because they are also confused or because they want to share the burden. I am telling you now that there is no pain, sorrow or anxiety if you decide to return to the golden era. If you believe that there is a golden era on Earth and you are going to accept it as reality, you will have no pain and suffering only love and happiness. Now, you are creating the golden era and this is the place where you should be.

Wisdom of Thoth: Suffering

People that see their lives as a list of unsolved problems do not necessarily have to be in a war zone or a hospital bed. Suffering affects people's lives when they are not able to connect to their true-self and open themselves up to growth. What will you give to your children to see them grow?

Most people live in illusion and artificiality and they tend to feel sorry for the ones that do not have what they have. But do you really know why you are on Earth right now? Are you able to create a life of growth for you and the people who connect to you or you are just following what is acceptable and right according to social expectations?

Have you ever taken responsibility when you feed your children poisonous substances that can lead to early death? If all people on Earth were free from mind manipulation, you will all know that you are here to grow and this will be your intention. There are many obstacles on people's path to truth and purpose; there is also a route that can take you there and this route's starting point is within you. Everybody can suffer and everybody can be fulfilled, this is a choice that you have to make.

Questions

1. Does suffering affect your life? How do you deal with this?
2. Why people on Earth are possessed with the idea of materialism and ownership?
3. What is your creation on Earth?
4. What are your obstacles to create a life of growth?

Introduction

All human beings can connect to the cosmic light. You can receive it when you accept that everything in the cosmos exists in unity. Human beings have also to accept that part of their purpose is to become a perfect receiver and transmitter of light and allow it to spread to humanity and Earth. The purpose of the light is to spread to all planes and living beings to maintain life.

Wisdom of Astaroth: Healing Yourself and Others

The support that the cosmic light can offer is present on Earth. There is a great force that spreads the cosmic light to the planet, transforming all creation. We want to inform humanity that the cosmic light is here with them right now and if they open themselves up, they will be able to receive it. We are showing you how to connect to your true-self and clear the multiple layers of imbalances that were created in you and your environment. Some of you may think that if you are able to purify yourself you have achieved the greatest reward; I see this as your first steps towards growth.

Your next task is to purify the people who connect to you. Who are they? Why do you feel connected to them? How do you exchange energy and how do you heal each other? What are your communities and what is your contribution? When you become a powerful receiver and transmitter of light, you will be able to heal yourself but you can only fully heal when you heal others. All beings are united and each other's growth affects the whole.

This is why we are connecting to you right now and we are opening you up to cosmic growth. We are not here to support distortion and illusionary mind structures where criticism, judgement, artificiality and illusion are blocking your way to truth. We are here to help you experience freedom and truth, becoming a creator of your own life, leading you to transformation and growth. The light of the cosmos surrounds Earth and as she opens up, great healing is taking place. This will affect all creation and the light will be transmitted to the cosmos.

Questions

1. How can you become a receiver and transmitter of light? How can this support your growth?
2. How can you affect the growth of others when you connect to the cosmic light?
3. How can you become a creator of a life of purpose?

Introduction

The unity that exists in the cosmos is contained in the light of our creator and is spread to the creation through our creation code. Our unity with our creator is a high truth and when we are able to understand the wisdom, we will open ourselves to the possibility of being a creator.

Let's take our intention away from the outer planes which we always think as separate from us and responsible for our limitations. We are all part of the unseen, formless, all-contained, all-created power of our High Creator and we are going to start our quest to high truth and knowledge from this point inside us which unites generates and contains all: our creation code.

Wisdom of Astaroth: You cannot Control the Cosmic Light, Let it Heal you

You are not able to control the cosmic light. You can only create a space in you and allow it to enter your being and heal you. The cosmic light is not man-made or man-directed. You cannot know the way it presents itself, works and creates. You cannot see its limitless abilities to create life and its countless ways to unite all with the Source.

You cannot experience the light's transformation but because of the light you can experience your own transformation. There is no need to try to control, plan or have expectations of your connection to the cosmos; these are diversions that take you away from your path. Empty yourself, observe your own purification and experience unity with all that exists. We are all connected and we all support each other's growth. This cosmic law will set you free.

Some of you may ask: how can I be free in a space of distortion? How can I be free when the people I connect to and care about are distorted and confused? I am not going to share with you a great plan or a complicated method/theory/explanation/idea that you can accept as truth and perhaps experience. I will show you how to connect to the cosmic light right now and allow healing to take place.

The light of the cosmos is going to fall on you like a powerful rainfall and clear all impurities. Allow it now by connecting to your being and remain in a state of peace. Allow the light to go through you and help you disconnect from illusionary thoughts and mind tricks. You are free to choose: now is the time to experience cosmic creation.

Questions

1. Can you control the cosmic light to support your purification?
2. How can you experience transformation?
3. How can you be free from distortion?
4. How can you create a space of peace in you?

Introduction

People on Earth who want to grow have to disconnect from their distorted patterns of the past. This can be achieved by observing yourself; look at the link between past patterns and present ones, observe artificiality in your life and focus on your growth. You grow when all actions and thoughts are true to your life path and purpose. This should be your criteria when you are about to take a step in your quest for truth.

Do not be afraid of letting go of your current affairs, personal ambitions, competitions, anger, desires; all these can only lower your ability to transform and become one with your divine plan. We are part of a renewal process which has started already in some spheres and will finally affect all.

Wisdom of Thoth: Disconnect from Distortion and Connect to Growth

Human beings have ambitions and want to achieve what nobody else has achieved before. They want to be pioneers, to be celebrated and remembered for many generations. Some of you may ask: does ambition link to growth? My answer is yes, if you have pure intention. People who are giving unconditionally in order to support people's growth; help others find their path of truth and use this as their guide for their entire reincarnation, they have achieved their goal on Earth.

You need to ask yourself, does your ambition link to growth? Does ambition disconnect you and the people around you from your true purpose?

There are many examples that show how certain authorities control and manipulate your mind and body. Some forms of manipulation may seem extreme but when the human mind accepts them as truth, it becomes normal and ordinary.

Human beings have to observe their own lives and see how their own mind is manipulated, how they accepted illusion as truth and how it pollutes their own being. When you are able to see, understand and purify yourself from those imbalances then you are able to help communities disconnect from distortion and connect to growth.

Questions

1. What are your ambitions
2. Do your ambitions link to growth?
3. Have you experienced mind manipulation?
4. What is your next step towards growth?

Introduction

It is important that you discover your true purpose and have a good understanding of how to use your tools and special gifts. When you are purified from the illusion and you are able to see yourself in your pure state then you will instantly see your purpose and you will have instant access to all cosmic truths because it is your right. We want humanity to wake up in order to assist planet Earth to wake up too. The Earth and her creation suffer from the same disease and this is a schism of the true-self and the growth of illusion. When you awake to the truth you will be restored to your true-selves.

Wisdom of Thoth: Are you creating a space of peace?

There are people on Earth who are affected by the planet's low vibration and the illusion that is suppressing growth. Illusion can penetrate your being, pollute your mind and affect your everyday life. If you are aware of this, you are awake; you prepare yourself, going through a purification process and then you focus on your path of truth. It is important for human beings to exist in a space of truth and growth and if they cannot enter a space of truth they have to create it.

Can you describe your space of truth? What does it consist off and what is your contribution to keep it alive? How can you unite with other beings in this space and make it expand? Human beings have to take decisions about their own lives and be creators of their own growth. Information on Earth is often diversion from the truth or keeping the mind in a fantasy world while the rest of your being is following illusion.

I do not want you to see this teaching as information but as a guidance to help you act and move out of the maze of illusion and in a space of truth. Connecting to the cosmic light and purifying yourself are gifts you can give to others and together you can co-create this space of truth. Healing and unity are necessary for humanity and Earth's growth. Connect to your pure intention and you a space will be able to connect to your whole being and then to humanity and Earth.

Questions

1. How can illusion affect your mind and being?
2. Can you describe your space of truth?
3. How can you spread truth to others?
4. Explain the following phrase: "Healing and unity are necessary for humanity and Earth's growth."

Introduction

Human beings will need to create communities that allow them to experience growth. All people united connect to their purpose and develop new skills of transmitting and receiving energy. Earth supports healthy communities that are able to grow following the natural laws. Earth wants to be involved in our communities, she wants to offer her light but she also wants from us to generate light and feed the whole planet. These are the natural laws and Earth was created to fulfil her purpose of a god-creator-planet, supporting the light of her beings.

Our aim is to show you your purpose and unique abilities to help you grow. You are going to create your life by painting your own authentic picture of yourself and let your true purpose be revealed. We want you to detach yourself from the persona and connect to your true-self.

Wisdom of Thoth: Creating Communities of Truth and Growth

Creating communities of truth and growth is the ultimate goal. The more human beings are able to connect to truth the more clarity will receive, regarding the creation of communities that will heal the schisms and bring growth. There were and there are still, a number of individuals who want to build communities in order to gain power over their members.

An ideology cannot support those groups because they are a repetition of what already exists, the pyramid structure. If you are one of those people who want to join a community, you should go beyond the mind manipulation and try to detect a pyramid structure, being the leading force and purpose. If you want to build a community, you should first connect to people energetically and then try to understand and develop their skills, abilities and purpose.

You are helping them understand why they are here on Earth and what gifts they possess to fulfil their purpose. When you have created this connection with a small group you can allow your community to grow and become a bigger and more complex organism. This will be successful if you all learn to communicate and experience truth in your everyday life; have no expectation for social success and exist in constant growth; this can also become a collective experience. These are the first instructions as to how to build your community.

Questions

1. How can you create communities of truth?
2. Can you explain the following phrase: "If you want to build a community, you should first connect to people energetically and then try to understand and develop their skills, abilities and purpose."
3. Can you live a life without ambition?
4. What is the pyramid structure?

Introduction

People reincarnate wherever and whenever there is a need for this to happen. They are beings who have reincarnated many times on Earth and they are other beings who have reincarnated on many others planets, galaxies and universes. For every being there is a divine plan, a plan of evolution, and this is stored in its creation code and is manifested on its higher-self. According to this plan, human beings will go through a certain learning process that is tailored specifically for them.

Life and death are both parts of the journey and evolution of a human being. Life after death is not the same for every being but you have to see death as a new cycle of evolution connected to your life cycle. People reincarnate in order to achieve a high level of understanding and when they achieve that the physical body is resolved and all experiences and learning are stored in the astral body.

All of you who have reincarnated on Earth you are part of her creation and your duty is to bring the light of the cosmos to Earth and help her to transform. Living in harmony with the Earth's cycles and natural laws helps you connect to the planet.

Wisdom of Thoth: Near Death Experience

There are beings on Earth that experience what they call near death experiences. Human beings cannot die and come back to Earth. When a life cycle ends is not an accidental event. It has to do with the being's choices, growth and ability to fulfil his purpose but it is also a moment that is recorded in his divine plan.

All of you come on Earth to fulfil your purpose, this means to achieve growth and spread this growth to humanity and Earth. You will be given opportunities to achieve this and the events are recorded in your divine plan. There are people who are going to pollute their being with artificiality and distortion; this is their choice.

They are responsible for their own growth and when they go against their growth, their opportunities diminish. There is a divine plan that shapes a being's existence but human beings with their actions, thoughts and creation can increase or decrease their opportunities of growth.

Human beings on Earth cannot detect or measure their life force in them.

Bodily organs can stop working but this does not mean that the person has completed his life cycle. There are also people who are kept alive using artificial ways but they have already ended their cycle. Near death experiences are similar to a dream state. The people who experience this are still alive and what they describe has nothing to do with what happens to the being at the end of the reincarnation.

Questions

1. How can a life cycle end?
2. Why do you reincarnate on Earth?
3. How can you explain the following phrase: "Human beings are responsible for their own growth"
4. What is your understanding of the following phrase: "There are also people who are kept alive using artificial ways but they have already ended their cycle."

Introduction

Humanity is disconnected from the gods and their light of wisdom and oneness. Their signs of alienation reflect the state of the Earth as a whole. When humans are able to fight illusion and heal distortion, they will support the planet's growth and transformation. They are many people on Earth who are walking the path of awakening. Their numbers are going to grow; this is the divine plan.

On Earth we experience duality which is a separation of self from all that exists. There is always a fight of the opposites which is the cause of fragmentation and illusion. If you wish to evolve beyond polarity and fragmentation you have to disconnect from the idea of opposites. In nature there is no fight against two elements there is only a union of the elements, bringing new life. In this teaching we learn that if there is a fight this is a fight of life for the new born who is coming to take his place of power.

Wisdom of Thoth: Unity and Healing on Earth

The godly light that exists in the cosmos and creates life with the light of our Source has a different purpose than all life that exists in all solar systems.

If you want to understand people's intention, actions and thought you should perhaps compare them to other human beings. They enjoy fighting, claiming, owning and also healing, protecting and experiencing growth. The mind brings the idea of war and destruction. Human beings are not the mind they are the creation of light.

We created Earth, this was our purpose and our duty. We are protecting Earth the way your spirit guides protect you. We cannot interfere but when Earth is looking for the cosmic light, the cosmic light will instantly flow in her and bring her growth. Perhaps you should ask yourselves about your own intentions? How can you grow with Earth? What will be your contribution to bring unity and healing to Earth and humanity?

Questions

1. What is the cosmic light?
2. How do you connect to people's intention?
3. Can you explain the following phrase: "Human beings are not the mind they are the creation of light."
4. How can you grow on Earth?

Introduction

You are here to receive the light and heal yourself from the illusion of separation and polarity which has given birth to fear, confusion and survival. There are many human beings on Earth who are longing to achieve clarity, connecting to their true purpose, but they are entangled in the web of illusion and limitation. Thoth wants to nourish all beings with his light and his teachings: when people are able to empty their minds from all illusionary beliefs, aspirations, needs, suffering, pleasures and expectations, they will discover their creator. When humans are able to heal distortion, they will support the planet's growth and transformation. They are many people on Earth who are walking the path of awakening. Their numbers are going to grow; this is the divine plan.

Wisdom of Thoth: The Illusion of the Mind

The cosmic light is reaching Earth to help her disconnect from illusion and artificiality; this can happen when everything that exists on her opens up to receive the light and transmit it to others. Opening up to the cosmic light is a natural process available to all beings in all planes.

If you think that you are not able to connect to the light, it means that illusion, blockages and trauma have locked you in a space of non-clarity, non-truth and non-growth. Being in this space you cannot connect to your true-self and purpose; you cannot heal and experience growth but also you cannot offer the gifts of knowing and transformation to others. You can be free when you start observing yourself and go beyond the persona and the ego.

You can ask yourself: what are you trying to achieve in your life and how is this connected to your purpose? Is your life your own creation and expression of your divine plan or perhaps you are following others, supporting social expectations? Can you give to yourself what is needed in order to achieve balance? If you are able to experience growth and connect to your purpose, can you help others find their path?

Human beings need to look at their everyday life and see that not only they can be part of a state of distortion but they can also support it and spread it to others. Can you observe yourself supporting distortion?

Sometimes the mind will not give you clear and direct answers to the questions above because it has been infected by illusion.

If you carry on focusing on truth, the mind will play the game of weakness, guilt and fear. When you are affected by negativity, you are going to be locked in a space where there is no healing or knowing; it is a space of isolation and darkness.

Most human beings will allow the illusion of the mind to take them to another space where life seems to be more colourful and engaging full of choices, opportunities and multiple diversions. Any time you find yourself going on a diversion you can always find your way back to truth and connect to your purpose. You can connect to truth if this is your intention and you can clear distortion when you are able to follow your purpose.

Questions

1. How can Earth disconnect from illusion?
2. If you are able to experience growth and connect to your purpose, can you help others find their path?
3. Can you explain the following phrase: "When you are affected by negativity, you are going to be locked in a space where there is no healing or knowing; it is a space of isolation and darkness."
4. Can you explain the following phrase: "Most human beings will allow the illusion of the mind to take them to another space where life seems to be more colourful and engaging full of choices, opportunities and multiple diversions."

Introduction

Our purpose is related to the elements of the planet that we inhabit. If your true purpose is related to Earth, you are a force of stability and balance between the elements and the planet. You are going to help Earth recognise her true potential and support her creation, as well as being open to the guidance of the gods.

People are kept prisoners of a man-made illusion. Most of them are isolated from nature and the natural laws and have a false impression that they are superior. In reality they are prisoners and are kept away from the beauty, harmony and wisdom of the divine creation that exists on Earth.

In realms of high consciousness, the weak are immediately seen and truth prevails. However on Earth's low vibration, the manipulators have found their perfect home, where they can breathe, multiply and control all aspects of human life.

Wisdom of Thoth: Become the Womb for the Cosmic Light to Create

My light is reaching Earth's energies. I am here to connect to Earth and her creation with the cosmic light that is the highest creative force and brings life. Understand our Source, being the highest mountain where nobody can visit or live there.

The heavy snow that gathers in abundance on the top of the mountain gives birth to rivers and lakes. Even if you are not able to reach the top of the mountain, it seems that parts of it are connecting to you, bringing life to human beings and all Earth's creation. The wind, sun light and rain are also reaching the top of the mountain and then unite to all that exists at the surface.

All elements are connected to Earth and this is why they stay connected to you. If our Source has created Earth then your connection with our Source is direct and without boundaries. The only boundaries that block your way are the ones created by illusion and accepted by you.

If you were able to connect to Earth she could show you the connections between the elements, the creation being an extension of the cosmos and the cosmic light. The cosmic light is the essence of the cosmos. It is the seed of our Source that is planted in all beings and in all planes. Your being is created by this seed and becomes a womb to carry the seed for a new creation.

Life is growth and this is experienced in all planes. Earth will tell you this when you are able to connect to her and will show you that birth never stops and has no end. This is how you should see your lives; constantly growing, transforming, becoming the womb for the cosmic light to create and then experience growth around you. If you ignore this cosmic law then you exist in illusion and you are responsible for blocking your own growth and connection to the Source.

Questions

1. Can Earth and her elements affect your growth?
2. What is your connection with the Source?
3. Are you able to communicate with Earth?
4. Can you explain the following phrase: "This is how you should see your lives; constantly growing, transforming, becoming the womb for the cosmic light to create and then experience growth around you"

CHAPTER II

Thoth teaches us freedom and truth; these are our main tools to help us fulfil our purpose. When human beings connect to their true-self, they will be able to follow their purpose and have a life full of remarkable and liberating experiences. Human beings should take a step out from their current spot of illusion and start to see their life in its true authentic state. We can acquire awareness when we acknowledge the truth in us and use it as a guide.

Introduction

All beings that have reincarnated on Earth are connecting to her energies and bring light to her being. Remember that the human state that you are experiencing right now is not permanent; you are astral beings who are in constant evolution and will never be controlled by anything and anybody than the cosmic laws. When human beings are fully awake then they will connect to their true purpose and will allow the high energies to heal Earth. All creation is united to a common goal and this will bring awakening to planet Earth.

Wisdom of Thoth: Return to the Astral Plane

In higher planes, living beings receive everything they need to help them grow and stay in unity with the whole cosmos and the source. They have countless opportunities to grow therefore they never experience limitation. You also have countless opportunities of growth the only difference is that you are not open to growth.

Some of you may ask: how can we stay in a state of receiving the cosmic light and make this our focus when our communities and all structures and systems that control our lives are showing us a different way in order to achieve success? Yes it is true that all human beings suffer from illusion because your whole community is affected and exists in a diversion from truth.

But you still have the ability to disconnect from what is happening around you and connect to who you are and what you are able to achieve. When you connect to your true-self, you understand your divine plan, the purpose of your reincarnation, your abilities to grow and your unique way to connect to others and support their growth.

At the end of this life cycle, you disconnect from your physical body and you continue to exist in other planes. Your cosmic growth which is eternal and unlimited does not depend on your physicality. Your light body was created in the astral plane and this is your home.

At the end of your reincarnation you will focus on one duty and this is to prepare yourself to return back to the astral plane and continue your cosmic growth. Illusion, distortion and fragmentation will not follow you there. You will go through a purification state to help you observe your achievements during your reincarnation and during this time you will collect all the learning you have experienced and dismiss all artificiality and illusion that have affected your life on Earth. Becoming a pure light, connecting to the cosmos will enable you return to the astral plane and experience cosmic growth.

Questions

1. What have been your opportunities of growth?
2. How can you receive the cosmic light?
3. How can you connect to your purpose?
4. What will happen to a human being at the end of the life cycle and how can you prepare for it?

Introduction

When people open their eyes and start looking at the crossroads, they will see a path of truth. If you decide to take this path, you will have to be purified and disconnect from the old imbalances.

If you decide to go on a quest to discover truth, you will connect to your true-self. You will begin to experience your essence and divine plan in your whole being and create an effortless life of peace.

Wisdom of Thoth: The Purpose of Humanity

Humanity and Earth should unite in order to clear distortion and make the way back to the golden era. Human beings are not the rulers or the owners of Earth's recourses as they want to believe but they are the extension of Earth; they are receivers and transmitters of energy that can connect Earth to the cosmos.

Earth has given you your physical body and being a mother creator is able to nourish her creation and sustain life. Your physical body is part of your being whose purpose is to connect and support Earth's growth. Your physical body is surrounded by energies and those energies are the link between your physicality and your astral existence.

At the end of your life cycle your body returns to Earth and after a purification process you will return to the space of your creation, the astral plane. All living beings are created there by the light of our Source. Human beings have the ability to connect to the astral plane and their astral body; all parts of their being are connected, united by the cosmic light which goes through every being in order to bring life and growth.

If you understand this, you are able to disconnect from the distortion and the illusion that turn you away from your purpose. If you are able to connect to Earth and see your life as a service to her then you are free from limitation. Some of you may find it challenging to accept that your physical body is connected to an astral body and that you are able to communicate and receive information.

If you are able to connect to Earth and accept your purpose to become a receiver and transmitter of cosmic light in order to help her grow then you will instantly connect to your astral body. You will achieve this because you have connected to truth and you have purified yourself from illusion and distortion. This is the purpose of humanity and united you should experience it in your everyday life.

Questions

1. How was your body created?
2. Why should you connect to Earth and how can you achieve this?
3. What is the astral plane?
4. What is your purpose in this life time?

Introduction

Humans need to know how Earth was created and what her purpose is. We are all linked with Earth's growth and it is important to unite in order to save the planet and her whole creation.

In the physical plane the essence of Earth can be described as the golden era, a time of high creation.

Earth in the golden era was a luscious land with the most extraordinary variety of plants and animals, rocks and formations. All beings, animals and plants lived in harmony with each other and stay connected to the energies of the planet. Earth was a planet of balance, harmony and abundance and an ideal home for high vibrational races that could appreciate her treasures and wish to enhance her beauty. Most visitors who arrived on the planet, tried to get all Earth's resources, kill and destroy animals and plants and alter Earth's natural laws; she is still suffering from people in control who try to constantly dismantle her and block her light.

If we want the planet to grow, we have to contribute to the overall growth of the whole being, Earth. This is a very important truth and can help you expand your consciousness. Our purpose is to help Earth transform to her first form, as she was in the golden era.

Wisdom of Thoth: The Golden Age exists in the Inner Earth

The human beings that exist on the surface of the planet are not able to enter the hollow Earth and experience life there. This is caused by the difference in vibration and the types of growth. Signs of the golden age are still apparent in the inner parts of the planet and affect their growth. All beings who exist there are able to connect to high energies; this allows Earth to continue being a creator.

Many of you have reincarnated on Earth in order to connect to her energies and allow the cosmic light to heal the schisms. The human beings that are reincarnating on Earth right now are brought to create a bridge between the planet and the Source.

The bridge will be cemented by the cosmic light that is the extension of the Source and brings life to all beings in the cosmos. Unity brings life to all. This is why all parts of Earth need to be united and exchange energies of healing and growth; all beings should unite in order to start Earth's purification and transformation.

Human beings have to stop seeing Earth as a piece of land whose resources can be taken and used any way they please. They have to stop seeing themselves as the owners and rulers, supporting Earth's distortion. When humanity knows the truth about Earth and accepts that their purpose is to become receivers and transmitters of cosmic light then Earth will understand her purpose and this is to bring the light of the golden age to every part of her creation. You can help Earth when you are able to connect to your truth and allow your own purification to take place. When you receive the light it can become a creator.

Questions

1. Is Earth experiencing the golden era right now?
2. Is your purpose related to Earth's purpose and in what way?
3. Can you explain the following phrase: "Unity brings life to all. This is why all parts of Earth need to be united and exchange energies of healing and growth; all beings should unite in order to start Earth's purification and transformation."
4. Can you explain the following phrase: Unity brings life to all. This is why all parts of Earth need to be united and exchange energies of healing and growth; all beings should unite in order to start Earth's purification and transformation.

Introduction

All planets go through a transformation which can affect them in many ways: their creation abilities; the quality of light that they can produce and receive; all their connections with the different electromagnetic fields including their own as well as their physical body. The transformation affects the rotation, position and physical size. Also planets can be moved from one galaxy to another when great imbalances take place. Earth was created to bring balance to a galaxy that had suffered destruction and great upheaval.

The galaxy which is supported by the Earth, Moon, and Sun alignment is a low vibrational space and attracts predators from other planes. This galaxy was formed many thousands of years after the golden era. There were destructions and planets had to move in order to maintain some balance. Earth is protecting her resources in the inner body because the surface is suffering from constant destruction. She tries to protect herself but at the same time there is very little nourishment for the beings there and this affects life and growth. In the core, Earth regenerates herself. The growth that takes place in the core and the lack of growth on the surface create many imbalances which lead alienation within the planet. It is important to be aware of Earth's condition because you are a reflection of this condition.

Wisdom of Thoth: Earth's Position in the Galaxy

Earth is an organism that follows the cosmic laws by design. Her size and position in the galaxy support the planet's link with the sun and allows some expansion. A galaxy does not exist separately from other planetary systems; it is a microcosm within a macrocosm, a receiver and transmitter of light.

Galaxies experience growth and this depends on all planets acting as a unified force connecting to the sun and having the ability to receive and transmit cosmic light. It seems that the planets are trying to stay connected to the sun but also the sun's quality to transmit light strengthens this connection with the planets.

The sun receives cosmic light when it is connected to other suns and then transmits it to the planets that form a galaxy around it. This is an important duty; when the sun transmits light to the planets it also teaches them not only to receive it but also to transmit it to everything that connects to them. Planets grow individually and transform physically and energetically.

All planets carry life in them because they are living beings. When human beings are wondering about life on other planets, they are affected by fear and their focus is on colonization and ownership. If you want to grow you should focus on your being and allow Earth, the planets, the sun and cosmos to nourish you, clearing all distortion and fragmentation.

When you are able to understand and develop your ability to become the receiver and transmitter of light then you will experience a type of growth that connects your true-self with the cosmos and the cosmos with your true-self; similarly, to the sun's quality to maintain life in the galaxy.

Questions

1. What is Earth's role in the galaxy?
2. What is the role of the sun in the galaxy?
3. Can you explain the following phrase: "When human beings are wondering about life on other planets, they are affected by fear and their focus is on colonization and ownership."
4. Can you explain the following phrase: "When you are able to understand and develop your ability to become the receiver and transmitter of light then you will experience a type of growth that connects your true-self with the cosmos and the cosmos with your true-self; similarly, to the sun's quality to maintain life in the galaxy.

Introduction

Thoth teaches us freedom and truth; these are our main tools to help us fulfil our purpose. When human beings connect to their true-self, they will be able to follow their purpose and have a life full of remarkable and liberating experiences. Human beings should take a step out from their current spot of illusion and start to see their life in its true authentic state. We can acquire awareness when we acknowledge the truth in us and use it as a guide.

There are many people who find it hard to connect to their purpose and this is because they cannot accept it. When we cannot accept our purpose, we create many false representations of it, often related to social ideals. These false representations are created by us and function as diversions. Some would ask why people do that, what they have to gain from it. There is nothing to be gained. If you follow your true purpose you follow truth and freedom and this is not promoted by your society. Your society teaches you a life of restriction where the individual has to restrict others too. A life of truth and freedom can only be a wild dream for most people on Earth and this is why they do not accept the true purpose. This happens to most people, even the ones who claim to be awake or aware or even enlightened.

Wisdom of Thoth: The Path of Perfection

My light is connected to those human beings that want to disconnect from illusion and purify themselves from stagnation. Often people who deceive are being deceived themselves and often they accept both roles which become their driving force. What growth opportunities does a seed of truth have when is planted in a space of illusion to grow and fulfil its purpose on Earth?

This is an important question for all fighters of truth whose pure intention is to purify themselves and humanity. First of all you have to be determined to see yourself as a receiver and transmitter of light. You can achieve this by purifying yourself, balancing the mind and the ego, disconnecting from the persona and focus on growth and healing that can be achieved when you receive and transmit the cosmic light. In this state you have achieved to have an effortless life, experience growth and walk the path of truth and purpose.

The warriors of truth know that they have an important task and this is to transmit the cosmic light. When you purify yourself and receive the light then you are able to connect to your essence and clearly see your purpose on Earth. When you are able to transmit the light, then you are fulfilling your purpose and you are able to expand even more.

Transmitting light to humanity and Earth should not be overlooked because it is the path of perfection. Some of you may say: transmitting light to others and helping them to grow is a difficult task because humanity is suffering from distortion and illusion. How can humanity wake up and experience truth? How can you help them purify themselves and show them ways to become the perfect transmitter and receiver of light? If you are able to connect to a number of people who are waiting for you to help them receive the cosmic light then you have achieved to experience being the transmitter as well the receiver.

Questions

1. Can you explain the following phrase: "Often people who deceive are being deceived themselves and often they accept both roles and become their driving force."

2. What chances does a seed of truth have is when is planted in a space of illusion to grow and fulfil its purpose on Earth?
3. How can you purify yourself?
4. How can you transmit light to humanity and Earth?

Introduction

Earth can provide nourishment for all her species including healing, purification, energy and resources in order to bring balance and harmony and encourage communication between all bodies. Earth can provide you with all the nourishment you need but you prefer the artificial substances that have no life in them. People who are addicted to contaminated food are not awake. They exist in a hypnotic state and illusion becomes the controller of the mind. People who are addicted are caught into the web of illusion. They want to be free but illusion creates many visions and thoughts related to happiness when you use a certain product you are addicted to.

You have to wake up if you want to stay alive. You have to take responsibility of your own everyday life if you want to be enlightened. If you are blocked, poisoned, confused, and fragmented because of your life style you cannot achieve enlightenment. Nature and the cosmic laws will teach you that your body is a tool and the gods created on Earth's numerous resources to help you maintain balance and harmony to your whole being.

Wisdom of Thoth: Addictions

What is it that you cannot live without? Some people will answer: my life, experiences and connection to others; others will say my connection with the Earth and the cosmic light that connects me to my astral body. Some of you will express that you cannot disconnect from imbalances and fears, therefore you cannot live without them.

Human beings have experienced imbalances controlling your mind, becoming blinded to truth, accepting distortion and illusion creating imbalances in them. Are your addictions, imbalances? If you observe yourself you will understand that an addiction causes confusion and self-harm. People who are addicted to contaminated food are not awake. They exist in a hypnotic state and illusion becomes the controller of the mind.

People who are addicted are slaves of the illusion. When your mind is occupied with multiple thoughts it is hard to be in a peaceful state and connect to your true-self. In this confused state you are going to follow illusionary beliefs and practices that are supported by your society and rulers. Then addiction becomes an ordinary pattern that is followed by many.

In some cases, people have addictions and cause self-harm in order to follow social expectations. Observe yourself: if you are harming yourself try to find peace; disconnect from illusion and connect to your true-self that is nourished by the cosmic light and astral growth connect to your true-self and allow clarity to enter your being and illusion fade away.

Questions

1. How can you disconnect from imbalances?
2. Are you able to observe yourself?
3. What are your addictions?
4. Can you explain the following phrase: "In some cases, people have addictions and cause self-harm in order to follow social expectations."

Introduction

The purpose of this teaching is to wake you up to your true purpose which has nothing to do with materialism, consumerism and manipulation but it is a life of truth, higher consciousness and supporting others to rediscover their true-self. If you wish to be a creator that is the path you have to take.

All beings that reincarnate on Earth are responsible for connecting to her energies, help the vibration to rise and the trauma to be healed.

We are all here to receive, share and grow.

Our light is connected to higher light and when we connect to it we receive guidance in relation to our purpose and our tools. Our spiritual quest is a path that cannot be taught or dictated by other humans because they are on their own unique paths and their understanding is formed by their own unique purpose. The heart often needs inspiration but this does not affect the process of enlightenment. Our true purpose is bare of feelings and logic. It is our inheritance from the astral plane where we exist in a pure form.

There are parts of our being which can show us the way to empowerment and our achievement is always linked with somebody else's growth. The hands of a healer know the healer's journey and as he/she empowers others with healing, the healer receives light, clarity and greater abilities. Our transformation is part of a chain of events that involves us and others. When you are a pure channel of the gods' light, you are going to connect to people who can help you with your transformation and you give this great gift back to them.

Wisdom of Thoth: The Light of the Cosmos is a Great Guide and Healer

People on Earth are surrounded by clouds of distortion and often this is a state they experience every day. Some of them are not aware of this and others are looking for remedies, healing, relaxation or enjoyment to help them disconnect from it. The cloud of distortion will not go away if you are not able to connect to your true-self and understand your purpose.

You have the tools to purify yourself and exist in a space of peace and growth. Your tool is your connection with your true-self. This connection will help you clear limitations, restrictions and boundaries given to you by your community and start having true goals which are linked to your purpose and divine plan.

If there is work to be done this is connecting to your true-self, recognizing your abilities and finding ways to fulfil your purpose. When you connect to your true-self, see your purpose and follow your path, your life will become a straight line of wonder, growth and transformation. This is how you can become the creator of your own life and purify your whole being from the distortion that exists on Earth. The light of the cosmos is a great guide and healer and when you connect to it. Humanity and Earth can find their way back to the golden Era.

Questions

1. Why people are not aware of distortion affecting their growth?
2. What are your tools to help you purify?
3. What is your true-self and why should you connect to it?
4. How can you become a creator?

Introduction

Human beings are seeking inner peace in a space of distortion. You have probably realized that you cannot be in peace when your family, friends and neighbours follow the path of illusion and insist on you and other members of your society to do the same. We are trying to warn you and give you a chance to escape what is coming to you. We want people to stand up and step away from the illusion. Connect with each other, support and teach each other truths and wisdom. If you have a better understanding about balanced life on Earth you have to share it with your friends and family. Truth can create miraculous bonds and everything will fall in its right place.

In some cases, people have to become slaves for their family, for social and financial success, to attract others, to follow what others do. They are people who think that being a slave will bring them freedom and happiness. The result of all this is an imbalanced life full of disease, confusion and dissatisfaction.

You are diseased if you allow yourself to become a slave; your true nature and purpose is to be free and connect to cosmic laws. You can go against the plan of slavery any time you wish. You just have to wake up to the understanding that most people's lives are formed by a contagious disease called illusion. You have the power to escape; remember that illusion has no life or true power over you. Now is the time that people on Earth have to take responsibility for their lives and wake up to a new and meaningful existence. If you are seeking enlightenment, purifying yourself from illusion is your first challenge.

Wisdom of Thoth: Creating strong bonds with your family

The light of the gods is reaching humanity and many of you will experience growth and transformation. People who are seeking truth will look at themselves and observe the many layers of distortion that were created for many years. Fear, judgement, limitation, ignorance are not natural qualities of a human being. They are impurities that were created by external forces.

People on Earth are not aware that they minimize their growth and are not able to help others grow. Part of your purpose is to connect to others, pass the cosmic light and assist them to connect to their true-self and fulfil their purpose. It is very clear that most people are struggling to support family and friends because they are not able to connect to their true-self.

Most actions and thoughts bring distortion; People appear to be selfish were in reality they exist in distortion. The family that you are born to on the Earth plane consists of energy beings that are connected to you in the astral plane. There are group reincarnations that are happening on Earth to offer support to all human beings involved.

Members of your family who pass away or others who are born when you are older, they often become your guides and support you on your path of truth. Creating strong bonds with your family experience your true-self with them, allowing them to step out from distortion and have a balanced state are great gifts for all of you to enjoy and share.

If you are able to disconnect from your artificial need to control, possess, ignore, separate, and judge or feeling weak and limited then together with you family you are going to blossom to a flower of truth and growth. This is something that you should all try to achieve; it will help you connect to your true-self and experience walking the path of truth with people who are connected to you energetically.

If you are able to grow with them in the astral plane you should allow this to happen on Earth and enjoy the fruit of this connection.

Questions

1. Can you explain the following phrase: "Fear, judgement, limitation, ignorance are not natural qualities of a human being."

2. Are you aware of your limitations?
3. How do you understand the following phrase: "Creating strong bonds with your family experience your true-self with them, allowing them to step out from distortion and have a balanced state are great gifts for all of you to enjoy and share."
4. Are you able to grow with your family and friends?

Introduction

Energy flows through all beings throughout the cosmos. Energy is information and the purest way of communication. Everything in the universe is in constant transformation and movement. When there is transformation, the universe is alive and produces high energy able to sustain life.

There is a constant movement of energy and this is responsible for creating and maintaining life on Earth. All beings are open to the cosmic evolution which is supporting their own growth and vice versa. The lower planes staying distant form the highly productive astral plane. The cosmic growth has very little effect on them and as a result their growth is very low.

The cosmos seems to have a very complex structure, mainly because of its vastness and the multiple reflections of it, co-existing at the same time. Life moves in a circular movement of growth and this movement is repeated. Every successful repetition traverses the astral body to a higher vibrational state. When a body is in a process of evolution, it is going to receive and generate more light. All beings are connected to a large group of astral beings. Your creation code is also communicating with their creation codes.

Wisdom of Astaroth: Your True-Self will Become Known to you

The intention of the cosmic light is to travel to all beings and give them the clarity they need to continue with their growth and fulfil their purpose. The cosmic light is the extension of our Source that connects to all beings in all planes; this is how unity is experienced in the cosmos.

In higher planes, there is a great movement of energies, connecting to the cosmic light and also connecting to other beings and energetic forms. The movement supports growth and creation. All human beings are naturally connected to the cosmic light and part of their purpose is to grow and create but often the blockages in them restrict those abilities; human beings are not even aware or understand that they can create and grow.

People on Earth focus on illusionary success criteria or negativity and limitation in them or others. They accept limitation as truth and they live a life of limitation. They also try to convince others by judging and criticizing them; they see it as their duty to infect people with limitation and take them on a diversion.

Some may ask: Why human beings cannot connect to truth and why do they go against their purpose? It has to do with being passive, not taking responsibility of their own lives; in this state they trust illusion more than truth. Illusion is a stranger that knocks their door and being in a hypnotic state, they will open the door to receive whatever stands there in front of them.

Truth is not a visitor, an external force or an intruder. Truth is part of your being and is waiting for you to connect to it. People do not know truth because they exist in a fragmented state. If they are able to experience unity and balance in all parts of their physical and energetic existence on Earth then they will be able to see truth and understand the importance of growth and connection to the cosmos and how it can be achieved.

The first step to connect to your true-self is to disconnect from distortion and be in a state of peace and then connect to your whole being, experience unity and allow the cosmic light to go through you. You will receive healing and knowing and your true-self will become known to you.

Questions

1. How can the cosmic light support your growth?
2. What is your understanding of the following phrase: "In higher planes, there is a great movement of energies, connecting to the cosmic light and also connecting to other beings and energetic forms."
3. Why human beings cannot connect to truth and why do they go against their purpose?
4. How can you disconnect from distortion?

Introduction

For life to be sustained on the planet, different types of transmitters and receivers of energy are needed to help the cosmos grow and maintain a good balance of energies. All beings that are created in the astral plane and are able to reincarnate on Earth carry the cosmic light in them. They are created to be receivers and transmitters of the cosmic creation force and experience accelerated growth. The unity of all creation brings energy, balance, strength to receivers and transmitters and more opportunity for further growth and creation. Earth is waiting for humanity to wake up from illusion and become true receivers and transmitters of cosmic light. Earth is waiting for humanity to wake up from illusion and become true receivers and transmitters of cosmic light.

Every living being, including the planets and the universes are surrounded by an aura. An aura is the energies of the being supporting electromagnetic fields. All beings that are connected to you receive and transmit energies to your aura. These electromagnetic fields are used as receivers and transmitters of energy as well as balancing and regulating the inner and outer light. What you call matrix is an artificial copy of the aura which was made to control and suppress the light.

Wisdom of Thoth: Receivers and Transmitters of the Cosmic Creation Force

Earth is waiting for humanity to wake up from illusion and become true receivers and transmitters of cosmic light. You may ask why is Earth waiting for humanity, a small part of her creation to wake up and why is it important?

You must know that a single imbalance can affect the whole being; an organ's failure can bring the end of a life cycle and a single process of purification can allow the cosmic light to go through and trigger healing and transformation.

All beings that are created in the astral plane and are able to reincarnate on Earth, carry the cosmic light in them. They are created to be receivers and transmitters of the cosmic creation force and experience accelerated growth. Their purpose on Earth is connected to the astral growth that is not terminated or restricted when they reincarnate on Earth.

They consist of physicality as well as an astral body that are both connected to the cosmic light which flows through them. If human beings on Earth did not experience distortion and fragmentation and were free to exist in a pure state, then they will have an effortless connection with their astral body. Distortion, fragmentation and illusion are three main reasons that can cause an astral paralysis.

This is why many human beings exist in a hypnotic state far away from their purpose. It is time now for humanity to understand that their astral growth and their purpose on Earth are connected and when you are able to understand and experience your purpose on Earth you are instantly connected to your astral growth. This is a great gift and gives humans the opportunity to exist in two different planes and because of that they are the perfect receivers and transmitters of light. Earth's creation includes many receivers and transmitters of cosmic energy that need to wake up and fulfil their purpose.

Questions

1. Why is it important for Earth's growth the awakening of humanity?
2. How is Earth affected by the imbalances of human beings?
3. What is your experience of distortion and illusion?
4. Are you a receiver and transmitter of light?

Introduction

Human beings on Earth have the ability to connect to the Source through their creation code. They are able to connect to the astral plane and be part of the astral growth. This is a cosmic law shared by the whole creation. Human beings have great capabilities to fight fragmentation, but the low vibration on Earth which is becoming constantly lower, does not help them to grow and evolve. Due to the distortion and fragmentation on the planet, the astral knowledge cannot penetrate the physical plane and human beings exist in isolation surrounded by the veil of illusion. It is important that we clear the channels of communication and connect to the astral plane as well as the Earth's energies.

The imbalances in our physical body are caused by the lack of communication between the physical and astral body. This communication can be done by allowing your bodies to connect and regulate the light and energy that flows through them. The dialogue between all planes should be clear, constant and truthful. Different planes converse through the creation code which unites all. Communication is energy which flows through to assist with balancing, strengthening and creating. Listening to the communication between your bodies is a very special skill practiced by masters on Earth plane.

Wisdom of Thoth: Effective Communication

There are certain life patterns that are shared by many people on Earth. Their inability to take responsibility and the lack of communication and understanding are very common patterns among humans. Those two patterns can grow, transform and take many different forms. If you are afraid of taking responsibility you may be the one who is waiting for guidance that never comes; you are not opening yourself up to others because you do not want to be responsible for any exchange.

A person who takes this path is not able to expand but stays disconnected from his purpose and all skills and abilities that can serve him to fulfil his purpose. When you do not take responsibility of your own well-being, growth and purpose on Earth you exist isolated, ignoring the vastness of the cosmos and the countless opportunities for growth. You think that you are protecting yourself by avoiding challenges but in reality the challenges are the open doors that connect you to your purpose.

When you do not take responsibility of your own growth and prefer to stay passive, you are not protecting yourself; you live in fear. When fear is experienced constantly, it becomes a blockage that is too hard to be removed. Fear and negativity can also be linked to lack of communication.

There are many ways to communicate; ignorance and ego are not part of them. An effective communication should consist of a preparation, trying to understand the imbalances and distortion in a being as well as their unique abilities, understanding, purpose and essence. If you are not able to go through this first step and connect fully to the person, the communication should not take place. Words and the intention of a confused communicator support the distortion on the planet. This teaching should be studied and people who understand it should take responsibility and use it to connect to their growth.

Questions

1. Can you explain the following phrase: "The inability to take responsibility and the lack of communication and understanding are very common patterns among humans."
2. Can you explain the following phrase: "You think that you are protecting yourself by avoiding challenges but in reality the challenges are the open doors to connect you to your purpose."
3. How can you communicate with your own being, humanity and Earth?
4. How can you connect to the cosmos and your astral body?

Introduction

The gods want to communicate and share their light with all human beings on the planet and heal all imbalances and blockages. The light of the gods is transmitted to Earth and we have to become pure channels of the cosmic energy for our own healing and purification as well as the Earth's.

When human beings connect to their true-self, they will be able to follow their purpose and have a life full of remarkable and liberating experiences. Human beings should take a step out from their current spot of confusion and start to see life in its true authentic state. We can acquire awareness when we acknowledge the light in us and use it as a guide.

Wisdom of Thoth: On your Path of Growth

Earth currently experiences high levels of distortion and people find it very hard to connect to truth. Some may think that the distance between their current state and the path of truth is too long and unclear, full of obstacles and secret dangers. In reality the path is only a step away if your intention is pure and unaffected from illusion. There are also people who think that they are walking the path of truth but in reality they are on a diversion. For them truth is a fantasy, a dream state of wellbeing, an excited concept or an attractive idea that may bring clarity and wisdom.

When people fantasize or have ideas about enlightenment, they avoid looking at themselves. Connecting to their true-self, purifying themselves, accepting their imbalances and open up to the cosmic light to receive healing are duties that people will not be reached. Sometimes being intoxicated by those great ideas of freedom, truth and enlightenment, people may experience illusionary pleasures but they do not lead to growth; they are still in a space of distortion.

Human beings on Earth talk about mysteries, hidden truths and secret formulas but they have to understand that the only way to growth is by connecting to their true-self. This natural process of growth becomes a mystery for human beings because their intention is not to connect to their true-self. Diversions take many forms; they may appear as consumerism, having an artificial lifestyle; being attached to certain institutions; having social and financial expectations or even seeking fantastic truths and wisdom.

If you want to connect to truth, connect to your own being, starting from your physical body. Allow the nourishment of the cosmic light to go through you; experience healing and rebirth. Experience your physical body in unity with your whole being, helping you connect to your astral body and the astral plane. The cosmic light can unite you to all that you are and help you on your path of growth.

Questions

1. Why is Earth suffering from distortion and how does this affects your life and grow?
2. What is your true-self and how can you connect to it?

3. How can you purify yourself from distortion?
4. Can you explain the following message: When human beings connect to their true-self they will be able to follow their purpose and have a life full of remarkable and liberating experiences. Human beings should take a step out from their current spot of confusion and start to see life in its true authentic state. We can acquire awareness when we acknowledge the light in us and use it as a guide.

Introduction

Due to Earth's polarities and fragmentation caused by high distortion, people can take a role or a persona and live an artificial lifestyle. This phenomenon happens repeatedly on planet Earth and has caused multiple schisms of the true-self. It seems that people are born to fulfil their path; they start their journey with great hope and often with pure heart and soon they are lost.

Truth is one path and is not related to one's ideas or thoughts. Truth is your unique path that was given to you from birth. It is connected to a greater path, a collective goal of transformation and growth. The divine plan is not concerned with survival. It is concerned with acceleration of growth and your ability to receive and transmit the high light. Those who know truth and have purity as their driving force they will be able to see the sun and they will have their ears open to experience unity with the cosmos.

Wisdom of Thoth: An Act of Life and Creation

There are people on Earth who are suffering from depression. It seems that black clouds are constantly over them and they feel more trapped, confused and limited than other human beings. Their reality and life experiences are affected strongly by the schisms in them. These schisms can produce low energies that can affect the physical body and the mind.

People who suffer from depression feel very weak physically; they may have physical pain that cannot be diagnosed. They have mood swings and feelings of deep suffering. People in this state have a busy mind that generates fear, rejection, loneliness and death. Depression can be healed when the schism is healed and the new being is ready to be reborn.

This can be achieved by either connecting to the cosmic light or achieving a connection with other human beings that have pure intentions and want to heal and support the person that is suffering. It is important for all of you who are connecting to my light right now that you support the weak with your light of purity and connect them to the cosmic light.

Perhaps there are not many people who are able to disconnect from illusion, connect to their true-self and allow the cosmic light to go through them. They have a very important duty and this is to heal humanity and allow the healing to grow on Earth. Many of you probably know people who need your help; do not be afraid to show your purity, acceptance and gratitude for healing humanity and Earth.

It is a task that brings you closer to your essence and also your cosmic growth. You will also experience people going to transform around you and finally you will be able to help others to transform too. Receiving and transmitting, growing and supporting people's growth, allowing the cosmic light to heal you and then allowing other beings to be healed by the cosmic light, are laws that affect Earth and the cosmos. A cosmic law is not enforcement but an act of life and creation.

Questions

1. How can you heal yourself from depression?
2. Why people are not able to disconnect from illusion?
3. How can people transform?
4. Is healing available to all humanity?

Introduction

Many people on Earth confuse the natural life style with a healthy life style. Natural is to live close to Earth, eat what grows on the ground you walk, be part of the planet's growth and detach yourself from all artificiality. A healthy life style prescribed by another human being does not connect you to Earth. You are still a consumer of man-made products and you depend on them.

You are responsible for your current state because you allowed it to grow in you and make strong roots. At your birth you were given all the tools you needed for this journey. You were born with a healthy body and a clear mind, you had passion for life and you were able to share your light with others. The purity of your childhood was given to you as a gift for your entire life cycle. What happened to you? How did you lose your purity and clarity?

If you want to be fully awake you have to be courageous and fight for life.

Wisdom of Thoth: Ignoring your Life and Purpose

Why people on Earth are consuming substances that were made in a factory or a laboratory and they think that this way they can boost their immune system? Do they ever think of their immune system and how to maintain it or they blindly consume what is given to them by the hand of institutions and organizations. Why do people not go directly to Earth in order to receive their nutrients? It is Earth's divine plan to feed her creation; animals and plants are following this natural law. On the other hand, humans not only do not follow it but they try to disconnect from Earth.

There are people on the planet that do not understand that the only way to bring health, longevity and balance is to abandon the man-made chemical substances and processed food and allow Earth to show them the way to nutrition. Some people may say that they have no time for this; they have to eat convenient food.

Why people do not have as their priority their well-being? If you are not able to look after your physical body when Earth is providing everything for you and it is all available, how will you be able to connect to the cosmic light, heal your imbalances and experience life as a cosmic being? Earth is sharing with you her light, her creative power, her ability to sustain life. If you ignore this then you ignore your life and purpose.

Allow truth to find a place in you and with its guidance you will receive clarity and you will reconnect to Earth and the cosmos.

Questions

1. Why people pollute themselves and how can this affect your growth?
2. Can your body show you your purpose?
3. How can Earth heal your being?
4. How can you explain the following phrase: "Allow truth to find a place in you and with its guidance you will receive clarity and you will reconnect to Earth and the cosmos."

Introduction

Escaping the illusion can be a hard task if you want to maintain your passive state. But you have to realize that your current artificial state is affecting every part of your life and will finally lead you to destruction. You are being emptied from all the gifts given to you from birth and you become a controlled being of low light.

Illusion is here and is affecting you right now. What you have to do is to stand up and take your first courageous step out of it. You have the power in you and you can win this battle. The gods are supporting those who are actively seeking true enlightenment. When you are in a passive state, even if you understand that awakening is necessary, you are still asleep and you are supporting the illusion. Clarity will not come to those who know but to those who are stepping out of it.

Truth is one path and is not related to one's ideas or thoughts. Truth is your unique path that was given to you from birth. It is connected to a greater path, a collective goal of transformation and growth.

Wisdom of Thoth: Accept Truth

You have accepted truth and you now you understand illusion; this is the first step to heal yourself and fulfil your purpose. Truth is your purity, your ability to receive and transmit cosmic light, to grow and support others to do the same, to fulfil your purpose on Earth and accept that your physicality is not your only body; your whole being is your astral body, higher-self and creation code.

When you are able to connect to the higher parts of your being, you will be able to transform your existence on Earth, having more clarity and experience unity with the cosmos. You have to erase everything that blocks your growth. You do not do this with fear but with great happiness, seeing yourself free, healthy, able to connect to the cosmic light, allow it to heal you and also to transmit it to other beings. When you meditate, focus on the cosmic light going through you; this way you connect to the cosmos and the cosmic growth. Everything else is illusion and should not occupy your mind.

When you have clarity, you will take the right decisions and you will be ready to move forward successfully. Do not act on impulse because often what you experience is not an expression of your true-self. Allow the cosmic light to go through you and see your impurities, blockages and imbalances leaving your body and make room for transformation and re-birth.

Questions

1. Can you describe the illusion that exists around you?
2. What blocks your growth?
3. Can you explain the following phrase: "Do not act on impulse because often what you do is not an expression of your true-self."
4. How can you purify yourself?

Introduction

There are many spiritual teachers who try to reassure their followers that enlightenment is available to all even if there is a clear division between the enlightened teacher and his/hers students who are desperately trying to receive enlightenment, often unsuccessfully. Human beings have blocked the high energies to grow in them because they are focusing on the five senses stimulation and other artificial sources. They never question and passively follow the social criteria of success and happiness.

Illusion is easily accepted by human beings because by remaining passive they are spoon-fed any false reality. They enjoy when they have to do nothing and on the other hand they are presented with many choices and opportunities which are all illusionary. Humans are an easy target for those who create illusion; they are the type of consumers who will buy everything at any price. There is a reason for that: it is their trauma and the fear of survival which have taken away the clarity.

Wisdom of Astaroth: A Pure State of Existence

There are people on Earth who are celebrating a new shift of consciousness and Earth's ability for rebirth and moving on to a higher energetic state.

Those people want to connect to the cosmos and the message is one of hope. On the other hand there are many people on Earth who are struggling to survive because of poverty, bad health, abuse and destruction or being completely lost in an artificial reality. How can two polarities co-exist and what is the true state of humanity and Earth? Both those states are illusionary because they are supporting duality. Hope and pain are man-made illusions that were created to keep people in a low state. They both teach you that you are not in control of your growth and you cannot be the creator of your purification and transformation.

When you are waiting for the pain to go away or for the wish to come true then you are allowing external forces to take you on a journey that does not lead to your purpose. You are not responsible for other people's growth even if they are your family or close friends because what you know is only your own divine plan and purpose.

Therefore you are only responsible for your own growth and it is your duty to connect to your true-self to help you find your way. If you experience upheaval and turbulence in your life, you have not reached your path yet. Following your path will bring you peace and clarity. You will understand that the challenges are helping you to grow and all your achievements should be shared with others. In this state you do not have fear and pain but you also do not have hope and expectations. When you know what your purpose is, you allow yourself to experience a life being a receiver and transmitter of the cosmic light. In this state of knowing and experience, your true-self and purpose can grow. This is a pure state of existence.

Questions

1. What are the schisms of humanity?
2. Can you explain the following phrase: When you are waiting for the pain to go away or for the wish to come true then you are allowing external forces to take you on a journey that does not lead to your purpose?
3. Can you explain the following phrase: "If you experience upheaval and turbulence in your life, you have not reached your path yet."
4. What is your pure state?

Introduction

We are all connected to each other and energy, which is information, passes from one being to another. Your intention should be to connect to your true-self and fulfil your purpose.

The cosmic light will flow in them and offer them healing and knowing that will clear imbalances. Opening up to the cosmic light will help you become a receiver as well as a transmitter of light. All human beings should spread the light and enable Earth and the rest of the humanity.

We can acquire awareness when we acknowledge the light in us and use it as a guide. When human beings connect to their true-self they will be able to follow their purpose and have a life full of remarkable and liberating experiences.

Wisdom of Thoth: Your True-Self is Part of your Divine Plan

Your true-self cannot be seen or touched because it is not part of Earth's creation but it is related to your divine plan for this reincarnation. Your divine plan was created in the astral plane and you were aware of it before your reincarnation; this means that you did not have a physical body yet to help you experience your reality. The divine plan is part of your astral growth and your true-self and purpose for this life time is just an expansion and growth towards the physical plane. Your true-self and purpose are energy fields and they exist close to your physicality.

If you try to understand your purpose with your mind or senses you will probably get confused because man-made theories will take you on a diversion. If you want to connect to your true-self you have to experience a state of peace where physicality, mind, senses, energies, Earth and the cosmos are all balanced in you and are united.

In this state you can experience the interaction of your physicality with the cosmic energies and you will reach to your true-self and purpose. This state can be achieved by all human beings when you block the manipulation of the mind. Human beings have the ability to perceive life beyond the five senses but illusion and distortion have created a matrix that keeps people in a low state, suffering from imbalances and limitation.

People are forced to be in a state of fear and dissatisfaction and they are reinforced by the media information, consumerism, art, work and even people's thoughts and actions. Human beings are not allowed to be free to experience reality on Earth as their true-self and this is why people find it hard to reach clarity. On the other hand, you are free when you decide to step out from the distortion and have a meaningful life as a receiver and transmitter of energy. When you are able to experience peace in you will also be able to experience a great opening that can make you connect to the cosmos.

Questions

1. Can you explain the following phrase: "Your true-self cannot be seen or touched because it is not part of Earth's creation".
2. How can you connect to your true-self?

3. Why human beings are restricting themselves from experiencing truth and freedom?
4. Can you observe your fears and blockages? What have you learnt from this?

Introduction

On Earth, beings seem to forget their astral existence and this is because they are focusing on the body time-line and the physical reality that surround them. As the physical being grows it becomes affected by the polarities, the fear for survival and the traumas which affect Earth and her creation. If you wish to evolve beyond polarity and fragmentation you have to disconnect from the idea of opposites. In nature there is no fight against two elements there is only a union of the elements, bringing new life.

People on Earth who want to grow, have to disconnect from distorted patterns and illusionary beliefs. This can be achieved by observing yourself. Look at the link between past patterns and present ones, observe artificiality and connect to your true path of growth. Be happy from within. This type of happiness is constant and everlasting but the artificial one fades away quickly and leaves a gap of dissatisfaction and longing. You grow when all actions and thoughts are true to your life path and purpose.

Wisdom of Thoth: Allow Earth's Healing to Reach You

Some of you may ask: Why many human beings cannot connect to Earth and they keep on bringing imbalances and destruction?

Earth has grown to be afraid of her own intention. She has allowed beings that are not part of her creation to connect to her energies use her resources and become part of the life that exists in her. Accepting alien energies was what led Earth to schisms and major imbalances.

When Earth's balance was affected then polarities were created that brought fragmentation and distortion. Earth lost her place in the high realms and her ability to connect to the cosmic light was limited. For Earth to move on to a higher vibrational reality, she will need to detach herself from all alien existence and create a stronger connection with everything that exists in her.

The same fight that blocks Earth's growth is also experienced by humans, animals, plants and other elements. Many animals and plants are already extinct and the human beings are sacrificing themselves in order to get power and control over the planet's resources.

There is a strong belief in humans; they are all fighting for ownership; this idea is illusionary. It is taking over people's minds; this is because beings that do not exist on Earth want to take over people's minds. Many human beings were reincarnated to heal Earth. Many of you were created to be Earth's receivers and transmitters of energy and heal the planet and humanity.

Some of you experienced her Golden age in previous reincarnations and you are coming back to prepare Earth to experience her new golden era. I want to help humanity disconnect from illusion and give them clarity to fulfil their purpose. I want them to see Earth not as a piece of land that can be bought or sold but as a powerful goddess that can create life and can connect directly to the Source. Allow Earth's healing to reach you and be part of her creation.

Questions

1. Can you explain the following phrase: "Earth has grown to be afraid of her own intention."
2. Why do human beings fight for ownership and what effect has this in their lives?
3. What is your purpose on Earth?
4. Can Earth heal humanity?

Introduction

We are the extension of our Source and our essence is the presence of its creative light.

Our High Source has no form, personality or characteristics. Our High Creator is the perfection in the cosmos where everything is effortless, whole and limitless. High Gods can only dream to be in this state of absolute perfection, where there is nothing to see and yet everything exists simultaneously. Let's connect to this high state of perfection and expand ourselves to a limitless, eternal state by connecting to our creation code and the whole creation.

Wisdom of Thoth: Our Source's Intention

The cosmic light is our Source's intention to bring everlasting life and growth to all creation. The Gods do not produce it; their purpose is to direct it and make it spread to all planes, reaching all energy points. We connect to the Source by receiving the cosmic light and allow it to create and maintain life through our being.

The Source is unseen and everything related to its birth and existence is not known to us. This is because our Source is not a being but is a cosmic force for creation. We know that this force is an open and unstoppable flow of energy that constantly generates itself in a speed, quantity and quality that cannot be experienced in any realm. The Gods exist to reach our Source's high light and experience unity with it. Our purpose is to exist in the highest plane and maintaining life throughout the cosmos.

I want you now to look at your purpose and observe your connection to the cosmic light, the Gods and the Source. If you are looking for truth you should accept that the unity in the cosmos is responsible for your own life and growth. Our Source's intention is our purpose, a purpose that is shared by all beings in all planes.

This is why we are united and our existence supports the existence of the cosmos. When this becomes your reality you will be able to disconnect from illusion and fragmentation and have meaningful lives. Connecting to Earth can bring you peace and clarity; this is because you are allowing the cosmic light to go through you and connect to the planet and her creation. Connecting to Earth with pure intention will enable you to exchange energy and experience healing. Unity with Earth and humanity is an important task for all those people who have reincarnated on the planet. This will lead you to your own growth.

Questions

1. What is your understanding about the existence of the Source?
2. What is the intention of our Source?
3. How can we connect to the Source?
4. Does humanity exist in unity with Earth?

Introduction

When we cannot accept our purpose, we create many false representations of it, often related to social criteria and expectations. These false representations are created by us and function as diversions. Some would ask why people do that, what they have to gain from it. There is nothing to be gained. If you follow your true purpose you follow truth and freedom and this is not promoted by your society. Your social expectations teach you a life of restriction where the individual restricts others too. A life of truth and freedom can only be a wild dream for most people on Earth and this is why they do not accept the true purpose. This happens to most people, even the ones who claim to be awake or aware or even enlightened. It is your responsibility, your lesson and study in this life time, to escape the restrictions' plan by nourishing your body and protect your light.

Wisdom of Thoth: How Can You Win the Battle against Illusion and the Control Mechanisms

Human beings are fighting for freedom, truth and growth within the political, social and economic systems that they do not control. They are systems created to control humanity and keep people in a low state of survival. There are many layers of this control: there are rules to control your recourses, giving to you by Earth unconditionally; there are rules to control your understanding of yourself and purpose as well as connecting to others and support their growth.

There are also restrictions to control your expression, tools, connection to your physical body, purification, growth and creation. There is one more layer of control and this has to do with the manipulation of your energy.

This is the highest control and it can be done by manipulating the mind in connection to other energy centres in the physical body. When people are fighting for truth in this system of control, they can only achieve illusionary victories because their energy is feeding the control system and supporting its games.

There is a simpler way to connect to truth and this is to disconnect from all illusion, artificiality, fear, distortion and fragmentation. This can be achieved when you are able to empty your mind, disconnect from social expectation, abandon polarities and connect to your true-self. Your true-self will show you the way to connect to Earth and the cosmos.

This connection and understanding is vital to your growth. When you open up to this experience all layers of control will start to drop. You will be able to connect to the cosmic light and this way you will connect to your whole being that expands in many realms. Instead of giving your power away and exist in a diversion away from your purpose, now you will fully experience your physical body and the energies that connect you to the Earth and the cosmos.

When you are able to exist in this high state, you become a perfect receiver and transmitter of cosmic light and you are able to offer healing to humanity and Earth. This is how you can win the battle against illusion and the control mechanisms. It is time now for humanity to connect fully to the cosmic light and bring growth on Earth.

Questions

1. What are the control mechanisms that cause restrictions in your life?
2. Can you explain the following phrase: "here are many layers of this control: there are rules to control your recourses, giving to you by Earth unconditionally; there are rules to control your understanding of yourself and purpose as well as connecting to others and support their growth."
3. There is one more layer of control and this has to do with the manipulation of your energy. What is your experience?
4. How can you connect to truth?

CHAPTER III

Let's take our intention away from the outer planes which we always think as separate from us and responsible for our limitations. We are all part of the unseen, formless, all-contained, all-created power of our High Creator and we are going to start our quest to high truth and knowledge from this point inside us which unites generates and contains all: our creation code.

Introduction

The High Creator decided that Earth had to be set free to create her path in order to become a living creator. A major gift was given to Earth; she was to become a creator and a god, acting as a meditator of the High Source. Earth went through a transformation when she was not protected anymore and had to cope balancing the rules of creation. Many races, travelers from other star systems, came to Earth to examine and experiment with all that existed and gradually the planet became a low vibrational wasteland; the land of the weak.

Wisdom of Thoth: Earth's Creation and Position in the Galaxy

Many of you want to know about Earth's creation and her position in the galaxy. There are more planets not known to you that are connected to the sun; there are planets that have moved to other solar systems and there are more solar systems connected to each other. When Earth was created, she was designed to support a large planetary system with many suns that worked together to receive and transmit energy to the cosmos.

This planetary system expanded through different planes and was created to connect and bring balance and growth to different energy bodies. This was a time that the different planes were less distinct and cosmic creation had a higher vibration overall. Receiving the cosmic light and connecting to the Source was possible to many beings, including planets and energy fields.

Larger planetary and energy systems were able to experience growth and evolution because they had direct connection to the Source and did not experience limitation and distortion; this was the Source's divine plan. Certain planets, energy fields and energy bodies lost their ability to connect fully to the cosmic light and imbalances were created in them.

Purification was not achievable and they slowly disconnected from the high light. Many planes were created to help parts of creation adjust to a slower pace of growth. Solar systems had to be divided, planets had to be removed and at times their physical form had to change. Earth had to be separated from the planetary system that she belonged to initially and moved to a lower plane. The divine plan is to restore Earth to her higher energetic state and heal distortion and fragmentation that exist in the lower planes.

Questions

1. What do you know about Earth's creation?
2. Can you explain the following phrase: "This planetary system expanded through different planes and was created to connect and bring balance and growth to different energy bodies. This was a time that the different planes were less distinct and cosmic creation had a higher vibration overall. Receiving the cosmic light and connecting to the Source was possible to many beings, including planets and energy fields."
3. What is your understanding of the following phrase: "Many planes were created to help parts of creation adjust to a slower pace of growth."
4. What is Earth's divine plan?

Introduction

When one reincarnates, a life-line is designed. The beings that reincarnate have a specific purpose and were put in the right physical, intellectual and social position to fulfil their purpose. All beings, often without knowing, are attracted to their life purpose and take a parallel route. When they are able to see clearly and find their way then they are awakened, enlightened and connected to their true-self which expands from the physical to the astral plane. When the connection is made, those beings will receive enormous amounts of light to help them deal not only with their physicality but also to help others find their path. All our special tools and talents are stored in the body and are waiting for us to discover them. When you know your body, you understand that is a microcosm of high creation and a link to all life. Your body is your temple and path for growth and expansion to other realms.

Wisdom of Astaroth: Earth's Growth

If you want to know about Earth's growth you should look at the growth of human beings. Most of them are waking up and they already understand that illusion forced on them an artificial reality to be seen as experienced as truth. They understand that they cannot fulfil their purpose if they live according to illusionary ideals. Human beings want to escape their illusionary life patterns and connect to their true-self. Most human beings are comfortable accepting an illusionary lifestyle and illusionary beliefs because this way they do not have to deal with their traumas and schisms. They think that by choosing to disconnect from truth, it will make their life easy and pleasant, hoping for a happy ending. Truth is a great cleanser but you can only connect to it if you are willing to face everything that you are including imbalances and schisms. Earth is divided into different areas of growth and this is why she suffers from imbalances and schisms. She is a Goddess planet; therefore, she has the ability to connect to the Source and create life. This ability is responsible for high growth and there are certain parts of Earth that experience high growth. These parts exist separately from what you know as Earth and have high vibration. The beings who exist there are also high vibrational beings and their way of existence is very different from yours.

Human beings on Earth cannot enter the high vibrational areas. The technology you have is created by your mind and your mind is limited. Your technology tries to conquer and control Earth's creative powers but you will never achieve that and all your attempts will fail. If you were able to see Earth as a high vibrational creator who is able to give you life according to our Source's intention, then you would be able to focus on your own growth which depends on your ability to know your true essence. Why do human beings want to own Earth? Why do they want to create life when this is not their purpose? If you wish to grow, you have to disconnect from illusionary beliefs of authority and see yourselves as part of the link between Earth and the Source.

Questions:

1. How does illusion affect one's growth?
2. What is Earth's ability to grow?
3. How can technology support your growth?
4. Why do human beings want to own Earth?

Introduction

In higher realms life is not the physical body but it is a unity of energies that it is part of a complex electromagnetic field. An astral body cannot be seen or measured by your Earth understanding and criteria; it is a very complex unity of energies which is in constant movement and in connection with our Source.

All living beings are united with the cosmic light and are part of the vast creation of our source. All beings receive guidance to help them grow and evolve and the ones who are chosen to reincarnate on Earth are guided in order to fulfil their purpose, bringing the astral light to the physical plane.

Wisdom of Astaroth: Cosmic Laws

All cosmic laws support growth and evolution. In the higher realms, life is not the physical body but it is often a unity of many energies that it is part of a complex electromagnetic field. An astral body cannot be seen or measured by your Earth understanding; it is a very complex unity of energies which is in constant movement and in connection with our Source.

In the cosmos there is unity and every being is in constant transformation. This can be achieved by receiving and transmitting cosmic light, experiencing uninterrupted growth and supporting other beings and fields in the cosmos. In high realms there is no personal gain because there is no ego; there are no imbalances because there is no distortion and fragmentation.

Existing in the high realms as an energy-body, you do not have to learn, understand and expand your consciousness. You are created to grow and this is what you experience. One of the natural laws on Earth is the end of a life cycle; in high realms, life is eternal. On Earth, the cycles of growth have to do with the movement of the planets and the elements.

This has inspired human beings to create the idea of time which is another illusionary aspect of the present time. There is a cosmic law that is also a natural law on Earth and this is life and creation. Earth is able to create and maintain life and this is an ability that she carried with her from her golden era. We want to teach humanity about cosmic life and laws because this will help them disconnect from illusion and purify themselves.

We want humanity to grow not as a parasite but as a cosmic creation on a planet that is going through a transformation. You can all support this by disconnecting from illusion and artificiality and connecting to the cosmos and the Source. We are all part of our Source's high light; we unite and support each other's growth that feeds the whole creation.

Questions

1. What is an astral body and how it experiences life?
2. What is your understanding of the following phrase: "In the cosmos there is unity and every being is in constant transformation."
3. Can you explain the following phrase "We want humanity to grow not as a parasite but as a cosmic creation on a planet that is going through a transformation."
4. How can you exist in unity with humanity and Earth, supporting growth on the planet?

Introduction

In this teaching, Thoth teaches us about the connection between the natural and cosmic laws and how they support life in all planes.

Wisdom of Thoth: The Difference Between the Cosmic Laws and the Natural Laws

When people exist in artificiality and distortion they are not fully connected to the natural or the cosmic laws. Instead they are connected to social mechanisms and rewards systems that encourage them to exist in a maze of confusion. If people were able to connect to their physical bodies, they will be able to heal every disease and also support the healing of others. Healing is a natural law. Your body has the ability to heal and renew itself. It also has the ability to connect to the cosmos and Earth for nourishment and healing. If you want to discover more natural laws you have to look at processes that involve the whole being and are constant because they bring growth. Some of you may ask: what is the difference between natural and cosmic laws? They are linked and support each other, allowing the cosmic light to enter all parts of creation. The cosmic laws can transform in order to support life in different planes. In the astral plane they are cosmic laws supporting high growth and on Earth become natural laws to support Earth's growth.

Questions

1. What is your experience with artificiality and distortion?
2. Is healing a natural law?
3. What is the connection between cosmic and natural laws?

Introduction

The astral plane is an enormous, multidimensional space of transformation which is divided into many sub-planes of various energetic structures. The people of Earth have a great deal of support and guidance coming to them from the astral plane but they choose not to communicate with the light in you.

Wisdom of Thoth: The astral plane

The astral plane is a complex electromagnetic field and its energy occupies the greatest part of the cosmic creation. It is divided into sub levels that have different vibration and growth. A simple way to explain this in Earth terms is that the lower sub levels are closer to the lower energetically planes of the cosmos including the Earth plane and the more you go higher the vibration changes and beings can move to these different levels when they are able to go through different growth cycles.

Reincarnations are part of these cycles for beings that exist in the lower sub levels in the astral plane. The greatest space of the astral plane is its core where energy and cosmic creation is being produced. There are also sub planes in the astral plane that have higher vibration than the core and the beings that exist there are responsible for regulating or directing the process of cosmic creation, maintaining life in all planes. The higher self exists in these sub planes. Your true and permanent body is your astral because it was created to exist being limitless and eternal. The physical body is Earth's creation to help you exist on the planet during your reincarnation. Within your physical body there is the light of the astral body. This is because you do reincarnate on Earth to support the planet's growth but you also have a divine plan that is supporting your astral growth. Your astral body's light can enter different bodies during different reincarnations.

The higher self can be seen as a guide or as a connector between the astral body and the source. The astral body cannot connect to the source without connecting first to the higher self. So the higher self can also be seen as the highest energetic reflection of the astral body which also has a permanent state.

Questions

1. What is the astral plane?
2. Can human beings connect and experience astral growth?
3. What is the purpose of reincarnation?
4. What is the higher-self?

Introduction

Earth is able to create a great variety of plants, animals and other substances in order to nourish her creation. In ancient times, human beings were connected to nature and were aware of all the different plants and how they can be used for nourishment and healing.

The wisdom of the plant is part of the wisdom of the culture and outsiders do not have this wisdom. Human beings were connected to nature and were aware of all the different plants and how they can be used for nourishment and healing.

Wisdom of Thoth: The Use of Ancient Psychedelic Herbs

All planets are alive. Earth is a unique planet with a unique creation. Life can exist in different forms. Most planets have many resources eternally and there are different types of beings who exist there. Life is abundant in the universe and there are many lifeforms different to the ones that exist on Earth and other times they are life forms with no physical existence and cannot be detected by your five senses.

Earth is able to create a great variety of plants, animals and other substances in order to nourish her creation. In ancient times, human beings were connected to nature and were aware of all the different plants and how they could be used for nourishment and healing. Earth has created plants and other substances to cure all imbalances and this is the true practice for well-being. People from many different parts of the world were aware that plants could be used to help them escape reality and connect them to beings from other planes. Local people knew how to use them and were aware of the outcome and how to avoid imbalances. Those plants were only to be taken by people who were trained and serve a certain purpose such as a healer, a priest, and oracle and so on. There were also ceremonies to prepare the users and enhance the effect. It is important to understand that the beings that use these plants have a special purpose and already have the ability to receive information from different realms, cure or pass information to others. This cannot be achieved by all, only by those who have the tools and qualities to serve their communities. When these people connect to different realms this does not mean that they have high consciousness or they have achieved high growth.

There are people from the west who want to experiment with these plants and they do. It is possible that you will have unusual experiences with beings from other planes and perhaps receive some information or you may even have a horrific experience that can lead to imbalance. Westerners are very curious but they never takethe time to understand that these plants grow in certain areas for a reason and people who live there are aware of their power and how to use them. The wisdom of the plant is part of the wisdom of the culture and outsiders do not have this wisdom. My advice is that people from other parts of the world should not rely on stimulants to expand their consciousness. Growth can be achieved by following your path and connecting to the cosmic light.

Questions

1. What is your connection with Earth?
2. What is your understanding of Earth's creation?
3. What is your experience with healing plants?
4. Can a healing plant define your human experience?

Introduction

Earth in the golden era was a luscious land with the most extraordinary variety of plants and animals, rocks and formations. The gods created mountains of crystal to be used as receivers and transmitters of energy and maintain the planet's state as a high vibrational being. Gods intended Earth to be a planet of many colours and shapes for the countless plants, animals and other species.

Wisdom of Astaroth: Animals and their process of growth and evolution

During the Golden Age many animals and plants were created and when Earth became a god creator planet, she was able not only to nourish but to create more animals and plants as well different elements. Humanoid beings were not part of Earth's creation, even though there were many gods, demi-gods and their helpers who had a form similar to humanoid and existed on the planet. The ancestors of the human beings on Earth were different astral races who visited Earth in different times and created civilisations. During the golden era, all beings lived in harmony and existed in a high dimensional plane.

The cosmic light was able to nourish them and connect them to other beings on Earth and other planes. Animals that had a short life, they also had a slower growth. But there were also animals that had a long lifecycle and were part of the astral plane as well as the Earth atmospheres. Not all animals had the same consciousness or life purpose. Certain species had an astral body and were able to evolve. Being an animal it meant that they had a different form. Our form affects our growth and gives us certain characteristics, tools and qualities to help us learn lessons about creation and continue to grow.

Animals may not understand your language, your manners or your civilisation but they are also in a process of growth and evolution. They receive light, connect to astral beings and follow guidance from the astral plane. Animals have fewer imbalances than human beings and demonstrate purity and truth in their actions. They also think but because they are connected to their true-self they do not need to speculate, plan and imitate truth. However, because of the fragmentation and distortion of the planet, they are also affected and have lost some of their powers. Animals are connected to Earth and understand that healing is needed for her to continue to grow. They are also aware of the imbalances carried by human beings and many of them want to heal humanity and see themselves and as the protectors of the planet. Animals live according to cosmic laws and they can be your teachers to help you escape illusion.

Questions

1. What is your understanding of the golden era?
2. Can you see balance and unity in all Earth's creation?
3. What is your understanding of the following message: "Our form affects our growth and gives us certain characteristics, tools and qualities to help us learn lessons about creation and continue to grow.
4. "Animals live according to cosmic laws and they can be your teachers to help you escape illusion." What is your experience?

Introduction

Is your life toxic? Observe your patterns, purify and grow.

Wisdom of Thoth: The toxic invasion

There are people on Earth who are supporting the idea of poisonous substances entering the body and allowing pollution to enter all parts of their being. Many people on Earth are not aware that the food they eat, the water they drink, the air they breathe and even their actions and thoughts are polluted by forces of destruction and illusion. Some of you have started to wake up and want to disconnect from destruction and illusion and create better life conditions for yourselves and others. This is a good step forward for the people who live in societies that restrict them from following growth. People who have lived in a state of illusion and have been disconnected from truth, they intent to accuse certain groups or forces for bringing destruction but they never observe themselves supporting illusion. This way they allow it to grow in them and others. It is important for all human beings to be nourished by Earth and protect themselves from all toxic substances, to guide others to do the same and live a life without fear.

There are people on Earth that are not affected by the toxic invasion, the illusion and the distortion that thrives in your western society. There are groups of people that are connected to Earth and live in peace with everything that exists. They are not suffering from pollution and they constantly experience regeneration in themselves and the planet. Are you ready to disconnect from all illusion and follow the footsteps of the groups mentioned? By being a channel of cosmic light you can regenerate your whole being and help others do the same including the whole planet. Earth and her creation are able to sustain life because they are constantly transforming, growing and evolving. For this to happen in a more effective way, Earth and her creation need to connect to the cosmic light, purify themselves from all imbalances, transform into a new being and transmit the light of the cosmos to the planet and her creation. If you are able to achieve this task which is a fundamental cosmic law then all fear, destruction, manipulation and pollution will disappear. There is not darkness when the sun shines; there are no imbalances when you complete a purification process; there is no fear when you know your purpose; there is not anxiety when you are creating truth and growth in others. Your being is the microcosm that effects the macrocosm; therefore you have to focus on its growth and start a process of purification.

Questions:

1. What is your understanding of wellbeing?
2. Are you receiving nourishment from Earth?
3. What is a toxic invasion and how can you heal yourself?

Introduction

I want you to experience your physical body as a unity of all different parts and that there is a collective purpose and growth. If you accept that then you will also have to accept that the energy structure that supports your physical body works as a link between your astral existence and your physicality. You are connected to your astral body because your whole being is a unity. If you are able to disconnect completely from your astral body then you do not exist as part of the cosmic creation.

Wisdom of Thoth: Experience Growth and Unity with the Cosmos

Many people on Earth are trying to explain their energy structure. There are people in your time that have used ancient wisdom to explain energy and the way it forms each being. Some people talk about chakras and their relation to different parts of the body as well as different dimensions. The human mind's intention is to divide and give distorted meanings to most experiences and ideas. I may surprise you with I what I am going to say but I do not want that people focus on the division of the body even though it consists of different organs that have their own qualities and purpose. I want you to experience your physical body as a unity of all different parts and that there is a collective purpose and growth. If you accept that then you will also have to accept that the energy structure that supports your physical body works as a link between your astral existence and your physicality. You are connected to your astral body because your whole being is a unity. If you are able to disconnect completely from your astral body then you do not exist as part of the cosmic creation.

Some of you have questions about different dimensions and they want to know what dimension they are experiencing right now. Being in a physical body you can only experience the third dimensional reality however, when you connect to your astral body you are able to experience life in higher realms where there is no limitation or distortion. If you are aware of your whole being including your astral body, your higher-self and your creation-code then you can experience life in different realms and you can bring high wisdom to your third dimensional reality. The purpose of all human beings is to connect to the cosmos, experience high growth and transmit cosmic light to Earth and her creation. The different realms are not in a certain numerical order; they cannot be defined and distinguished by your mind/logic. You should not follow the limitation of the mind but allow yourself to experience growth and unity with the cosmos.

Questions

1. Can you experience your energy?
2. Is your physical body a limitation?
3. Are you aware of your being?
4. What is your purpose?

Introduction

The purpose of Earth's creation was to bring stability to a galaxy that suffered destruction and great imbalances. At that time, a number of planets experienced imbalances and had to alter their rotation. The only way to bring harmony to this galaxy was by creating a creator planet that will be able to produce life and energy. The moon was not part of the galaxy but it was brought to secure the alignment of Earth and sun and also support life on Earth. The moon gave protection to Earth but it also operated as a barrier and blocked energies from the high realms to come to her and the planet's vibration became lower. The gods' intervention on Earth was also blocked. The moon attracted low energies from the lower spirits who were able to intervene on Earth's energetic fields.

Wisdom of Thoth: The Existence of the Sun in Earth's Galaxy

I will explain to you the purpose of the Sun in connection to the Earth and the galaxy. There are many planetary bodies similar to what you know as the Sun, in different planes in the cosmic creation. They were created before all other planets and there are centers of high creation similarly to the creation of the Gods.

The Sun is the highest receiver and transmitter of energy in your galaxy and all life is supported, linked and created by the Sun's high energy. There are Suns in higher vibrational planes that are able to connect directly to the Source; their light can reach vast cosmic areas of growth. Suns are able to receive and transmit light to each other and often experience high growth that is not shared by other planets.

In many of your mythologies, the Sun was believed to be the highest God and the life bringer. This is because the Sun is not planet as science tries to explain but is a high energy body which is purified and has a constant and uninterrupted connection to the cosmos and the Source.

The Sun does not exist in your third dimensional reality but expands in different planes; its energy is able to reach Earth but in order to bring life, it connects to higher realms too. The Sun cannot be touched by human beings; its high energy does not match the third dimensional reality. Similarly, to the cosmic light the Sun's energies can reach you and create life on Earth.

It is the Sun's sperm that makes Earth fertile. There are planetary bodies who were created to be Suns but there are also others who became that. Earth was created to support the Sun to bring life to a much bigger planetary system, galaxy, and be the connector between lower and higher planes. The connection between planets is quite complex.

Their growth affects a great number of beings and energies and this can bring evolution, stagnation or destruction. The movement of the planets and their co-existence are affected by various changes. The planets are in constant connection with the energies of the Sun for guidance and support in their path of growth and evolution.

Questions

1. What do you know about the Sun-Earth alignment?
2. Can you explain the following phrase: The Sun does not exist in your third dimensional reality but expands in different planes; it energy is able to reach Earth but in order to bring life; it connects to higher realms too."
3. How does your growth support humanity's growth?
4. How your growth can be affected by your unity with Earth?

Introduction

All living beings are united with the cosmic light and are part of the vast creation of our source not aware of it. All beings receive guidance to help them grow and evolve and the ones w\ho are chosen to reincarnate on Earth are guided in order to fulfil their purpose, bringing the astral light to the physical plane.

The gods' project is to awake the inhabitants of Earth; disconnect them from the illusion; pass the divine light to them which will help them connect to their true-self and recognize their tools and purpose; enable them to heal Earth and the rest of the humanity. The gods want to communicate with all beings on the planet and heal all imbalances and blockages. The light of the gods is transmitted to Earth and we have to become pure channels of the cosmic energy for our own healing and purification as well as the Earth's.

Wisdom of Thoth: Connecting to the Cosmic Light

Many of you are connected to the cosmic light and this helps you to maintain life in all realms and go through a process of purification to clear the imbalances that you experience on Earth. The cosmic light is the essence of our Source. Our Source is not divided into different bodies, higher self and creation code. Exists as one state-force-light and unstoppable/boundless/eternal creation.

Our Source connects to everything that exists and a simple explanation of this connection is that the cosmic light is our Source's intention, creativity and also the hands that want to reach out and create in all beings. The cosmic light travels to all planes and its ability to create varies according to growth.

The Gods can maintain and create life when the cosmic light goes through them. This is how they connect to the Source and become a creation tool. When the cosmic light travels to the astral plane, it helps beings grow and transform constantly and without interruption. When the Gods receive the cosmic light, they direct it to the astral plane because not only it is the largest plane but also is an energy space of high growth.

It is the birth place of all beings. The cosmic light continuous its journey to all the other planes.

Due to limitation and distortion on Earth, the creative abilities of the cosmic light are restricted. When more people are able to connect to their true-self and know their purpose the more cosmic light will enter humanity and Earth. When you are disconnected from illusion and experience truth, you will purify yourself from imbalances but you will be helping others to do the same.

When you experience growth, you will realize that you cannot fulfil your purpose if you do not help others to achieve this too. We want to unite humanity and connect them to Earth. We want to disconnect you from fragmentation that keeps you divided. All beings have a purpose, special skills; they are able to receive and transmit light and connect to Earth. When you experience unity you will understand that there is not superior or inferior being only ignorance.

Questions

1. What is your understanding of the following phrase: "Our Source is not divided into different bodies, higher self and creation code. Exists as one state-force-light-eternal and unstoppable creation."
2. How can you transmit cosmic light to others?
3. What does restrict your ability to understand your purpose?
4. Can you explain the following phrase: "When you experience growth, you will realize that you cannot fulfil your purpose if you do not help others to achieve this too."

Introduction

All human beings have a unique path leading to a unique purpose and have their own unique tools. When astral beings are selected to reincarnate they go through an intense preparation. While they are in the astral plane, they study the purpose of their reincarnation; they connect to their guides who will help them reincarnate and guide them when they are on Earth.

Reincarnation is often a challenging experience for astral beings and this is why they need to prepare themselves and make the connections with their guides. When they are finally on Earth, they still have access to the astral knowledge, but because of the low vibration on the planet, their connection with the astral plane can only be achieved in certain states like the dream state.

Your spirit guides support your growth and their intention is to help you escape the maze of distortion and illusion. They can see your purpose and want to pass this knowing to you.

Wisdom of Thoth: Spirit Guides

All human beings on Earth have guides. They exist in the astral plane and they are the ones who are first informed about your reincarnation and its purpose. They receive the divine plan which is a guideline of the main events in your life. Before you reincarnate you connect to your guides in order to look at the plan and make an agreement regarding your reincarnation.

You then become aware of your purpose, the reason of your reincarnation, your special tools and abilities and the opportunities that will be given to you to develop them and use them in order to fulfil your purpose. Your guides help you during your transformation, becoming a physical being and support you to stay alive and balanced in your early days.

Getting older, human beings are affected by illusion and with their mind disconnect from their guides. This is happening because the mind is manipulated to accept only the five-sense-reality as true. Your guides are always connected to you and this can be experienced when you follow your intuition or synchronicity.

Accepting your guides, you reopen the connection with them and you are able to receive guidance. When you are able to clear distortion and illusion, your connection with your guides becomes stronger. When you are able to be in state of peace and not being affected by negativity, anger and disappointment then you will connect to your guides' support and knowing.

They are observing you and they want to help you find your way to your true-self and purpose. They want to help you avoid diversions and open up to the cosmic light that will heal your imbalances and bring you clarity. When you are on your path, you will be able to connect to them and receive direct guidance. This is a connection worth maintaining.

Questions

1. What support you can receive from your guides?
2. How can you connect to your guides?
3. How can your guides help you clear distortion?
4. Can you explain the following phrase: "When you are on your path, you will be able to connect to them and receive direct guidance."

Introduction

Let's take our intention away from the outer planes which we always think as separate from us and responsible for our limitations. We are all part of the unseen, formless, all-contained, all-created power of our High Creator and we are going to start our quest to high truth and knowledge from this point inside us which unites generates and contains all: our creation code.

It seems that truth seekers exist in a labyrinth of ideas, words and visuals and they are desperately looking for a way out but without success. There are many beings on Earth who are longing to achieve clarity, connecting to their true purpose, but they are entangled in the web of illusion and limitation. Thoth wants to reach all beings with his light and this is his advice: when people are able to empty their minds from all beliefs, aspirations, needs, suffering, pleasures and longings, they will discover their creator.

Wisdom of Thoth: Energy Centres

When you experience truth, you connect to the cosmic light and bring healing to your whole being. Your physical body consists of different organs that they are vital for keeping you alive and receiving the cosmic light. There are many centres in your body that receive and store energy; on the other hand every cell is a centre able to receive and transmit light.

Your heart is a communicator and creator. It creates a connection between your being and intuition. It also allows feelings to transform into great tools such as acceptance, kindness and love. These tools can help you connect to your true-self but when they are distorted they connect you to fear, anxiety and limitation. When you are able to connect to truth, you are able to heal the heart centre and use it great gifts for healing and creating life structures on Earth.

Questions

1. How can you connect to the cosmic light?
2. Can you explain the following phrase: "There are many centres in your body that receive and store energy; on the other hand every cell is a centre able to receive and transmit light."
3. How can your heart support your growth?
4. Can you explain the following phrase: "When you are able to connect to truth, you are able to heal the heart centre and use it great gifts for healing and creating life structures on Earth."

Introduction

This teaching explains the use of prayer and the way it can affect your growth. Religions encourage their believers to pray to God and ask to forgive them or to empower them. Can a prayer disconnect you from illusion, teach you truth and freedom and help you connect to your astral body?

Wisdom of Thoth: Prayer

It is common for human beings to try to connect to cosmic existence through prayer. Some of you may ask: how effective is prayer and who do you connect to when you pray? This has to do with your intention, your ability to connect to the cosmos and your ability to purify yourself, disconnect from illusion and be able to transmit and receive light from the cosmos and the Earth.

For some people, prayer is an energetic communication between them, their astral body and all beings that are connected to their growth such as their guides. These people have pure intention; they are focusing on their growth on Earth in connection to their astral growth.

This form of prayer is normally non-verbal because the being is focusing on receiving and transmitting light, connecting to high planes and supporting the growth of Earth and humanity. This communication when it is done with purity and clarity is very effective. There are people on Earth who are praying to a certain God that has a persona and an ego.

Your religions want you to prey to Gods that have a human understanding and often a human body, this way they can understand and carry your imbalances and limitations. Praying to achieve illusionary goals that are linked to social expectations is often expressed in prayers to the Gods of your religions.

Praying in order to stop the suffering, the fear and pain is totally acceptable and recommended by your religions. When you do this, you accept illusion as truth, you do not experience purification and you give your power and ability to grow away. Prayer becomes a bondage which will lock you to a low state of limitation. This way, illusion can take over and manipulation can affect your being. People are able to transform their lives and it is their responsibility and duty to grow and fulfil their purpose.

Questions

1. How effective is prayer and who do you connect to when you pray?
2. Can you explain the following phrase: "Praying to achieve illusionary goals that are linked to social expectations are often expressed in prayers to the Gods of your religions."
3. Can you explain how a prayer becomes a bondage that can lock you to a low state of limitation?
4. Are you responsible for your own growth?

Introduction

When people start to wake up and observe the effect of illusion in their lives, they become angry and frustrated. They want to fight injustice, destroy the social pyramid, demonstrate against the social systems of illusion and perhaps create a new existence on Earth. Thoth is teaching us that by fighting an enemy we create an enemy. Fighting is an illusionary process that takes us away from our truth and leads us to a fragmented state. By fighting illusionary enemies with illusionary weapons, we do not disconnect from illusion and distortion. We are here to support ourselves and others to grow to our pure state and follow our divine plan. For this to happen we have to live in a state of peace.

Wisdom of Thoth: Fighting for Injustice

The people of Earth are divided and remain divided, fighting for their rights. There is a race, some call it fight for truth and equality and many people are involved in it. There are genuine people who want to see the poor having enough resources to survive and continue their life cycle. There are humans who want to wake up others but they use their ego to achieve this.

I know that many of you are passionate about justice and equality but I have to say that your path leads to diversion. You may be surprised if I say to you that by fighting you are supporting illusionary divisions and fragmentation. You are fighting an enemy therefore you are creating an enemy. You have anger and negativity regarding your situation and you make them your weapons; this way you spread negativity to others instead of releasing imbalances.

By fighting illusionary enemies with illusionary weapons, you tie yourself even more to illusion and distortion. My advice to you is to remain in a peaceful state and observe yourself and the situation you are in. Try to answer the following questions: who are you fighting for and what will be the outcome of this? Is this fight part of your experience of true-self and does it guide you to your purpose? Is this fight related to the ego and the persona?

Does it help you restore clarity and heal your imbalances?

You are here to support yourselves and others grow and this is your only fight. If you give yourself to this duty, you are going to be a winner; it is part of your divine plan and it follows the cosmic laws.

All human beings who are fighting for justice they should connect to Earth instead. They should allow her energies to connect to them and become the great receivers and transmitters of cosmic light. Earth has created you to be a transmitter and receiver to help her connect to the cosmos and complete her transformation. This is your challenge and your reward.

Questions

1. Can you explain the following phrase: "The people of Earth are divided and remain divided, fighting for their rights."
2. Should you fight for injustice? Will this help you grow and create a community of truth?
3. Can you explain the following phrase: All human beings who are fighting for justice they should connect to Earth instead."
4. How can you stay in a peaceful state?

Introduction

All living beings exist in unity with the vast creation of our source. Humans who exist in third dimensional Earth are connected to all parts of their being such as the astral body, higher-self and creation code but due to distortion and fragmentation are not aware of it. All beings receive guidance to help them grow and evolve and the ones who are chosen to reincarnate on Earth are guided in order to fulfil their purpose, bringing the astral light to the physical plane.

The physical body connects you to the Earth's energies and shows you how to create with your limited resourses. Your five senses are also messengers of information and humans on Earth have almost exhausted all different ways of experiencing life with their senses.

Create the balance needed for all your bodies to grow and live a life of truth and purpose.

Wisdom of Thoth: Understanding the Connection between the Physical and the Astral Body

Some people may ask: if I do not sense or understand that the physical body is connected to the astral how can I experience it?

The process is simple. Connecting to your true-self is your first step; that will give you clarity, connect you to the cosmic light and help you to follow your purpose.

People who are able to follow their purpose, they are connecting to their true-self. Many human beings on Earth are not able to achieve that because they accept illusion as truth and live a life with a social purpose. All beings need to start experiencing truth and freedom in their lives because the unity of the two is a driving force that can lead you to your true-self and guide you to fulfil your purpose.

Existing in a peaceful state means that you exist in unity with your whole being and you allow the cosmic energy to go through you connecting the astral and the physical body. When you are in a meditative state and you are able to disconnect from all illusion, negativity and artificiality, you exist in a space that is limitless.

You experience constant growth that has nothing to do with challenges and obstacles and it is experienced by you like a flow of immense power of transformation. When you are in this state you connect to the astral plane. You are opening up to unlimited opportunities of cosmic existence and this knowing is transferred to your physical body.

When you are able to achieve this, your imbalances will be diminished and illusion will not be strong enough to affect you. Knowing and exercising, truth, freedom and unity between your astral and physical body will transform you to a high receiver and transmitter of light. You will be able then to achieve your purpose and transform humanity and Earth.

Questions

1. Are you able to connect to your physical body and what have you learnt from this connection?

2. Is distortion blocking you from connecting to your physical body and how do you experience this?
3. How can you disconnect from distortion?
4. Can you explain the following phrase: "Knowing and exercising, truth, freedom and unity between your astral and physical body will transform you to a high receiver and transmitter of light."

Introduction

Some people may be wondering: why do we need to have a body and live with the fear and limitation of death? Believe me; your bodies are very precious. A living being consists of many different bodies and all of them are messengers of information. The physical body connects you to the Earth's energies and shows you how to create with your limited recourses. Your five senses are also messengers of information and humans on Earth have almost exhausted all different ways of experiencing life with their senses.

Human beings have many chances in their lifetime to evolve and connect to their astral body. Evolution is taking place on Earth but is not helping the planet's vibration to rise. All beings that reincarnate on Earth are responsible for connecting to her energies, help the vibration to rise and the trauma to be healed.

You either choose truth or illusion; anything in between leads you straight to illusion. Some may ask: how can we escape what we know as normal life when we have allowed illusion to form every single aspect of our lives? My answer is this: if you are so entangled in the illusion, why are you seeking awakening and enlightenment? If your life can give you all the nourishment that you need why are you still looking for your path and purpose? The illusion can trap you to support your own enslavement; the truth is transparent and is part of your astral evolution.

Wisdom of Thoth: Understanding the connection between the physical and the astral body. Part 2

Many of you may have questions about the connection between the physical and the astral plane; the astral body and its connection with the physical body. The astral plane is a space of creation and life transformation. All beings that exist in the cosmos have a creation-code and this is the seed of our Source that created your being and exists in a plane that is higher than the astral plane.

The creation code exists as part of the Source and is able to generate different forms of life that can expand and transform. These forms of life are created in the astral plane with the light of our Source when it connects to the creative powers of the Gods, working together as one.

The astral plane is divided into different sub-planes and this has to do with the type of growth and purpose of the beings that occupy it. At the same time all sub planes are connected by cosmic laws and by the light of creation. Your astral body is not solid but it is an energy form that cannot be described by your five senses.

This energy form is in constant transformation and experiences everlasting growth. For this to happen, the astral body needs to connect to the cosmic light. Your astral growth affects your physical growth because the physical is an extension of the astral energy transformed into a physical body. If you are able to connect to your true-self, fulfil your purpose and support transformation experienced by Earth and humanity then you have achieved high growth.

You are able to receive the light from the astral plane to your physical reality and you are able to create with it. At the end of a life cycle your physical body returns to Earth and you gradually return to the astral plane. You already exist in the astral plane and you have to go through a process of purification and detachment from the persona and imbalances that were created during your reincarnation.

Questions

1. What is the connection between your physical and your astral body?
2. What is the creation code?
3. Can you describe the astral plane?
4. What happens at the end of a reincarnation?

Introduction

Human beings on Earth, even if they live a tormented life, they can still connect to the creator. The difference is that the knowledge does not penetrate the physical plane but mainly stays in the astral plane. They have great capabilities but the low vibration which is becoming constantly lower does not allow any evolution to take place. Currently on Earth there are many groups which try to promote spirituality and wellbeing. This is a sign that Earth's vibration is very low and the living conditions are very poor even for the people who live in the privileged parts of the Earth.

Many leaders and practitioners of the arts of manipulation were attracted to sacred knowledge that they though it will help them empower themselves and connect them to high beings. Many expeditions and wars of destruction took place on Earth to help the leaders acquire sacred knowledge. This caused the end of the mystery schools.

Wisdom of Thoth: The Enormous Potential of Self

Human beings tried to safeguard sacred knowledge in order to protect it from distortion, destruction and death. Many leaders and practitioners of the arts of manipulation were attracted to this knowledge that they though it will help them empower themselves and connect them to high beings. Many expeditions and wars took place on Earth for people of power to acquire sacred knowledge.

The place of The City of Shambhala (Tibet) was a mystery school connected to other mystery schools that existed in the areas of Europe and Asia. Many of those mystery schools were invaded and destroyed and their members had to take sanctuary in remote areas that were less accessible. The people who lived in there were students and teachers of cosmic truth.

They were all connected to the high energies of Earth and this made it possible for them to connect to the cosmos. All people who lived there understood cosmic truths and they participated in rituals. Wisdom was not a privilege but a gift to all beings that are able to connect to the light of the cosmos and understand their purpose.

The purity and connection that those people were able to experience then are now diminished and altered because they accepted visitors who were against growth. You are asking me if there is an entrance in this area that leads to the hollow Earth. Human beings cannot enter the hollow Earth. You can use telepathy to connect to beings that exist there; you can have visions of it.

Some of the first races that came to Earth and experienced the Golden age, they now live in Earth hollow to protect themselves from destruction. Many people are interested in reading about mystery schools and the knowledge and growth they shared with their members. I will advise you not to follow illusion by fantasizing what you cannot experience yourself. Do not divide people into masters and students; you cannot be a master if you are not a student. Growth is constant and mastery is an illusion. Everything that exists on Earth and the cosmos is in you and you have to focus on the enormous potential of self. Allow transformation to take place, allow your light to transform others.

Questions

1. What was the work of the mystery schools?
2. What is your understanding of cosmic truth?
3. Can you explain the following phrase: "Wisdom was not a privilege but a gift to all beings that are able to connect to the light of the cosmos and understand their purpose."
4. Is fantasy illusionary? What is your experience?

Introduction

When you are purified from the illusion and you are able to see yourself naked and pure then you will instantly see your purpose and will have access to all cosmic truths. We want humanity to wake up in order to participate in Earth's growth. Earth and her creation suffer from the same disease and this is a schism of the true-self and the growth of illusion.

Wisdom of Thoth: Earth's Purification

Earth has been going through a long process of purification which was interrupted because of the great schisms that were created every long time ago.

Our Source has allowed us to support Earth to complete her purification, in order to transform to a goddess of high light and re-experience her golden era. You have to understand that Earth's cycles of growth are much longer than what you experience as a human being on Earth and may take thousands of years. It is important that you are supporting Earth's purification by receiving and transmitting cosmic light and teaching new generations to do the same. This way you will create a constant flow of energy between the cosmos and Earth which will support her growth and evolution.

When humanity wakes up and connects to the cosmos, becoming a transmitter and receiver of light, Earth will experience her connection to the Source and will follow the path of truth, leading to her purpose. When this happens all lower energies that are creating a low frequency matrix on Earth will have to be banished and all human beings who are supporting this will either purify and grow with Earth or leave the planet. A high vibrational planet cannot sustain fragmentation, distortion and destruction.

Some of you are wondering about disasters such as earthquakes. These disasters are caused by the greed of human beings to possess more of Earth's resources. Certain human beings do not understand that Earth is not a possession that will bring them more wealth and power over humanity. She is a living goddess and a creator of life and was created according to cosmic laws and with the light of our Source. If human beings helped Earth purify, the whole planet could regain balance and what you call Earth disasters will occur to support growth; it will be an interaction between the inner core and the surface which will bring Earth great abilities to create life. Humanity should wake up to this challenge and support Earth's transformation and growth.

Questions

1. Can you describe Earth's purification process?
2. How can you support Earth's purification?
3. Can humanity and Earth connect and grow together?
4. What is your understanding of the following phrase: "She is a living goddess and a creator of life and was created according to cosmic laws and with the light of our Source."

Introduction

What separates you from your true-self? Why can you not see your purpose clearly?

The gods' project is to awaken the inhabitants of Earth; show them the way out of the maze of illusion, help them to connect to their true-self and recognize their tools and purpose; enable them to heal Earth and the rest of humanity. The gods want to communicate with all beings on the planet and heal all imbalances and blockages. Their light is transmitted to Earth and we have to become pure channels of the cosmic energy for our own healing and purification as well as the Earth's.

We are all part of an eternal divine plan which is not limited to patterns and forms. All creation exists in unity. We all receive and transmit light. We are all creators and we have the tools to maintain balance not only in us but also in all beings that are connected to us. When humanity suffers from imbalances and distortion, the planet is also suffering from the same imbalance. The illusion and fragmentation are the symptoms.

When a planet is not able to receive cosmic light because of blockages, it has a slow growth. This affects the balance of many other beings as well as other planets. The light of our creator should shine on Earth, purification and transformation should take place now.

Teaching of Christian Rosenkreutz: Challenges and Growth

All beings who reincarnate on Earth will meet obstacles on their way to growth. Blockages, imbalances, confusion and separation from their true-self are challenges you all have to face. This is how you connect to Earth and the third dimensional reality. You are all united with Earth. She supports your existence; the challenges you have to face are part of your growth not only on this plane but also on the astral plane.

People on Earth wish to have a good life; a comfortable and prosperous life.

I was once interested in being prosperous and having power over others. I wanted to possess all wisdom, unique gifts and superhuman abilities. I wanted to be the master of all kings and have the grace of the Gods. In this state of illusion, I disconnected from my true-self and purpose and I created obstacles everywhere I turned. My success turned into a great challenge and I was not able to see where my route was leading to. I made people believe in me but my weaknesses affected their lives too.

Suddenly I realized that my life was going to end soon and all my plans would never be realized. As I was very close to death, the light of my own existence reached me. I stood naked in front of the light of my higher-self without plans, ambition and superiority. I was empty of the persona, the social status and the power that was hidden in ambition. I had clarity and, for the first time, I experienced what the Gods describe as "diaphanous". I am energy and I can reach other energetic points in the cosmos. In this state you have no limitations, blockages or imbalances.

There are no hidden mysteries, dark paths and confusion when you understand yourself as pure energy that exists and grows in many planes. This was my rebirth on Earth; a new being who is able to bring the light of the Gods to Earth, heal and enlighten humanity and prepare the way for others to heal Earth and restore her to her Golden Age.

Questions

1. What are your challenges, experiencing growth?
2. What is your understanding of humanity's growth?
3. What is your experience of your own energy?
4. Can your energy connect you to Earth's golden era?

Introduction

We have to unite and connect to the light of our source which is the life-giver. We all have to work against the illusion that has taken over the planet and our weapon is truth. Truth can create miraculous bonds and everything can fall in its right place.

When human beings connect to truth, they will be able to see their purpose. You will connect to your true-self by observing your life patterns and understanding the different ways illusion affects your life.

When people unite and are able to realise that growth is an experience and not a doctrine, not a distant goal that only a few have experienced, growth can be part of your everyday life. When you disconnect from all artificiality and be your true self, you are transforming humanity and Earth.

Wisdom of Thoth: A Faithful Representation of a Human Being

A faithful representation of a human being, on Earth in this time, a person who is blindfolded, his ears are blocked by social messaging, his hands are tied behind his back and his feet are also tied together leaving him with no freedom, purpose or growth.

In this state, the being is forced to walk on a tight rope; this means receiving no nutrition from the Earth or connecting to the light of the cosmos. Do you recognize yourself in this representation?

Your body is the meeting point and the receiver of Earth's light and nutrition as well as the cosmic light, our Source's high creative force. Your body can connect you to your astral existence; after all they are both reflections of your creation code. Existing in a third dimensional reality, you should be able to connect to your physicality which is part of your body and support its rebirth and growth. You can achieve this by consciously using the best nutrients for your body's growth.

This is an opportunity for you to act with your eyes and ears open.

In a world of illusion you are convinced that you have choices but in reality you have been chosen to accept a certain lifestyle that often goes against your essence and growth. If your intention is truth, you should be able to decide about your own lives and safeguard the precious gift given to you, your physical body.

It is important to take action and clear all illusion that affects your everyday tasks and responsibilities. If you are addicted to an unhealthy lifestyle this means that there are imbalances in you that connect you to illusion and when this happens you are not able to see truth or act with truth. Imbalances are common phenomena and when you are able to purify yourself and experience balance then you will be able to receive the light of the cosmos. Enlightenment is a lesson learnt that opens you up to cosmic light. Everything that you are affects your ability to achieve clarity and walk the path of truth and wisdom. Connecting to your body is the first step towards enlightenment.

Questions

1. What is a faithful representation of you?
2. How can your physical body guide you to your true-self?
3. What happens to your physical body when you are affected by distortion?
4. How can you heal yourself and bring balance to your being?

Introduction

The light of the Earth in the golden era had high vibrational qualities and was used as a high vibrational tool. It allowed Earth to be a creator planet responsible for healing and nurturing as well as a pure channel for transmitting large quantities of high light to her own creation and the cosmos. This enabled her creation to exist in a high vibrational state and allow the cosmic light to create in them.

Earth was created to be a perfect receiver and transmitter of cosmic light, a planet of creation, growth, healing and nourishment. All Earth's creation supported her growth and was given nourishment and healing to help them grow with Earth as receivers and transmitters of cosmic light. Ancient civilizations were aware of this and kept observing Earth's energies and healing qualities.

Wisdom of Thoth: Healing in Ancient Times

I was asked to give information about healing in ancient times. There are two ways to heal: with the healing and nurturing resources that can be found on Earth and with the cosmic light. In the golden Era, Earth was a planet of healing and high nutrition and all beings were fed with the high living energy of Earth and the cosmic light which brought eternal life.

There were many natural devices on Earth which were used to collect light and then it was shared with all creation. Earth enjoyed an abundance of cosmic light which helped her to create new species and develop a great range of nutrients to support their well-being and growth. Her energies were very powerful and beings could connect to them instantly and experience immediate results. There was no suffering because there was no disease. In the golden era, beings were concerned only with growth and this could be achieved by connecting to high energies.

In ancient times people were already lost and well-being was not a common quality of humanity. They had already experienced fragmentation and the illusion brought to them negativity, pain and disease. What made a difference was their ability to connect to the Earth and being aware of her healing abilities and great range of nutrients which were still growing on the surface of the planet. People were aware of the healing properties of plants and their different uses. Priests combined herbal remedies with energy healing in their ceremonies. The sun, the life giver, was also used for healing as well as the energies of the moon.

Many priests and mystery schools tried to connect to the Earth energies, the ones that come from the core of the planet. Ancient societies carried a higher light than present human civilizations because, even though they were distorted, they maintained their connection to the Earth and the cosmic light and this was an everyday practice. Modern people see themselves as superior; I will say that they are experiencing the most complex and advanced system of illusion that controls every aspect of their lives.

Their attachment to illusion is so strong and complete that they are unable to care about their basic needs; instead they are happy to poison themselves every day. Awakened human beings should observe themselves and answer the following questions: are you looking after your body and what does this mean to you? How many times do you have to inject poison in yourself by eating artificial substances? How often do you connect to the Earth energies and what does this mean to you?

You cannot receive or transmit healing energy if you are fragmented and distorted. Earth's power to produce living nutrients has been reduced from the time of the golden era but there is still a great range of plants, minerals and other healing nutrients that you can find on the planet. Now that you are aware of Earth's healing properties I want you to ask yourselves: is chemical healing and nutrition necessary to a living planet?

Questions:

1. What is your understanding of the golden era?
2. How were the healing energies of Earth transformed at the end of the golden era?
3. What was the purpose of the mystery schools?
4. How often do you connect to Earth's energies? What are your experiences?

What is your understanding of the golden era?
How were the healing energies of Earth transformed

Introduction

Distortion has made it very difficult for human beings to live according to natural laws. Connecting to your true-self is a natural law of life and creation. When human beings choose to live a distorted life they also block divine light and cosmic wisdom from coming to them. A true being has divine guidance naturally. This guidance will not only help them to grow, but it will also help them to connect.

We are not working only for our own growth, but we also exist to connect to other beings and help them grow. In other words we are all responsible for a large part of creation and our growth affects all. People on Earth live in a daze. They have no control of their lives and they are unaware of their light. Try to stand still and remain silent inside and outside; feel your own energy and as you become this energy try to distance yourself from the illusion and see your true-self, accept it and be one with it. Now you are nothing else but except your true-self.

Wisdom of Thoth: What is distortion?

A distorted space is a space that is unclean, unpurified and the people who live there are affected by this pollution, mind and body.

When you are distorted you have no clarity, you have no connection to your true-self. In this confused state you cannot see your purpose; you cannot allow yourself to walk your path and live and effortless life according to your divine plan. When many people are affected by distortion they all exist in this space of confusion and they convince each other that this is a natural way to experience life on Earth. When you finally see truth, you will see distortion as a dark cloud that blocks your understanding. Opening up to the cosmic light, can help you blow this cloud away and heal the trauma, schisms and unpurified parts of your being. Purification will be the next phase of your growth.

Questions

1. What is a distorted space?
2. What blocks you from connecting to your truth?
3. What is your experience connecting to the light?
4. What is your experience with purification?

Introduction

In the following teaching, Thoth wants to connect to all those people who see spirituality/cosmic wisdom as a way to acquire special abilities that will make them superhuman. He wants to teach people to observe themselves and focus on their pure intention that leads to truth and growth. Question your thoughts and actions, observe negativity, illusionary fears in your mind; understand old patterns, blockages and imbalances by creating a space of peace and connecting to your true-self. Your pure intention is part of your true-self; it supports your growth and strengthens your connection with the cosmos and Earth. This is not a superhuman quality; it is a natural ability and a cosmic duty.

Do not allow illusion to take you on a diversion away from your true goal which is to fulfil your purpose. Your purpose is part of a divine plan that is transforming you and the cosmos. When you connect to your true-self, you have a pure intention and you are able to receive and transmit light to Earth; to heal and be healed; to grow and allow others to grow with you. This is the path of your enlightenement.

Wisdom of Thoth: Becoming Superhuman

Human beings that exist in a low vibration, are very interested in connecting to the higher-self and often speak about this as it is something achievable. This is a sign that most humans are confused. They want to learn, they want to know what is beyond the physical body. How can they acquire more power? How can they become superhuman? This idea is very attractive to humans: they enjoy power.

I will say to them that before you climb at the top of the steps you have to stand on the first step. Why do not you work your way up slowly? This way you will be learning, growing, receiving the light, clarity and healing. This is how you can become powerful.

The other way is the way of the blind. Observe your actions, thoughts and communications. How all these different expressions of you can help you rise and grow. What does growth mean to you? How do you connect the being that you are with growth?

If you have light what do you do with it? Do you spread it to other human beings that can benefit from you? In what way? Look at your life structures. Your life should be your creation, your true path that leads you to your purpose. For a true being everything is simple. Everything is clear and whole. When you are your true-self you unite with all your bodies, higher-self and all the other connections within the cosmos and the creation of our source.

Questions

1. Why human beings connect the idea of being superhuman with their need to connect to the higher-self
2. Observe your imbalances. What do you see?
3. How can you grow?
4. How can truth help you on your path?

Introduction

Have you ever observed yourselves? Were you able to see your imbalances, your layers of distortion, your limitation, fears, abilities to grow, unique gifts, truth and light. What are the ways to purify yourself and restore balance into your being?

Due to distortion on Earth, human beings find it very hard to escape the patterns of distortion which are created by beliefs, dogma and other types of mind manipulation. The way we understand growth is by knowing your true purpose, allowing yourself to act and think according to your purpose, be the ground where divine seeds will grow and enable you to become a creator of your own true path as well as assisting others to follow their paths.

Knowing yourself and clearing old patterns is an act of bravery and clarity.

Wisdom of Thoth: Observing Limitation

There are people on Earth who believe that the repetition of a thought, word, message or feeling will unblock the areas of stagnation in them and will finally be free to grow. Other people believe that by repetition they can achieve to hold in their hands the item they desire, to attract all types of social success or be in a certain state of peace and fulfilment.

I want you to observe yourselves and see that all repeated patterns in your life have brought you stagnation and distortion. During your purification process you will have to break the pattern; isolate the seed of its creation and observe its multiple transformations. When you are fully aware of how it was created and the different ways that can affect your mind, you accept it all and make space for the pattern to leave your being.

All repeated patterns where created at a young age. The limitation that exists in your environment and your ability to absorb it and store it in you will determine its birth and growth. When you are free from this pattern you will open up to growth and experience clarity. Being a creator of your own life helps you experience new abilities, new strength as well as truth and freedom.

It will be beneficial to you to see your life not as a cycle but to see it as a straight route that will finally guide you to a new reality away from Earth and your present physical experience. A straight route can only take you to new lands and new creation.

Questions

1. What is a repeated pattern and how it affects your life?
2. What is your understanding of the following message: "isolate the seed of its creation and observe its multiple transformations".
3. How can you interrupt the pattern?
4. What is your truth and how it can help you expand?

Introduction

Many human beings experience exchanges of limitation and distortion with people in their environment. Distortion can only exist when people accept it as truth and allow it to spread to their being and the being of others. You are not responsible for other people's growth; your highest contribution is to receive the cosmic light that flows in you, experience healing and knowing, connect to your truth and pure intention and share the light and the transformation in you with others.

The seeds of light and truth that can be shared with different individuals do not have the same path of growth. This depends on the ground where they are planted. You cannot restore balance in others; people may not recognize the light that you carry only if they become receivers and transmitters of light and truth.

Wisdom Astaroth: Low Energies

Low energies affect all human beings in different degrees. When people feel disconnected, having no clarity, not knowing their purpose and not being able to receive and transmit healing, they are affected by low energies. Your inability to connect to your true-self and develop your unique abilities and skills can be transferred to others in your environment.

Limitation can be transferred to others when you try to "protect" them, keep them in line with social ideals, make them happy by encourage them to follow beliefs, dogma and artificial life style. This type of behaviour needs to stop; allow yourself and others to be free and explore growth and creation. If you truly care about others you have to teach them freedom and truth by letting them go and become creators themselves.

You cannot teach others if you do not know your purpose on Earth. Looking after people's needs does not make them stronger; without knowing you are limiting their ability to grow. You are feeding them with your own fears, insecurities and limitation.

You can create connections that will bring light to people when you start purifying yourself and allow healing to bring balance into your being. Limitation is not a comfort zone; it is a burden you choose to carry. If you put it down you will realize that it was easy to be free from it. Pure intention can become your ally.

Questions

1. What is your experience with exchanging distortion?
2. How can you block distortion?
3. What is your understanding of the following statement: "If you truly care about others you have to teach them freedom and truth by letting them go and become creators themselves."
4. How can pure intention become your ally?

Introduction

Observing yourself can help you purify from imbalances and distortion. Your starting point for your purification process is your connection with your true-self. The true-self is never part of the illusion and it always exists in you. In order to reach the state of truth you have to question yourself: what is real in my life; what brings me pure happiness and growth; what is my true purpose and what do I need to do to fulfil my purpose? These are the questions that you have to ask yourselves if you wish to have a happy life and wake up to your true potential. It is natural that when you grow and you follow your true path you are euphoric, because your vibration rises and you are there supporting others to get on their path.

Wisdom of Thoth: Observe Yourself, Connect to your True-Self

People, who are suffering from illusion, accepting illusion as truth, will find it very hard to connect to their true-self. Illusion will take them on a diversion; will make them fearful or it will affect their ego.

It is important that you create a space of peace and truth by emptying your mind from thought, fear and limitation. Focus on creating this space, keeping illusion away from you.

When this happens, you will naturally connect to the cosmic light and you will be able to observe your imbalances, blockages and the layers of illusion in you. The cosmic light can offer you healing and knowing that will help you during your purification process. The more you observe yourself and accept the layers of distortion in you the more you understand the way they have affected you over the years.

When you observe yourself, do not have any emotions, fear, guilt or any other feeling that can limit your understanding of yourself. Accept all that you are and connect to your true-self. This will be a high point in your purification process. When you connect to your true-self, illusion will start to evaporate and this is how you will be able to understand your purpose.

Questions

1. What is a purification process?
2. How can illusion disconnect you from your true-self?
3. How can you create a space of peace in you?
4. How can you connect to the cosmic light?
   What is a purification process?

Introduction

This teaching explains the ability of human beings to move objects with their energy. The energy that gives life to your being can create and communicate the cosmic laws.

Wisdom of Thoth: Telepathy

Human beings have the ability to move objects with their own energy. Some people think that when they are in an uncontrollable state such as anger, fear and panic are able to move objects; so perhaps fear and anger are producing this effect.

When you are in an angry state you are in a limited state.

If you can see objects moving around you, this may mean that other energies or energy beings want to get your attention or they want to communicate with you. It may mean that they want to challenge you and this way help you get out of your state of limitation. This is not telekinesis but it is a communication between you and your guides or other energy beings who want you to disconnect from limitation and enter a space of growth.

Questions

1. How can you communicate energetically?
2. Do you experience a connection with low beings?
3. What is telepathy?

Introduction

All planets are alive. Earth is a unique planet with a unique creation. Life can exist in different forms. When human beings observe planetary phenomena, they should be able to understand and be part of the living experience of the galaxy. Humanity can observe and participate in life in the galaxy.

Wisdom of Thoth: Planetary Phenomena

The different planetary phenomena that can be experienced by people on Earth can have many different effects on them but also no effect at all. It depends on the energies of the planets in the galaxy and how they are able to affect human beings. It all has to do with the energies and the connections of a human being.

The movement of the planets is a sign of life.

When human beings observe planetary phenomena, they should be able to understand and be part of the living experience of the galaxy. These are positive events that can make humanity observe and participate in life in the galaxy.

If people are affected negatively by planetary phenomena, it means that planetary changes are supporting illusion that is already growing in them. It may also mean that they are experiencing an awakening to help them observe their imbalances and start their purification. The movement of the planets, which is constant, does not bring bad luck or unhappiness to people of Earth. When you connect to your own truth you can use energy to heal yourself.

Questions

1. Can planetary phenomena have an effect on the life of human beings?
2. How can you experience the movement of the planets?
3. Can the planets affect your growth?

Introduction

Every living being, including the planets and the universes are surrounded by an aura. An aura is the energies of the being organised in electromagnetic fields. All the beings who are connected to you add energies to your aura. These electromagnetic fields are used as receivers and transmitters of energy as well as balancing and regulating the inner and outer light. What you call matrix is an artificial copy of the aura which was made to control and suppress the light.

Everything that exists is light and energy and is constantly moving within the being, within the aura of a being, connecting to other beings, planets, planes and the cosmos. This is how we describe life, a constant flow of energy. Energy is moving in a circular motion and there is a certain pattern that is followed in order to maintain life and growth. When energies are moving in one's body are clearing, purifying old blockages and imbalances and rejuvenating the body. As energy flows from one being to another, it enables communication and connection and with this you exchange energy which is very important for your growth.

Wisdom of Thoth: Strengthening your Aura

Your aura is part of your being and you should nourish it the way you nourish your physical body. Imbalances can affect your whole being and this is when you experience limitation and separation from your purpose. It is important that you are able to experience life as a whole being and allow the cosmic light to heal you, bring clarity and sustain inner communication and energy exchange.

A way to help you practice this is to disconnect from the distortion of the mind, be in a state of peace and focus on how the energies of your aura are connected to your physical body. Understand that when your aura is connected to the cosmic light, the whole being is able to grow and transform. When you experience this sacred unity, you will be able to connect to the cosmos and the cosmos in you, your true-self. When you master this, you will be able to strengthen your aura and to unite your whole being through transformation and growth.

Questions

1. What is the aura?
2. How can imbalances affect your being?
3. How can you experience life as a whole being?
4. How can you connect the cosmic light?
   What is the aura?
   How can imbalances affect your being?
   How can you experience life as a whole being?
   How can you connect the cosmic light?

Introduction

Earth in the golden era was a luscious land with the most extraordinary variety of plants and animals, rocks and formations. The gods created mountains of crystal to be used as receivers and transmitters of energy and maintain the planet's state as a high vibrational being. When travellers from other planets were able to visit Earth, they saw the devices and realised that she was made of the godly elements which gave her a superior position in the godly creation.

The gods created mountains of crystal on Earth which brought the high energies on the planet. This led to the planet growing faster and occupying a high astral place; beings were able to feed from the energies, raise their consciousness and become gods themselves. Many of the mountains that existed on Earth were used as transmitters and receivers. The pyramids of Egypt which still exist today were covered with glass; they were only a small device of receiving and collecting information and it was built by visitors from other planets who inhabited the area.

All creation exists to maintain the cosmic laws. This is a very important truth and can help you expand your consciousness. Our mission is to help Earth transform to her first form, as she was in the golden era. If you are able to reach the planetary consciousness then you will directly help Earth to transform.

Wisdom of Thoth: Sacred Places on Earth

Most sacred places on Earth were created by human beings and the Earth's energies in order to help humanity and the planet receive cosmic light. During the golden era, the whole planet was sacred and all beings were perfect receivers and transmitters of light.

Earth was the creation of the Gods and their intention was to help her grow and become a high creator planet; the energy that was given to her should grow and spread to the cosmos. During this time, creation was taken place in all parts of the planet and all beings were able to enter the inner parts of Earth.

The inner parts were created first and all resources, high energies and Earth's creative force still exist there. After the golden era, beings created physical portals to allow them to enter the inner parts. Earth experienced multiple colonization that brought destruction and distortion. At that time, the portals kept a secret.

Human beings created temples and were drown to areas that had high vibration in order to connect to the cosmos and the living force. Many human beings tried to discover the portals but they were not successful because Earth does not wish intruders to enter the inner parts of the planet which are sacred, free from distortion and fragmentation.

If you want to create a sacred space it will be helpful to use Earth's high energies. You should exist in a high vibrational area and connect to Earth; allow her energies to nourish and purify you. If you are able to connect to Earth's energies then you are sacred and everything that exists around you is also sacred.

Questions

1. Have you visited any sacred sites on Earth? What was your experience?
2. Can you explain the following message "During the golden era, the whole planet was sacred and all beings were perfect receivers and transmitters of light."
3. Can you create your own sacred space?

Introduction

Planets are living organisms and when they are in an alignment they connect energetically and affect each other's cosmic laws and systems. There is unity and we are all part of this alignment able to strengthen the bonds and the energy that flows through it. Our duty as energetic beings is to strengthen and support Earth's alignment with our own light and the clarity of our intention.

Different races inhabited different parts of the planet and created advanced civilizations. Connecting to the Earth's high energies brought immense growth to the inhabitants; the study and practice of natural laws and cycles was a common goal. The beings that came from other planets to inhabit Earth multiplied and spread; beings of the same race occupied certain parts of the planet.

You have to use your energy to strengthen bonds on Earth: bonds between people, activities, spirits, energy fields, actions, thoughts and imperfections. Accept it all and then embrace it all. Also teach others to do the same, physically or energetically so we can all travel together and expand. This is a new era which will be embraced and celebrated by all.

Wisdom of Thoth: Transformations on Earth

Many astral beings that belonged to different races, visited Earth from the time of her Golden era to recent times. Some of these races did not make Earth their permanent home on Earth and others created civilizations that expanded not only on the surface but also in the inner parts of the Earth.

The planet went through several transformations including what you call catastrophic changes, disasters and mass extinction of a number of species that lived on the planet. Right now there is a distinction between animals and humanoid beings and this was the result of the changes of the planet and the low vibration of Earth.

The races known to you such as African, Caucasian and so on are related to different astral races that existed on the planet before Earth's transformation. The races known to you are the humanoids of Earth who were isolated and created civilizations similarly to what is described in your books about prehistoric times. Earth changes and transformations affected all beings; some became extinct and others reappeared on Earth having a different form, consciousness and light.

Questions

1. What do you know about the golden era and how this knowledge can affect your life?
2. What is your understanding of the following phrase: "Right now there is a distinction between animals and humanoid beings and this was the result of the changes of the planet and the low vibration of Earth."
3. What do you know about the astral races that visited Earth?
4. How can Earth's transformation affect your life?

Introduction

Living a life of limitation and confusion does not allow human beings to grow and fulfil their purpose, becoming a perfect receiver and transmitter of the cosmic light and heal humanity and Earth. Perhaps some of you believe that your purpose is to reach the highest zones of the pyramid; the higher you can get the better. All these people who are obsessed to be on the top of the social pyramid of success they will be very disappointed to find out that their quest are an illusion.

Wisdom of Thoth: The Darkness of Confusion

There are many people on Earth that are not aware of their purpose in this life time; their actions, thoughts, experiences and connections do not reflect their purpose and their divine plan that was created before their reincarnation. Other people are able to catch a glimpse of their purpose occasionally but most of the time they exist in the darkness of their confusion.

Some may ask: is there a natural law on Earth that makes humans unaware of their purpose? Perhaps there is a cosmic law that makes humans experience life being blindfolded and confused. Some of you may be surprised when you hear my answer to your question: Beings who experience life and not being able to connect to their purpose are going against the cosmic laws; are going against growth.

Living a life of emptiness and confusion does not allow you to grow and fulfil your greatest task which is to become a perfect receiver and transmitter of the cosmic light and heal humanity and Earth. Perhaps some of you believe that your purpose is to reach the top levels of the pyramid; the higher you can get the better.

There are people who depend their lives on this quest and eagerly try to convince everybody around them to do the same. I call this the darkness of confusion. It is a darkness that expands beyond the life cycle and affects the being even after his death. Some of you may experience the darkness of confusion on Earth when you had a physical body and connected to Earth's energies but your inability to connect to the cosmic light during your reincarnation will make you carry the darkness of confusion even after the end of a life cycle when you have no body and you are not connected to Earth's energies.

At the end of a life cycle, beings are able to go through a purification process and experience all the opportunities of growth and non-growth that they had during their life time. They are able to learn from their purification and this way clarity and knowing is coming back to their being. Beings that carry the darkness of confusion even after death they will stand at the crossroads without knowing where to go and what to do. Purification is a great gift given to the ones who are willing to experience growth, transformation and being supported by the cosmos.

Questions

1. What is your understanding of your purpose?
2. Is your purpose related to social expectations?
3. How can you regain clarity to help you understand your path and purpose?
4. Can purification help you to connect to your purpose?

Introduction

There are many beings on Earth who are longing to achieve clarity, connecting to their true purpose, but they are entangled in the web of illusion and limitation. When people are able to empty their minds from all beliefs, aspirations, needs, suffering, pleasures and longings, they will discover their creator.

There are many people who find it hard to connect to their purpose and this is because they cannot accept it. When we cannot accept our purpose, we create many false representations of it, often related to social ideals. These false representations are created by us and function as diversions. A life of truth and freedom can only be a wild dream for most people on Earth and this is why they do not accept the true purpose. This happens to most people, even the ones who claim to be awake or aware or even enlightened.

Your body is a microcosm of the cosmic creation. You consist of countless energy points and they are all united with ropes of energy. They all communicate with each other and they are able to receive and transmit light which helps them to stay alive and grow. All energy points in your body are part of a collective operation.

They all belong in your body but they have not been created in your body; they were brought together by the cosmic ropes that connect cosmic creation. What we are able to create in all different planes was first created in the limitless light of our source and then through us was directed and given a form in different planes. This is our duty, to give form to the light of our source and create the ropes that maintain a connection with the cosmos and other energy beings.

Wisdom of Thoth: High Creation

When we want to show you the way to grow, we always point at truth because this is your best ally. Truth can be part of you but it is also an extension of the cosmic light. It is the rope that connects your whole existence with the cosmos, the creation of our source. It is our duty to create new life and also create the ropes that connect every single energetic point in the cosmos.

Your body is a microcosm of the cosmic creation. You consist of countless energy points and they are all united with ropes of energy. They all communicate with each other and they are able to receive and transmit light which helps them to stay alive and grow. All energy points in your body are part of a collective operation.

They all belong in your body but they have not been created in your body; they were brought together by the cosmic ropes that connect cosmic creation. What we are able to create in all different planes was first created in the limitless light of our source and then through us was directed and given a form in different planes. This is our duty, to give form to the light of our source and create the ropes that maintain a connection with the cosmos and other energy beings.

Looking at Earth, we can see that the ropes are strong enough to help her connect to the high light. Different parts of the Earth's body consist of energy points that are not connected and this is why there are imbalances. Humanity is one of Earth's energy point and it is obvious that humanity and Earth cannot fully communicate.

Their ability to receive and transmit the light of each other is very weak. People on Earth find it hard to receive and transmit light to each other. Humanity is Earth's blockage and needs to be purified. What is your connection to Earth? Are you able to communicate with her? Are you able to receive and transmit light? What is your intention when you connect to other human beings? We are waiting for you to connect to truth and then we can help you transform.

Questions

1. Explain the following phrase: "Truth is the rope that connects your whole existence with the cosmos, the creation of our source."
2. How does Earth connect to the cosmos?
3. Explain the following phrase: "Humanity is one of Earth's energy point and it is obvious that humanity and Earth cannot communicate."
4. Are you able to communicate with Earth? Why is this important and what have you experienced connecting to Earth?

Introduction

God simply means creator of the cosmos. If any living being is an open channel to the light of our high creator and is able to receive its creative force and direct it to create is a god. All gods have unique qualities and attributes and there are chosen to participate in creation due to their uniqueness. All planes are regulated by cosmic laws. When these cosmic laws are not followed we have high levels of distortion and imbalances similarly to what Earth is experiencing right now.

The gods' project is to awake the inhabitants of Earth; disconnect them from the illusion; pass the divine light to them which will help them connect to their true-self and recognize their tools and purpose; enable them to heal Earth and the rest of the humanity. The gods want to communicate with all beings on the planet and heal all imbalances and blockages. The light of the gods is transmitted to Earth and we have to become pure channels of the cosmic energy for our own healing and purification as well as the Earth's.

Currently, people on Earth are trapped in a low vibrational reality because of the high level of distortion. Imbalances appear in all expressions of their lives and they are unable to heal themselves because they are unaware of their true state. Ignorance and confusion will not lead you to harmony and fulfilment. You have to be pure and true to your calling and purpose.

Wisdom of Thoth: Symptoms of Imbalance

It is important to understand that purification can support your health. There are many forms of purification and they all link with each other. Purification can target imbalances that were created long time ago and still exist in you, taking different forms. These imbalances are creating schisms within your being and lead to physical illnesses as well as a polluted mind.

When your mind is suffering from distortion, the body can become affected too. When human beings are not focusing on their wellbeing and allow dangerous substances to enter their being instead of Earth's nourishment, then there are imbalances in you that are affecting your mind. Having no clarity, no understanding of your purpose, no ability to connect to Earth and the cosmos are all symptoms of imbalance. If you are not able to heal yourself and heal others then you need to purify yourself, disconnect from distortion and bring healing into your healing.

Many of you are convinced that you are suffering, you are lost and you are helpless; this is communication coming from a fragmented mind. You are able to connect to high forces and bring healing into your being. These high forces are the Earth being a Goddess creator and the high cosmic creative force that supports life and maintains balance in the cosmos. Healing is something you seek and experience; it is not an idea or a thought. Connecting to everything that you are, accepting you imbalances and disconnecting from them is your path of growth.

Questions

1. What are the different ways to purify yourself? Can you purify your whole being including your physical body?
2. Can you explain the following phrase: "When human beings are not focusing on their wellbeing and allow dangerous substances to enter their being instead of Earth's nourishment, then there are imbalances in you that are affecting your mind."
3. What is your understanding of the following phrase: "Having no clarity, no understanding of your purpose, no ability to connect to Earth and the cosmos are all symptoms of imbalance."
4. How can you heal yourself?

Introduction

There was a time that gods were able to communicate with the people of Earth and sacred wisdom was passed down to them. It was necessary that the Earth should return to her first phase of growth, her golden era. Gods shared sacred knowledge and high light with the priests and wise men of different communities to help people escape survival and return to effortless growth. The priests created temples which had high energies for people to visit and receive healing, acquire knowledge, restore balance and connect to the gods' energies. The ceremonies and rituals often took place in rural areas in order to heal Earth from her trauma. The teachings of the gods were communicated to people energetically; musical harmonies and dance were also used, imitating the harmonies of the cosmos.

Earth in the golden era was a luscious land with the most extraordinary variety of plants and animals, rocks and formations. The gods created mountains of crystal to be used as receivers and transmitters of energy and maintain the planet's state as a high vibrational being. When travelers from other planets were able to visit Earth, they saw the devices and realised that she was made of the godly elements which gave her a superior position in the godly creation.

Wisdom of Thoth: Sacred Temples

Human beings have created a number of temples that can be found in all different continents. They are called sacred and some of them have existed for many years and nobody on Earth knows when, how and why they were created.

During the golden era, devices existed on Earth to receive and transmit the light of the cosmos. These devises were spread all over the planet and supported the creation of star gates and other forms of electromagnetic fields that helped Earth to fulfil her duty being a creator of life.

Those devices were seen by the astral races that visited Earth. They understood their purpose. Some of your sacred temples are placed in the areas where the devices existed so they can continue receiving and transmitting light. There are also temples on Earth that were created for the same reason in different parts of the planet. The distortion on Earth has affected their ability to receive and transmit light. Distortion can be seen in your modern buildings: plurality and no high purpose is a life of restriction and separation.

Questions

1. What is your experience of Earth's sacred temples?
2. What do you know about Earth's golden era?
3. How did Earth receive and transmit cosmic light?

4. Can you explain the following phrase: "Distortion can be seen in your modern buildings: plurality and no high purpose is a life of restriction and separation."

Introduction

There are so many people who wish to be sold and bought in the name of power. There are people who call themselves masters and they teach that anybody can achieve enlightenment if they follow a certain life style or have certain beliefs. They are offering a tailor-made product of illusion ready to be bought by minds of physical orientation. People who buy this product are not naive. They just respond to the transaction, the same way they buy an exotic fruit they have never eaten before. The people who are attracted to these "teachers of enlightenment" do not just accept illusion but they celebrate it.

Wisdom of Thoth: Mind Manipulation

There are people and groups that are trying to convince you of the superiority of the mind. You can achieve everything by keeping your mind busy with thoughts and fantasies; you can acquire goods and lock yourself into a relationship with desirable partners, have recognition, power and be successful professionally and socially.

You are told that you can attract wealth and furthermore all your wishes will come true. There are people who call this spiritual advancement and a great way to live a balanced and successful life. I have a question for you: if your intention is to acquire goods and to be socially and professionally successful and you are trying to use your mind to achieve this, are you still on your path of purpose or perhaps you are lost in a maze of distortion?

There are people who go against the social expectations but happily they accept that by thinking of a certain luxury item this can become theirs; this will bring them the happiness and balance they seek. Mind manipulation can take many forms. There are people that will accept mind manipulation because there is a reward attached to it.

For other people it needs to be disguised into a positive idea or method and take a different name such as enlightenment, spirituality, empowerment, self-realization and many more. If you are able to observe all different types of manipulation, you will see that they want you to focus on artificiality and illusion and then they want you to have needs; to be affected by criticism, follow a leader; join the competition and exist in fragmentation. If you want to escape the maze of manipulation then you should always connect to the truth within you.

Questions

1. Can you explain the following phrase: "There are people and groups that are trying to convince you of the superiority of the mind."
2. What is your understanding about mind manipulation and how does this affect your life?
3. How can you escape mind manipulation?
4. How does artificiality and illusion affect the mind?

Introduction

Structures are necessary when they support truth and growth for all.

We need communities where people are supported in their evolution, developing their skills, studying true methods and fulfilling their purpose. With our whole existence, we support and complement each other inventing new ways of transmitting and receiving energy.

There is a miraculous way of living and this is being detached from beliefs, dogmas and archetypal behavior. All the above have been created to help you focus and sustain a certain consciousness and life experience. We are asking you now to abandon and destroy the persona and the life style. Our aim is to give everybody the tools they need in order to paint their own authentic picture of themselves and let their true purpose be revealed. We want you to detach yourself from all that you are, right now and connect to your true-self, the one that is known to the masters and gods.

Christian Rosenkreutz's Teaching: Reincarnating in the Lower Spheres

Reincarnating in the lower spheres is like leaving a toddler in a thick jungle of many shapes, colours and expressions of life. Many of you are disconnected from the divine plan because you are surrounded and controlled by social structures. Your starting point on Earth is related to social structure. Some of you also receive the light of the beings that bring you up but you also inherit their own limitations and imbalances.

The social structure plays a very important role in your understanding of yourself and its main aim is to support your separation from your divine plan and purpose. When society loses its humanity and compassion for others then it becomes responsible for the creation of an invisible but thick web of control and manipulation.

If you travel around the world, and focus on exploring different types of social structures you will discover that there are different forms and have their own rules. Societies that have followed ancient practices, allow the members to grow and give them some support to follow their path. If you decide to visit big cities around the world, you will discover that they share similar social rules.

People who live in the cities have the illusion that a successful job is the only way to fulfil their purpose. They believe that the farmer who works hard and understands the natural laws is not privileged or successful because he does not meet the social criteria of success. Life on Earth is a journey for learning and growth.

There are people who are suffering, trying to fight their imbalances; trying to disconnect from artificiality and connect to Earth; going against the social criteria of a successful life and focusing on bringing balance and harmony to their lives. All of you are great warriors and collectors of cosmic light. You will be the first to be called in order to help the Gods to build bridges between the Earth and the cosmos. You are the strongest and the purest and connecting with the Gods is a gift given to you to be shared with the rest of humanity. Your bravery will be rewarded.

Questions

1. Can you explain the following message: "Many of you are disconnected from the divine plan because you are surrounded and controlled by social structures."
2. In what way you are connected to illusion?
3. Can acceptance help you grow?
4. What can you are taught by your pure intention?

Introduction

Do not miss the opportunity to experience life using your physical body; however you do not need to diverse from your true purpose, getting lost in the five-sense reality. If you are not wise you can find yourself in a five-sense labyrinth with no way out. I hope that you follow my teaching and create the balance needed between all bodies and all their expressions.

When you have a body you have to use it to help you receive light. It is a wonderful and versatile tool to help beings in lower vibrations expand and grow into higher planes. You can be truly free if you achieve to depend on nothing than your light which is a connection between the physical body and all the other bodies and expressions of true-self. Our purity will help us connect to higher realms and become a living uninterrupted cycle of evolution.

You can heal yourself by exploring the life of your body through movement. If you wish to escape the restrictions placed on you by your social expectations, you should connect to your body and allow free movement to take place.

There are people on Earth who enjoy a guided type of movement; a teacher or an expert will show you the steps or the movements and teach you techniques to help your body develop certain qualities. This can be useful but should be combined with a free flow of movement which is an expression of your true-self connecting to the cosmos.

Wisdom of Thoth: The Movement of the Body

The movement of the physical body is a great way to express cosmic truth. You may be able to move your body in different ways but you really do is imitating the movement of Earth and the cosmos. So human beings can experience stagnation when their body does not express the cosmic movement daily.

You can heal yourself by exploring the life of your body through movement. If you wish to escape the restrictions placed on you by your social expectations, you should connect to your body and allow free movement to take place.

There are people on Earth who enjoy a guided type of movement; a teacher or an expert will show you the steps or the movements and teach you techniques to help your body develop certain qualities. This can be useful but should be combined with a free flow of movement which is an expression of your true-self connecting to the cosmos.

Some of you may also be interested in the martial arts. When martial arts teach you concentration, focus, inner communication, being in a state of peace, it will be very useful to you. It is a form of active meditation using your body, following the Earth and the cosmos and coordination with other beings through movement and energy.

When your intention is to hurt somebody in order to survive, your power of knowing and connecting to your true-self is not there anymore. The fear of survival should not enter your being if you are looking for truth.

Questions

1. What is your understanding of the movement of the body?
2. What is your experience connecting to your physical body?
3. How can you heal yourself?
4. Can you explain the following phrase: "The fear of survival should not enter your being if you are looking for truth."

Introduction

Your five senses are also messengers of information and humans on Earth have almost exhausted all different ways of experiencing life with their senses. The physical plane is a school of the five senses, learning to live with the limitations of a body which quickly decays and turns into a different substance. There are many beings that need to experience physicality and an astral existence simultaneously in order to advance to higher levels of learning.

Do not miss the opportunity to experience life using your physical body; however you do not need to diverse from your true purpose, getting lost in the five-sense reality. If you are not wise you can find yourself in a five-sense labyrinth with no way out. I hope that you follow this guidance and create the balance needed between all bodies and all their expressions.

If you were able to see beyond Earth and galaxy formations, you could understand that the physical body is a microcosm of the cosmos. There are countless galaxies joined together, affecting each other's growth; their movement is synchronized similarly to the movement in your own body.

Wisdom of Thoth: Galaxies

Human beings use the five senses to define and experience the world around them. If they were able to see beyond Earth and galaxy formations, they could understand that the physical body is a microcosm of the cosmos. There are countless galaxies joined together, affecting each other's growth; their movement is synchronized similarly to the movement in your own body.

The movement of a single planet supports the movement of all united galaxies. If you were able to see this, you will experience the unity and the movement, bringing life to countless points of cosmic energy. Some of you may ask: what is the purpose of this movement? It is the movement of life, growth to help you rise towards the cosmic purpose.

It is the way to attract the cosmic light which is the intention of our Source. It is also a way to support life within the unity of galaxies and the cosmos. Earth's energies support her movement and unity with other planets in the galaxy. The sun is a high point of energy that guides, nourishes and supports movement and life. When a planet no longer connects to the sun then there is no life in it. All planets that coexist with Earth and move together in a celestial sun dance are living beings in constant growth

Questions

1. Can you explain the following phrase: "The movement of a single planet supports the movement of all united galaxies. If you were able to see this, you will experience the unity and the movement, bringing life to countless points of cosmic energy".
2. What is the movement of life?
3. What is the intention of our Source?
4. Can you explain why the physical body is a microcosm of the cosmos?

Introduction

The energy in you creates channels of communication; you can visualise them as tunnels of light, similar to star-gates that exist on different locations on planet Earth. As energy flows from one being to another, it enables communication and connection and with this you exchange energy which is very important for your growth. If people on Earth want to experience an accelerated growth and fulfil their purpose, they have to allow their energy to connect them to many energetic fields not only on Earth but also in the astral plane.

Wisdom of Thoth: Strengthen your Bonds

You have to use your energy to strengthen bonds on Earth: bonds between people, activities, spirits, energy fields, actions, thoughts and imperfections. Accept it all and then embrace it all. Also teach others to do the same, physically or energetically so we can all travel together and expand.

There is a motion inside you that keeps you alive and anchors you to the physical plane; you understand that this corresponds to the vibration of your astral body and it is also linked to planetary motion. In the physical plane, beings learn to experience life through the five senses or the limitations of a physical body. Beings that experience an astral existence simultaneously with their physical reality are able to acquire knowledge leading to a new cycle of growth.

Questions

1. How can you use your energy to create bonds with Earth?
2. How can you experience unity with Earth and her creation?
3. What is the motion that keeps you alive?
4. Can you experience physical and astral growth all at the same time?

Wisdom of Thoth: The Anatomy of the Physical Body

If your scientists were able to go deeper into the different systems and ways of coexistence in the physical body, they would be able to see that there are unique points of life that are united to follow the cosmic laws. If you want to know the different blood types, I can tell you that your scientists cannot see the uniqueness of every human being but instead they create certain categories in order to find a definition that leads to fragmentation and limitation. The known blood types define certain characteristics of the blood stream but they also ignore many other characteristics that are unique to each human being.

Questions

1. Can you connect to your physical body?
2. Can you experience growth by focusing on your physical body?
3. Can science help you experience unity within your being?
4. Are human beings unique?

Introduction

When human beings experience distortion, they are connecting to low energies that exist on the planet. The low energies manipulate the mind, create physical imbalances and lower the ability of your energy to connect to the cosmos and Earth. Connecting to the cosmic light is a natural process that brings life, healing and knowing to all beings. When you share your light with others you accelerate growth, becoming a perfect receiver and transmitter of light.

Wisdom of Thoth: Space of Growth

Sometimes human beings are connected to certain forces without realizing and can have sensations that bring fear and uncertainty. Connecting to the cosmic light is a natural process that brings life, healing and knowing to all beings. Your mind is manipulated and this can cause fear that opens up connections between you and the forces that bring imbalance. You can find peace when you connect to Earth and act in a way that can benefit you and others. When you spend your day, helping other human beings, connecting to the cosmic light and true-self, disconnecting from fear and enjoying a life that brings you closer to growth and creation, you will be fulfilled. Fear is your enemy; positivity, fulfilment and growth are your allies. The space you need to be is a space that you can meet and co-exist with your allies.

Questions

1. What is your experience, connecting to low energies?
2. How is your mind affected by illusion?
3. Can you explain the following phrase: "You can find peace when you connect to Earth and act in a way that can benefit you and others."
4. How can you support your light and abilities to grow?

Introduction

You are here to receive the light and with it you will fight the low vibrational illusion of separation and polarity which has given birth to fear, greediness, survival and death of the real goal which is rebirth and transformation.

All beings that reincarnate have a path and a purpose to follow for their own evolution. All beings are given a task and at the end of a cycle their guides are going to evaluate their progress and decide where they have to go next. Human beings are affected by the overall growth of creation as well as the individual growth. This is the challenge they have to take when they reincarnate on Earth. We are aware of the distortion on Earth and the beings that are sent to reincarnate there, need to face this in order to grow.

Low spirits affect humans. They have a parasitic behavior, feeding from the energy of humans. When beings exist in a low vibration and experience fear, anger, insecurity and all the negative feelings, they have a slow growth and are more open to low spirits to connect to them. When you open to truth you are strong, responsible for your own life and your growth is effortless.

Wisdom of Thoth: Returning to the Astral Plane

There are many reasons why the essence of a human being can exist close to Earth and not being able to find its way to the astral plane at the end of a reincarnation. A sudden or violent death can cause the essence of a human being to remain on Earth and have a certain experience of limitation such as being angry, sad or just want to communicate with the human beings that currently exist on the planet and occupy the same physical space.

This does not take long and the human essence finally disconnects from the experiences of this reincarnation and enters a space of nothingness, getting ready for purification. Sometimes there are other forces linked to you that create different sensations to distract you. If you allow those entities to connect to you, this is not going to bring you any knowing or growth.

If you want to stay in this space you have to ignore the different sensations and fill the space with healing energies. If you find yourself being in constant battle, you have to seek shelter in a space that you can be in peace. You can help the essence of another human being return to the astral plane when you exist in a space of truth and connect to the cosmic light.

Questions

1. What happens to the essence of a being at the end of a reincarnation?
2. What is your understanding of Earth?
3. How can you disconnect from low energies?
4. Why is it important to create a space of peace?

Introduction

You were given freedom to choose different paths in order to gain experience and learn lessons from them. Your true life path is a single line without shortcuts and diversions and it is connected to both your essence and creation code. Once this is realized, you will not sway elsewhere. You will know that you have been here all along. All options, questions, uncertainties, dramas and failures in your life will fade. You begin to experience your essence, your divine purpose and your existence in all of its forms, physical and astral and you become aligned to your own essence.

Wisdom of Thoth: Connecting to your Essence

Your essence is a river flow that has no start or end. The river that flows gently and peacefully, bringing life to everything that connects to, cannot be restricted or exist in a limited state. You may be serious and dedicated to everything you do but sometimes this energy is not creation but it is the fear of failing or disappointing others. Your abundance is freedom to flow and co-create life. If you understand this and open yourself up to this experience then you realize that life can be effortless. All human beings have a different path and unique tools, so it is pointless to compete or compare yourself with others. Connecting to your essence will help you grow and purify yourself from fear and limitation.

Questions

1. Can you experience unity and cosmic flow?
2. Can you explain the following phrase: "You may be serious and dedicated to everything you do but sometimes this energy is not creation but it is the fear of failing or disappointing others."
3. How can life become effortless?
4. How can you purify yourself from fear and limitation?

Introduction

On Earth we experience duality which is a separation of self from all that exists. There is always a fight of the opposites which is the cause of fragmentation and illusion. If you wish to evolve beyond polarity and fragmentation you have to disconnect from the idea of opposites. In nature there is no fight against two elements there is only a union of the elements, bringing new life. In this teaching we learn that if there is a fight this is a fight of life for the new born who is coming to take his place of power.

People on Earth understand the world around them as a polarity of good and evil. This is a characteristic of the third dimensional perception. All beings are in a process of growing and evolving. Your path has challenges and you will be called to take decisions for your own life and focus on staying on your path. You can escape illusion, reclaim your power, connect to your astral body and raise your vibration. Some people choose to give up their powers, others prefer to ignore their true-self and follow the growth of the blind and the deaf. When you choose this path you are harming yourself and you become a victim of your own ignorance.

Wisdom of Thoth: The Hierarchy of the Gods

On Earth, people experience division, fragmentation and polarities. Your social structure is divided into many categories and sub-divisions related to status, life style, interests and other factors; this has affected your understanding of yourself and the cosmos. Division brings fragmentation which goes against the wholeness and unity that exists in the cosmos.

When people accept and experience division as well as the pyramid structure reward system, they exist in an illusionary state disconnected from themselves. In the cosmos we all experience growth and we all share the same gift of being the receivers and transmitters of energy. All contribution is necessary for the maintenance of life and the evolution of the cosmos.

All beings have a task and a purpose and they all have unique abilities to help them achieve their task. Beings that have reincarnated on Earth have the important task to overcome distortion, connect to Earth and the cosmos, receive and transmit light and support growth on the planet. Their task is not less important than the task of astral beings; if they achieve to fulfil their purpose, they will be supporting the growth of our Source's creation.

Beings that exist close to the Source were given the task to maintain life and create life through the cosmic light. In the cosmos there is not superiority or inferiority; low and high position of influence; possessions and power over other beings; ambitions, deceit, illusionary success and failure. In the cosmos there are no divisions; we all experience unity and our task is related to our essence and growth.

It is important that humanity experience cosmic unity and distance itself from divisions and fragmentation. This will bring healing to Earth and her creation, receiving and transmitting light, returning to the golden era and reconnecting fully to the Source's high light.

Questions

1. What is fragmentation?
2. What is the pyramid structure reward system?
3. What are your unique abilities?
4. What is your understanding of the following phrase: "In the cosmos there are no divisions; we all experience unity and our task is related to our essence and growth."

Introduction

When humans are able to fight illusion and heal distortion, they will support the planet's growth and transformation. They are many people on

Earth who are walking the path of awakening. Their numbers are going to grow; this is the divine plan.

When you are purified from the illusion and you are able to see yourself naked and pure then you will instantly see your purpose and you will have instant access to all cosmic truths because it is your right.

Wisdom of Thoth: Fighting Illusion

Fighting illusion is not a war against two opposite sides. Fighting illusion will connect you to your true being. This will bring you peace; will prepare you to become creator of your own life.

Before you enter this fight, you have to be aware that if you accept illusion as truth, you give it your power, you destroy your balance. Illusion is a great deceiver and if you accept it as truth, you give it power and part of your essence to form into a limitation that becomes your limitation.

Your lives are created according to the growth and imbalances that you may carry. When people have imbalances, they cannot absorb the cosmic light and they start having severe distortion and schisms. When this happens, they become attracted to illusion.

When you have accepted illusion as your true experience then it will grow in you and reshape according to your state. Needs, fears, disappointment, success, aspirations are illusionary and are affected by your relationship with illusion. To escape this gigantic monster, you have to disconnect from numerous layers of false existence and understanding.

Many of you are perplexed, you do not know how to go about it, and you need guidance. I will say to you that what you need most is the will to detach yourself from all artificiality. If you take full responsibility of your actions and thoughts and consciously decide to exist in unity with your true-self and purpose then illusion will not have a strong hold on you anymore.

You will have to examine your life and observe yourself; do not allow illusion to take different forms and come back to you. This happens because your society exists in illusion and being part of it you are affected. When you take the first step towards freedom, you concentrate on yourself and your abilities to grow. This should be your focus.

Questions

1. What is your experience purifying yourself from illusion?
2. What is your understanding of the following phrase: Illusion is a great deceiver and if you accept it as truth, you give it power and part of your essence to form into a limitation that becomes your limitation.
3. What is a schism and how it is created in a human being?
4. How can you observe yourself and purify from illusion?

Introduction

Observe a moment in your life that you were forced to act in a way that was destructive to yourself or others; you were being forced to act this way or accept certain actions from others and this has created a gap in you which can also be called a schism. You can heal yourself by start observing the schism and the distortion that feeds it. Create a space of peace in you and focus on your being and growth.

See yourself as a seed that grows because its existence is only linked to transformation and growth.

Wisdom of Astaroth: Coming Back to Life

Coming back to life is an easy process. Many of you were given a life time on Earth and during this time you may be disconnected from reality and exist in a distorted sub plane. This can happen to all of you. The ones who are able to observe themselves and see this pattern developing and repeating itself, may have the following question: why do I have to go through this and not being able to carry on following my path of truth?

There is a gap in you; there was a moment in your life that you were forced to act in a way that was unnatural and destructive to yourself or others; you were being forced to act this way or accept certain actions from others and this has created a gap in you which can also be called a schism.

Questions

1. Are you able to observe yourself and see your patterns?
2. What is a schism and how can you heal yourself?

Introduction

We believe that all people on planet Earth have the right to receive high light and should be connected to Earth. What kept Earth alive is her ability to create and nourish. Earth's transformation is going to affect the whole planet; you will all transform together. This can be successful if you are transforming in a space of creation, nourishment and healing.

There are many ways to experience growth. I share with you the easiest way and most effective. Connect to your true-self. This practice is related to personal growth as well as the collective one. It brings you clarity, healing and wisdom. You can clear you blockages and imbalances if you are able to observe them and understand the reason of the creation. Go deep in you without fear or criticism. When you are connected to truth you will be able to receive the light that will heal your imbalances.

Wisdom of Thoth: How Can you heal Yourself?

You have to look for peace within you and accept everything that you are including the schisms that you need to heal. People who need healing will receive cosmic light in great abundance. Being in a state of peace and acceptance, connecting to everything that was created in you in this life time and opening up to receive healing, will help you experience a strong connection to the cosmos.

If you focus on fear and limitation then you are going to experience the opposite effect; the schism will grow. Destruction is not a natural state for any being. Therefore you are responsible for bringing peace in you and to other beings around you. This can be done by releasing the fear and limitation that you have experienced in the past.

Your purity is your weapon and this weapon can only bring growth. So, do not hesitate to use it. Ask yourself, what are you longing for? What do you want to see on Earth? What should be Earth's transformation and how can you contribute? You are free to create and when you do you will be healed.

Questions

1. How can you heal yourself?
2. How can you create a space of peace in you to help you connect to your true-self?
3. Can your purity help you grow?
4. What is your understanding of the following phrase: "You are free to create and when you do you will be healed.

Introduction

The creator exists in peace, which is a space of growth, when does not follow competition, limitation, fear or survival. The creator knows that he does not own any of the qualities including the physical body. The creator is free from the need to own and possess. A creator is not affected by drama and artificial success. He is a person that connects to the energies and experience life as a learning process and connection to the astral plane, the true home of all beings. Human beings that want to be creators, have to purify themselves from all imbalances and then connect to the high light. All creation should be in a process of constant purification and transformation but this is not always possible because the light is not allowed to enter fragmented and distorted areas of growth.

Wisdom of Astaroth: Enter a Space of Peace and Truth will be Restored

It is important that people focus on healing their mind because distortion and illusion can create disease that can affect the whole physical body. If your mind is constantly occupied with thoughts you are already suffering from imbalances that can cause different illnesses.

If you live in a state of fear, the imbalances are growing and are affecting your physical body. It is not unusual that people feel very tired and exist in a survival mode most of the time. When this happens, you will accept everything that is presented to be good for you and you become addicted to artificiality and self-destruction.

If you want to live a long and healthy life, you have to heal your mind. A state of peace will bring you healing. If you truly want to clear your imbalances you have to observe yourself. Why your mind is constantly occupied with thought? Are your plans helping you to grow? Why is fear breading in you? How does this affect your everyday life?

Fear needs to be removed from people's minds only then they can connect to their true-self and fulfil their purpose. This is very important because you need to know why you are here on Earth and how can you use your full being to follow the divine plan that was created before your reincarnation.

The divine plan is your guide, your true-self is the path and the purpose is your destination. Fear has no place in you because it will only take you on a diversion towards limitation. If you allow fear to be your guide then you will experience suffering and disease will start affecting your body. Enter a space of peace and truth will be restored.

Questions

1. Why is it important to heal your mind and how can you achieve this?
2. Is fear affecting your mind?
3. What is your divine plan?
4. How can you enter a space of truth?

CHAPTER IV

Do not be afraid of letting go of your current affairs, personal ambitions, competitions, anger, desires; all these can only lower your ability to transform and become one with the gods and the divine plan. We are part of a renewal process which has started already in some spheres and will finally affect all. The main work will take place in the lower planes and will help people to adjust to the overall transformation where everything is linked and is moving together in a faster pace.

Introduction

It is important that Earth wakes up because she is the one who has to fight illusion and go ahead with a new transformation. When Earth is awake and able to look at herself she will realise that a transformation is absolutely necessary to help her stay alive but also to be able to go a step further and receive new light. I am ready to help Earth to transform; I am longing to see her experiencing a new golden era. For this to happen, all illusion, distortion and trauma needs to go away.

The schism which makes Earth weak needs to be cured. There is no other way to heal Earth than building bridges between the Pleroma and the planet. People of Earth, you are responsible for opening up to the light of the cosmos. This cannot happen if you are blocked by distorted thoughts and lifestyle. Free yourself from everything that holds you back. If you don't choose truth you have lost your chance to fulfil your purpose in this lifetime.

Wisdom of Astaroth: Transforming Planet Earth

There is a divine process that allows us to connect to Earth with her creation with the cosmic light. We are opening channels on the Aura of Earth and all her reflections in the cosmos, for the light to go through. We are recharging all relevant electromagnetic fields and we are transforming many parts of Earth's existence.

We also want to connect the outer with the inner parts of Earth and bring balance between them. We want to empower humanity and help human beings experience cosmic growth. This process has been applied to many planets of the lower plane. Earth however is unique because she was created to be a Goddess and a high creator.

Humanity is waking up but is not seeking truth and growth. Illusion, fear, negativity are still the driving force and the way they think and act. We want you to be brave enough to remove all garments of artificiality and fear and start observing yourself. The masks of the persona are not needed because they are not helping you to fulfil your purpose.

You can be naked and pure when you deal with your life challenges. This way you will understand that challenge is growth. There are also artificial challenges that are fed by the ego. When you are pure, you are able to recognize artificiality and this will help you diminish its power against you. We are all here to evolve and humanity's task is to evolve while is sitting on the back of a goddess. Transforming yourselves and the planet is a high goal that we all share.

Questions

1. How can you support Earth's transformation?
2. Can humanity transform with Earth and experience growth and unity?
3. What is the persona and how can affect your growth?

Introduction

In ancient times, young people were brought up to connect to their body, understand their skills and talents and try to master them. They knew that the path of truth is connected to their true-self and the divine plan. All people supported their community with their skills, were able to create in others and maintain a strong bond with Earth and the cosmos.

They recognized that they can only stay alive and grow if they were connected to Earth, the creator Goddess and allow the light of the cosmos to go through them. When you are aware of those cosmic laws and you experience them in your everyday life, you are already connected to your true-self and you have a clear understanding of your purpose.

Wisdom of Thoth: The Path of Truth or the Path of Chaos

All human beings are able to create and be part of their creation. In ancient times, beings on Earth did not have many choices and they understood that they can either take the path of truth or the path of chaos. Both paths were clearly understood and families, teachers and social structures made people aware of the differences between the two paths.

Young people were brought up to connect to their body, understand their skills and talents and try to master them. They knew that the path of truth is connected to their true-self and the divine plan. All people supported their community with their skills, were able to create in others and maintain a strong bond with Earth and the cosmos.

They recognized that they can only stay alive and grow if they were connected to Earth, the creator Goddess and allow the light of the cosmos to go through them. When you are aware of those cosmic laws and you experience them in your everyday life, you are already connected to your true-self and you have a clear understanding of your purpose. I do not see the people of your time having these experiences. This is because the distortion that is partly man-made has reached high levels and people are disconnecting from truth and are connecting to illusion.

Many of you believe that you have countless options: when you buy your food, it seems that there is not enough space to store the food products that you can eat. In reality most of your food options do not offer nourishment. If you take away the poisonous and artificial substances you are left with a small number of choices.

This number becomes even smaller when you try to answer the following questions; is the food produced locally and is it produced in a healthy and balanced way? Do not be surprised if you are left with no food choices. It is the same with your life style and achievement. How many of your choices bring you growth, support other people's growth and your connection to Earth and the cosmos? This will give you an indication as to what path you are following: the path of truth or the path of chaos.

Questions

1. Can you explain the following phrase: "All human beings are able to create and be part of their creation."
2. How did ancient people understand their path and purpose?
3. Why is it important to connect to Earth?
4. What are your choices in life?

Introduction

It seems that in the beginning of a life cycle you are working on your own for your own preparation. People on Earth who want to grow have to disconnect from patterns and cycles of the past. This can be achieved in different ways: observe yourself; look at the link between past patterns and present ones; observe artificiality in your life and connect to your true ambitions regarding your personal growth. You should be happy from within. This type of happiness is constant and everlasting but the artificial one fades away. You grow when all actions and thoughts are true to your life path and purpose. This should be your measurement when you are about to take a step in your quest for truth.

Wisdom of Thoth: Destructive Food and Lifestyle Patterns

I am here to share light with you, help you overcome illusion and find your way to your truth and purpose. Your food and lifestyle patterns can show clearly your path of growth. If you are one of those people who are attracted to globally advertised products and a life style that is an imitation of a social pattern then your growth is limited.

You have to look around you and recognize that artificiality can stop your growth and also harm your physical, mental and energy being. Your food affects your ability to grow and evolve, becoming a receiver and transmitter of light. You have to observe yourself and examine your eating patterns. What are your favorite meals?

What are your favorite products and where do you buy them? What are your expectations when you buy those products? Do you prepare your own food? How often and when do you eat? Do you share your food with others and what benefit do they receive from this exchange?

Eating the right food is receiving light that heals your being and passes information and guidance to your physical and energetic body. When you eat the right food and the right amount when it is needed, you give life to yourself; you can heal physical and mental illnesses, receive clarity, become grounded and you are also able to open up to the cosmos.

When you share this with others, your ability to receive and transmit light is multiplied. There are also people on Earth that are suffering from imbalances caused by excessive eating. This is linked to consumerism and destruction. Many beings are following an illusionary life style which supports self-destruction and living in a distorted state.

You have countless choices of harmful and artificial products whose only purpose is to be bought and sold. Nourishment and life choices can become great channels for the cosmic light to go through but if you pick the ones that are advertised then not only you are shutting down all entries but you speed up the end of your life cycle.

Questions

1. How can you overcome illusion?
2. What is your understanding of the following phrase: "If you are one of those people who are attracted to globally advertised products and a life style that is an imitation of a social pattern then your growth is limited."
3. Does your life style support wellbeing?
4. How do you nourish yourself?

Introduction

Human beings should celebrate their connection with Earth; connect to her creation and the energies of the planet. People should celebrate their ability to exist on Earth to know their purpose and tools and experience clarity and growth. Many of you relate celebration with excessive consumerism, feeding your body with toxic substances, disconnecting from your true-self and get attached to the persona and the ego, try to intimidate others and completely ignore your purpose, be greedy and unsatisfied because you are not able to reach illusionary goals.

All beings receive guidance to help them grow and evolve and the ones who are chosen to reincarnate on Earth are guided in order to fulfil their purpose, bringing the astral light to the physical plane.

The Gods' dream for creation is to restore Earth to her golden age by purifying her from all trauma, distortion and fragmentation. Once the elements of stagnation and imbalance are removed, the precious flower of light and wisdom that Earth once was will be revealed. Earth will be reborn from within and enter a new cycle of growth. She was created to exist for eternity and protect her creation to complete its life cycle. But as Earth loses control of her power and allows distortion to take over, the gods will have to intervene, connecting Earth to cosmic wisdom, healing and reminding her to exist as a creator once again.

Wisdom of Thoth: A State of Well-Being

Human beings on Earth exist in a fragmented state not being able to connect to the cosmos, the Earth, their physical body and energies. You have to fight fragmentation if you want to experience growth and your first step is to connect to your physical body and understand that it is an extension of cosmic creation.

The well-being of your body should be one of the priorities in your everyday life. You should fight artificiality and pollution and look for ways to consume less and receive more nourishment. Mental health can be healed when you are able to balance energies, thoughts and physicality. You are going to have a fulfilled life when you feel supported and free to experience your purpose; this is a state of well-being.

When you experience a state of expansion beyond fragmentation, you will realize that you have abilities and skills that can help you fulfil your purpose. The physical being is surrounded by energies whose function is to attract cosmic light, create a bond between your Earth-existence and your astral body and connect to the energies of Earth and humanity.

Beings on Earth are able to receive and transmit energy to one another, offer healing, maintain balance, pass information, guidance and cosmic wisdom. Living a healthy life and clearing imbalances. Being able to receive and transmit light is not a difficult task. It is a natural process of renewal which takes place in all cosmic beings.

Focusing on wellbeing, connecting to your body and clear all the energy connections will help you to experience growth. If this is your choice, you will achieve and experience unity. Some of you may need to take action in order to keep their body healthy and balanced. It may be that you need to change your life style, patterns and the time and effort that you dedicate to yourself in order to connect and grow. This is your challenge and it is also a great opportunity for individual and collective evolution. Do not stay passive but embrace your physicality because it is a cosmic tool.

Questions

1. What is fragmentation?
2. What is your experience of the following phrase: "The well-being of your body should be one of the priorities in your everyday life."
3. What is your understanding of the following phrase: "beings on Earth are able to receive and transmit energy to one another, offer healing, maintain balance, pass information, guidance and cosmic wisdom."
4. "Do not stay passive but embrace your physicality because it is a cosmic tool." What will be your next step?

Introduction

All of you who have reincarnated on Earth you should be aware that your connection to the planet is of great importance. You are part of Earth's creation and your purpose is to experience life as a human being, connecting to others and creating bonds of light between the cosmos, humanity and Earth. Your journey away from illusion is not supposed to be a solitary and painful event but a rewarding and joyous experience.

Everything you do in your everyday life should involve receiving and transmitting light to others. People on Earth have a great deal of support and guidance coming to them from the astral plane but they choose not to communicate with their spiritual guides. Everything that is pure in you, you hide away, you dismiss it, you disconnect from it. If you wish to find your path do not look at sparkling, inviting and deceiving mind-structures. Simply look inside yourself and find this sacred part of you, your purity, and make it your guide. Be diaphanous, exist and live as a diaphanous being.

Many of you say that you have to stay grounded. Do you understand what this means? When you reincarnate on Earth you travel from a different plane and your enter Earth's physical and third dimensional existence.

The cosmic light is your guide to a fulfilled and balanced life on Earth; to help you explore physicality and bring light to the planet. You cannot bring light to Earth if you do not have a bond with her and that is why being grounded is very important.

Wisdom of Thoth: Staying Grounded

All of you who have reincarnated on Earth you should be aware that your connection to the planet is of great importance. You are part of Earth's creation and your purpose is to experience life as a human being, connecting to others and creating bonds of light between the cosmos, humanity and Earth. Many of you say that you have to stay grounded.

Do you understand what this means? When you reincarnate on Earth you travel from a different plane and your enter Earth's physical and third dimensional existence.

It is very important that you see yourself as a human being on Earth who is also connected to the cosmos. The cosmic light is your guide to a fulfilled and balanced life on Earth; to help you explore physicality and bring light to the planet. You cannot bring light to Earth if you do not have a bond with her and that is why being grounded is very important.

If you are one of these people who do not want to focus on their physicality and you are attracted to unearthly energies, you are going on a diversion. This can cause a premature end of your life cycle. When you are embracing your physicality, looking after your body and trying to balance all energies then you will be rewarded to a long-life cycle.

If you go against your physical growth then you go against your life on Earth. Human beings are often unaware of the outcome of their actions and the mind is not able to maintain clarity. When the body is connected to energies from higher planes, the mind is not able to process this and then confusion and distortion can affect the being. Staying grounded and not relying on the mind-logic can help you balance your physical existence and your connection to your astral body and growth. You can always connect to Earth to help you maintain a physical and energetic balance in you.

Questions

1. Can you explain the following phrase: "You are part of Earth's creation and your purpose is to experience life as a human being, connecting to others and creating bonds of light between the cosmos, humanity and Earth."
2. What is your experience connecting to Earth and staying grounded?
3. How can human beings go against their growth?
4. What is your understanding of the following phrase: "You can always connect to Earth to help you maintain a physical and energetic balance in you."

Introduction

Human beings on Earth are connected to the light of the cosmos. All beings receive guidance to help them grow and evolve and the ones who are chosen to reincarnate on Earth are guided in order to fulfil their purpose, bringing the astral light to the physical plane.

Humans who exist in third dimensional Earth are connected to all parts of their being such as the astral body, higher-self and creation code but due to distortion and fragmentation are not aware of it. Beings, which are chosen to reincarnate on Earth in order to bring the astral light to the physical plane, can get lost in the jungle of physicality.

The physical body is the vehicle to help the being experience life on Earth. When the baby is born tries to balance the astral and the physical existence. It experiences a connection to the astral plane and it is still aware of the divine plan of this reincarnation. Earth's third dimensional reality weakens a being's ability to connect to the astral plane.

Wisdom of Thoth: Astral Beings Reincarnating on Earth

Human beings on Earth are connected to the light of the cosmos. This is a natural law and it is also a cosmic law. The astral being that is going to be reincarnated on Earth is aware of its past reincarnations, the lessons that need to be learned and the divine plan. When the being is in the womb, it is still an astral energy that is allowing the physical body to be created.

The physical body is the vehicle to help the being experience life on Earth. When the baby is born tries to balance the astral and the physical existence. It experiences a connection to the astral plane and it is still aware of the divine plan of this reincarnation. Earth's third dimensional reality weakens a being's ability to connect to the astral plane. However, the biggest obstacle is growing up among beings that are completely disconnected from their astral growth and the social systems that support illusionary beliefs and create distortion in people's minds.

Young children are forced to think of their future role in the society. They are programmed to accept illusion as truth and completely ignore their purpose and the divine plan of their reincarnation even if they decide to connect to their true-self at some point in their lives. They will have a hard time purifying themselves from the countless layers of illusion, distortion and artificiality that have affected them over the years.

Freedom and truth are stages of growth that not many people experience on Earth. If you connect to them and allow them to guide you, you will connect to your true-self and purify your imbalances. Knowing the divine plan of your reincarnation is your right and duty. You are all able to fulfil your purpose because the obstacles that stop you are illusionary and are not part of your divine plan. Allow truth to enter your house and be your guide and best friend. Then freedom will follow.

Questions

1. Can human beings stay connected with their astral body?
2. What is the biggest obstacle for you to connect to your astral body?
3. What is your understanding of the following phrase: "Freedom and truth are stages of growth that not many people experience on Earth."
4. How can you experience truth and freedom and become creator of your life?

Introduction

When human beings chose to experience a distorted life, they block the divine light and cosmic wisdom from entering their being. Divine guidance will not only help them to grow but will help them to connect to their true-self which is a natural law of creation. To know yourself, you have to go through a process of purification to help you disconnect from all artificialities in order to experience your true abilities, weaknesses, strengths, talents and skills. When you connect to your true-self you will become aware of your purpose in this life time. We are not working only for our own growth but we exist to support other beings and help them on their path of growth and evolution.

Now you have to empty yourself from the influence of distortion. Purify yourself in order to see your true-self. This is a hard task if you take different diversions but it is an easy task if you just follow your path and be ready to detach yourself from the false persona you created over the years. Truth is one; the way to truth is one and direct. Humanity on Earth needs to wake up to truth; it will be ideal if a collective purification and clearance of distortion can take place on Earth. This is why we are here and we want to communicate to you right now.

Wisdom of Thoth: Purification is a Process of Knowing Yourself

Purification is a process of knowing yourself and let go of your imbalances. There are many people who cannot connect to truth because illusion has taken over their being and imbalances have created schisms. If this is what you experience then your way to meet and accept truth will be long. All people on Earth have imbalances and purification is always needed this is how you are able to tune your energy to the high energies of your astral being and exist in harmony with the cosmos.

If you are new to purification, I advise you to start by getting into a meditative state, disconnecting from all thought and seek absolute peace in you and around you. When you are in a peaceful state you can ask yourself simple questions such as what is blocking my way to fulfil my purpose or what life experience has made me grow? When you ask this question for the first time you may not have an answer or the mind will try to interfere.

If you do not have an answer you can try again. If your mind interferes then you should try to disconnect from pattern-thinking and connect to peace again; peace leads to truth. If you start understanding the form of your imbalance, you can specifically ask a question related to it. When human beings examine their behavior, they are often affected by negativity that blocks the cosmic light to go through and heal them.

They feel guilty, sad, angry, weak or unable to face truth. This is a path you should not take if you want to complete the purification process. Observe yourself as an outsider, someone who is not affected by the imbalance; your role is to bring peace and create new life in a being that is suffering from a schism.

You can be an observer of your actions when you become your essence looking at the persona. Purification may seem to some not an easy task. However it is absolutely necessary to help you grow. When you experience purification, you will realize that is a natural process of cleansing all impurities of a distorted third dimensional reality and allow the cosmic light to create light and high energies. We are here to support you and help you open up to the laws of cosmic creation.

Questions

1. What is purification?
2. Explain the following phrase: "All people on Earth have imbalances and purification is always needed this is how you are able to tune your energy to the high energies of your astral being and exist in harmony with the cosmos."
3. What is your experience with negativity?
4. How can you disconnect from impurities and distorted patterns?

Introduction

People will experience true awakening and connection with Earth, when they are able to express truth in all representations of their lives. Earth will teach you that your body is a tool and the gods created on Earth's numerous resources to help you maintain balance and harmony to your whole being.

You can create a space of truth away from the tricks of illusion and you will be able to create your own life. This is not an achievement it is a natural process that you have forgotten. Your journey away from illusion is not supposed to be a solitary and painful event but a rewarding and joyous experience. Everything you do in your everyday life should involve receiving and transmitting light to others. Earth can provide for all her species not only food but also healing, purification, energy and resources in order to bring balance, harmony and encourage communication between all bodies.

Wisdom of Thoth: How Can we Support Earth and her Creation and How can we Escape Illusion and Return to Nature?

Most human beings feel hopeless when they attempt to escape illusion because they cannot see all the support they can receive to help them connect to Earth. Your journey away from illusion is not supposed to be a solitary and painful event but a rewarding and joyous experience. Everything you do in your everyday life should involve receiving and transmitting light to others.

This can be done constantly with whoever and wherever you are. When you have pure intention and you are able to share your light with others, you also have the ability to connect, heal, purify and transform others. Your genuine connection may not bring you a financial reward but it will open you up to the cosmic light and connect you to your true-self. All people have the ability to connect and heal others and themselves; when you heal others you also heal yourself because the cosmic light goes through you and brings transformation to all that it connects to.

Every day you are given the chance to heal yourself and others, to allow cosmic light to go through you, let go of imbalances and allow transformation to take place. You do not have to plan or try hard when you are healing a being. You just have to allow it to happen and it will happen when you have pure intention. Illusion creates fear in you and when you are in this state you block your light and instead of healing you are transmitting fear and distortion.

People are sometimes unaware of the healing they receive or they are not able to open themselves up to the cosmic light. Some people may go against you and this is when illusion fights back in order to spread fear and block your light. You have to create a space of peace where you exist in peace, truth and freedom. Truth is your armor and the cosmic light is your sword. You are not here to fight but to heal and create. This way you connect to Earth, support her growth and her connection to the cosmos.

Questions

1. How can you support Earth and her creation and how can we escape illusion and return to nature?
2. Can human beings escape illusion?
3. How can you receive and transmit light and why is it important?
4. Why should you create a space of peace?

Introduction

In the Golden age there was no separation between human beings and the animal kingdom. During the golden age, all beings, animals and plants lived in harmony with each other and stay connected to the energies of the planet. All beings contributed to the overall growth of the whole being, Earth. When the planet was colonized by the intruders, the balance and harmony on the planet were interrupted. Earth became a colony and the alien forces became the rulers.

Humanity is not in control and does not own Earth's creation. Human beings have their own cycle of growth and it is related to the cycle of other beings on Earth. You are all transmitting and receiving light to support your growth and Earth's evolution.

Wisdom of Thoth: Reincarnation of Human Beings, Animals and Other Species

Human beings on Earth have the tendency to separate themselves from the rest of the creation and see themselves as superior. They think that everything should belong to the human race: the riches of the Earth and the riches of the cosmos. You believe that you are the only living species in the cosmos and your creator that appears to have a physical body similarly to yours will reserve for you the best place in an unearthly "paradise" called heaven.

Humanity is not in control of Earth's creation. You have your own cycle of growth that corresponds to the cycle of other beings on Earth. You are all transmitting and receiving light to support your growth and Earth's evolution. There are certain types of species that are connected to Earth and they constantly reincarnate on the planet. Other beings including humans and animals they either reincarnate on other star systems or they exist in the astral plane.

In the Golden age there was no separation between human beings and the animal kingdom. There was no difference between humans and animals because they all knew their purpose which is to receive and transmit light, create balance and support others to follow their path. They were aware of their astral existence and their connection to the cosmic light. In the Golden Era there was a much greater and more intricate variation of species and there were beings that shared animal as well as human characteristics.

Currently on Earth, the human race, as well as the animal kingdom, has been reduced dramatically and the cause of this is a series of disasters that took place on Earth many thousands of years ago. The human superiority is illusionary and destructive to Earth's creation. People think that if animals were intelligent they could invent and develop language, social structures, monetary systems, science and politics. My answer to this is that animals have been protected by the energies of Earth and the cosmos not to follow illusionary paths and stay focused on the cosmic creation that exists around them.

Questions

1. Can you explain the following phrase: "Human beings on Earth have the tendency to separate themselves from the rest of the creation and see themselves as superior."
2. Can humanity control Earth's creation?

3. What is your understanding of the following phrase: "The human superiority is illusionary and destructive to Earth's creation."
4. Can human beings heal Earth and her creation?

Introduction

Every living being, including the planets and the universes are surrounded by an aura. An aura is all the energies of the being organised in electromagnetic fields. These electromagnetic fields are used as receivers and transmitters of energy as well as balancing and regulating the inner and outer light. What you call matrix is an artificial copy of the aura which was made to control and suppress the light.

Everything that exists is light and energy and is constantly moving within the being, within the aura of a being, connecting to other beings, planets, planes and the cosmos. This is how we describe life, a constant flow of energy. Energy is moving in a circular motion and there is a certain pattern that is followed in order to maintain life and growth. When energies are moving in one's body are clearing, purifying old blockages and imbalances and rejuvenating the body. Energy is always connecting you with other beings, planets and planes and this is because without unity we cannot achieve growth and evolution. It is not good enough to stay alive, your main purpose is to grow and with your growth you affect the cosmos.

Wisdom of Thoth: The Aura

People on Earth can see and feel the physical body but they do not know its function and purpose. Part of its purpose is to connect a being to the Earth's energies and allow the cosmic light to connect to Earth and her creation. The physical body is surrounded by what you know as aura which allows your physicality to receive and transmit energy.

Your aura is your energy body that has multiple functions. It helps you communicate energetically. It acts as a form of protection, supports the body to function, offers healing and connects the body to the astral plane. Your energy body is affected by your physicality, your interaction with others, Earth's energies and your ability to disconnect from distortion and open up to your true-self, the cosmic light and your astral body.

Distortion and fragmentation can affect your aura as well as your ability to connect to the cosmic light and your astral body. Your aura can suffer from imbalances which can affect the physicality. You cannot heal the physical body when there are imbalances in your aura. When you receive healing is directed first to your energies and then travels through them to the physical body.

Your physical body and aura should be seen as one being. When you are fully aware of this, you can function in multiple and diverse ways. Most human beings are limited because they do not use their body fully to achieve their purpose. I advise you to explore all abilities that you have as a being of both energy and physicality and allow yourselves to grow and achieve your purpose.

Questions

1. What is the aura?
2. Can your aura support your growth?
3. Can distortion affect your aura?
4. How can you explore the abilities that you have being energy and physicality?

Introduction

Transformation is a common process for beings in higher spheres and can take different forms: healing, connecting to gods/source, receiving knowledge/tools, sending and receiving messages to beings involved, adjusting your vibration and moving to a different plane where you can play your part. Transformation in lower beings is slower and therefore not easily detected; sometimes can take several life times. It is very important that beings that exist in lower spheres start their process of transformation now.

Often illusion tries to fight back and keep you in a low state. There is a possibility that you will be very confused and your transformation may not be completed; you may decide to follow a diversion or you will not be able to fight illusion. Your ego can go against you. Ego is a great weapon for illusion and is used to attack and pollute your mind. When humans are able to fight illusion, they will support the planet's growth and transformation.

Wisdom of Thoth: Standing at the Crossroads During a Transformation

In every transformation, the being stands at the crossroads and has to choose between the path of truth and the path of distortion. During a process of transformation, imbalances will come to the surface and you may experience illusionary thoughts, you may have visions about going on a diversion or you may experience confusion.

Often illusion tries to fight back and keep you in a low state. Whatever happens to you during this process, I see it as a learning curve and an opening towards the path of truth. Fighting illusion gives you clarity. There is a possibility that some of you will become very confused and your transformation may not be completed; you may decide to follow a diversion or you may not be able to fight illusion. Your ego can go against you. Ego is a great weapon for illusion and is used to attack and pollute your mind.

When the ego goes against your being, a great imbalance is created. Many of the imbalances have very deep roots and when you transform and you are able to move on towards your purpose you may not have achieved to totally purify yourself from imbalances and their roots.

This is why beings on Earth need to go through a series of transformations to bring some balance into their being. There are many ways to disconnect from illusion and you can pick any way suitable to your needs and tools. You all have to recognize illusion; this is the first step. Recognizing illusion is your first victory but is prepared to be attacked again. It is always good to exist in a state of peace where you can connect to the cosmic light; the only truth.

Questions

1. Can you describe the process of transformation?
2. Can you explain the following phrase: "Fighting illusion gives you clarity."

3. How can you purify yourself from imbalances?
4. How can you connect to the cosmic light?

Introduction

People on Earth understand and connect to the physical body and the mind. They understand their body as a group of separate organs that have an individual purpose and exist in isolation; they are not able to communicate or support each other. You understand growth as a competitors' race that will take you to the highest part of a social-pyramid structure.

You were all given a body, mind, heart, soul and spirit to be used as vehicles in order to get to your final destination. You were given freedom to choose different paths in order to gain experience and learn lessons from them. Your true life path is a single line without shortcuts and diversions and it is connected to both your essence and creation code. Once this is realized, you will not sway elsewhere. You will know that you have been here all along. All options, questions, uncertainties, dramas and failures in your life will fade. You begin to experience your essence, divine purpose and your existence in all of its forms, physical and astral and you become aligned to your own essence.

Wisdom of Thoth: Your Intention and your Guide in this Reincarnation

People on Earth understand their existence, being the physical body and the mind. They see the body as a group of separate components that are not able to communicate or support each other grow. They see the body as a machine that is controlled by a device, the mind, which is supposed to be able to gather information and send instructions to all parts of your being-machine. You understand growth as a movement that will take you to the highest part of a social-pyramid structure.

For many of you there is no higher power than what exists on the top of the pyramid. For people who accept this as truth and dedicate their lives to serve and support the social structures, I know that they will never fulfil their purpose and will never achieve growth. Illusion supports the ego, false authority, social success, consumerism and money-orientated life styles and all aspects of negativity such as anger, greed, fear and limitation.

You probably know people who are accepted by others as superior. They appear to you wearing the garments of power and having unlimited resources that can be used to control the mind of humanity. If you are able to turn these people inside out and try to connect to their light and essence, you will find that not only they are not able to fulfil their purpose but they block many others to achieve their purpose too.

I am here to connect you to the light of the cosmos, to Earth and experience cosmic growth. Being your true-self will lead you to an effortless life. Connecting to your astral body will help you receive the cosmic light and transmit it to Earth and her creation. When you exist in unity with the cosmos, it will help you disconnect from your imbalances, all illusion and fragmentation on Earth and help others do the same. We all have an important duty and this is to fulfil our purpose and growth. This should be your intention and your guide in this reincarnation.

Questions

1. What is your understanding of your being?
2. What is your connection with your physical body?
3. Can you explain the following phrase: "Being your true-self will lead you to an effortless life."
4. What is your duty and how is this connected to your purpose?

Introduction

People on Earth understand the world around them as a polarity of good and evil. This is a characteristic of the third dimensional perception. All beings are in a process of growing and evolving. Your path has challenges and you will be called to take decisions for your own life and focus on staying on your path. You can escape illusion, reclaim your power, connect to your astral body and raise your vibration. Some people choose to give up their powers, others prefer to ignore their true-self and follow the growth of the blind and the deaf. When you choose this path you are harming yourself and you become a victim of your own ignorance.

Wisdom of Astaroth: Separation and Polarity

In lower planes, separation and polarity are apparent and are often viewed as natural laws. You understand yourselves as being a single unit of physicality and energy that came to Earth to exist and function as one single being. This is happening because transformation and growth are not constant.

Your understanding of higher planes and the beings that exist there are related to what you experience in your reality. You accept a masculine or feminine god with a physical form that is surrounded by physical objects or Earth like nature. You imagine that high beings have technology and physical needs as well as personality and character.

The high gods of the Pleroma are a unity that is able to connect to the source and bring its light to the cosmos. They cannot be seen or touched; I can simply describe them as an unseen electromagnetic field whose purpose is to create. This electromagnetic field does not experience creation by expanding but by connecting to the cosmos and transmitting light to it in order for the cosmos to expand.

There are beings that exist in high planes and they go through a transformation in order to connect to the gods' energy field. These beings exist in a lower plane and have special duties; often they are the connectors that help the cosmic light travel to all planes. The gods' energy field cannot be broken or altered; it is one being connecting to the source. When this takes place, the being becomes part of the source and as the cosmos is connected to the gods, the whole of creation becomes part of the source.

I have to explain that everything that exists is created by the light of our source and this connection cannot be diminished because if it is then life will stop. When the Gods connect to the source, all creation codes are energized and the connection between the source and all beings in all planes becomes stronger. The creation gods are part of our source's existence and this is how all creation is connected to the high light and is able to transform.

Questions

1. 1. What is your understanding of separation and polarity?
2. What is your understanding of the higher planes?
3. What happens when the gods connect to the source?
4. What is your connection to the source?

Introduction

There are many beings on Earth who are longing to achieve clarity, connecting to their true purpose, but they are entangled in the web of illusion and limitation. When authority gives you a role/social status they only try to empower themselves and continue to exist and rule. So if you are surrounded by the tight control of different hierarchies you have to look in yourself and find your true purpose and path. This is not an easy practice and it takes time to be accomplished but when you are finally awake to your true potential you will be empowered.

Many people on Earth never get to that level of understanding because they allow limitation, fragmentation and distortion to block their way. There are other beings that are able to disconnect from all negativity and live a life that is truthful and free. Those people know their path, have a good understanding of their purpose and have a deeper understanding of life. At this advanced stage, human beings need to connect with their teachers and masters of the higher realms in order to expand and grow beyond Earth's limitations.

Wisdom of Thoth: Limitation

In a low vibrational reality, human beings accept and believe that they are limited. They have many unanswered questions; they do not have clarity. They identify themselves with the physical body and the decay that takes place during their life cycle. There are people who want to be the leaders and want to control Earth and humanity.

The ones who experience weakness and the ones who want the power are going to find ways to empower themselves but they do not know that they both go on a diversion away from the truth. There are people who think that if they are surrounded by certain crystals, burning oils and incenses, praying, wearing certain clothes and holding certain objects are going to experience growth that will unite them with their astral body.

Eating healthy food is important to keep your body alive and balanced but is not helping you to fulfil your purpose. There are many treasures on Earth to help you feed your being but purification, transformation and growth help you understand your true-self.

Surrounded by powerful crystals that can receive and transmit light can help you meditate but purification is your task and duty. There are people who depend on different material objects and they think that they can be responsible for healing and growth. There are people who give their powers away to forces whose intention is not known. If you wish to know yourself, to fulfil your purpose and grow you have to disconnect from illusion and be brave to face your imbalances and limitations.

Questions

1. What is your experience of Earth's low vibration? How does it affect your growth?
2. What is limitation?
3. How can you empower yourself and focus on your growth and path?
4. Can you face your imbalances? How can you achieve this?

Introduction

The gods' project is to awake the inhabitants of Earth; disconnect them from the illusion; pass the divine light to them which will help them connect to their true-self and recognize their tools and purpose; enable them to heal Earth and the rest of the humanity. The gods want to communicate with all beings on the planet and heal all imbalances and blockages. The light of the gods is transmitted to Earth and we have to become pure channels of the cosmic energy for our own healing and purification as well as the Earth's.

Some of you may ask: why people on Earth go against their own growth and healing? We all exist in unity and growth. This is our driving force to help us connect to the Source. When you understand that all beings are created to experience unity by receiving and transmitting light then you will experience the cosmos being part of yourself.

We are all connected to each other and energy, which is information, passes from one body to another. If you have the skill to translate the cosmic information and bring it to your own plane then you are a creator.

Wisdom of Astaroth: If you Wish to Experience a Cosmic State

Some of you may ask: why people on Earth go against their own growth and healing? We all exist in unity and growth. This is our driving force to help us connect to the Source. When you understand that all beings are created to experience unity by receiving and transmitting light then you will experience the cosmos being part of yourself.

The process of your birth, entering a new life cycle, is designed by the cosmic light and what you truly are at the very first stages of your formation in the womb is cosmic light being transformed into physicality. Your body is alive because you are connected to the light and support your ability to be a receiver and transmitter of energy.

Connecting to other beings with your light is a natural process; connecting to your astral body is also a natural process. Visualize yourself being part of a vast electromagnetic field and your only experiences are unity, transformation and growth. See yourself as the light bringer and the one who supports life and creation in all planes.

This is your essence and your life on Earth should demonstrate this. Now you can observe yourself and look at your life experiences. Do you exist in unity with Earth and all beings around you? Do you support their growth? Do you support your own growth by eliminating negativity, illusion and fragmentation? Do you support healing for yourself and others? Do you exist in a space of peace connected to your true-self and are you aware of your purpose? These are the questions you should ask yourself if you wish to experience a cosmic state. You can find your path when you have pure intention. You will never find your path if you cannot connect to your true-self.

Questions

1. Why people on Earth go against their own growth and healing?
2. Can you explain the following phrase: "Your body is alive because you are connected to the light and support your ability to be a receiver and transmitter of energy."
3. Do you exist in unity with Earth and all beings around you? Do you support their growth?
4. Do you exist in a space of peace connected to your true-self and are you aware of your purpose?

Introduction

You can achieve growth by connecting to your own body; understand it as a unity of your astral body, higher-self and creation code. When you understand the unity of your bodies then you have to accept that the cosmos unites all beings with the source. Fragmentation on Earth is supported by certain forces who do not want humanity to follow its true purpose, grow as a cosmic being and connect Earth with the cosmos.

Fragmentation has transformed your life experience on Earth. You see your physical body as a machine of separate components and you accept the mind, being the superior tool. Your whole physical body is not in balance because you do not understand its true function; you have allowed your mind to be manipulated and often go against your physical body. Illusion has taken over your whole being by using fragmentation and distortion.

Wisdom of Thoth: Your own Existence

Your science has developed the ability to explain your mind functions through separation and fragmentation. You have invented many terms, characteristics and explanations to describe a fragmented mind. There is a force on Earth that is allowed to shape or limit your consciousness and this force wants to convince you that fragmentation is truth.

You also have a very distorted idea about your own existence: you believe that if you constantly use your mind you are intelligent and when you connect to your heart you are kind and compassionate. I want to say to you that the above statement is not true, it is illusionary. I understand growth as the only purpose of any being in the cosmos.

You can achieve growth by connecting to your own body; understand it as a unity of your astral body, higher-self and creation code. When you understand the unity of your bodies then you have to accept that the cosmos unites all beings with the source. Fragmentation on Earth is supported by certain forces who do not want humanity to follow its true purpose, grow as a cosmic being and connect Earth with the cosmos.

Fragmentation has transformed your life experience on Earth. You see your physical body as a machine of separate components and you accept the mind, being the superior tool. Your whole physical body is not in balance because you do not understand its true function; you have allowed your mind to be manipulated and often go against your physical body. Illusion has taken over your whole being by using fragmentation and distortion.

If you want to fight this and focus on your true purpose, you have to connect to your whole body and allow it to show you your purpose. Experience balance by maintaining a state of peace and focus on what you are experiencing at this moment. Connect to the cosmic light, see yourself as part of cosmic creation that is constantly growing and transforming. Experience freedom by blocking illusion to influence your mind. Following your path of growth, you will experience freedom to exist as a whole being.

Questions

1. Can you explain the following phrase: "You can achieve growth by connecting to your own body; understand it as a unity of your astral body, higher-self and creation code."
2. Can you explain the following phrase: "Fragmentation has transformed your life experience on Earth."
3. How can you experience balance and maintain a state of peace?
4. What is your path of growth?

Introduction

You, who are looking for your purpose, what is your strategy in your quest? For some people, purpose is just a word, an idea. For me purpose is a living being, much higher than the human being itself. A purpose of a being stays the same in all different realms and all reincarnations. It is a part of the higher self and perhaps it is the only part that stays close to the being in all different realms. Your purpose is a versatile instrument which was created with great effort and skill. You can always reach your purpose wherever you are because it is your compass through your whole growth.

All beings that exist on Earth including animals, plants and minerals are created to receive and transmit light and support Earth's connection to the cosmos. Being a creator, Earth gives life to countless receivers and transmitters of light. If you were free to connect to Earth and fulfil your purpose, she will also be free from her own imbalances, trauma, distortion and fragmentation. Reincarnating on Earth, you are given a difficult task, going through all different types of illusion and distortion and follow your true path.

Wisdom of Thoth: Staying on the Path of Truth is the Highest Reward

We are helping you understand your connection with Earth and the rest of the cosmic creation. All beings that exist on Earth including animals, plants and minerals are created to receive and transmit light and support Earth's connection to the cosmos. Being a creator, Earth gives life to countless receivers and transmitters of light.

You can see yourself as her extension and tool to receive and transmit light to the cosmos. You have a physical body to help you connect to the energies of Earth but you also have an astral body which is eternal and it is directly connected to the Source. Therefore, you are an astral being that was placed on Earth given a physical body and connected to channels for the cosmic light to go through you and reach Earth.

If you were free to connect to Earth and fulfil your purpose then she will also be free from her own imbalances, trauma, distortion and fragmentation. Reincarnating on Earth, you are given a difficult task, going through all different types of illusion and distortion and follow your true path.

You all focus on this and ignore your true purpose which is to connect the Earth with the cosmos. The ones who focus on illusion and the ones who passionately fight illusion are both disconnected from their true goal and the purpose of their reincarnation.

Being successful and popular is an idea that takes many forms in people's minds but it also causes fragmentation and confusion. What will happen to you if you are not successful? How will you feel if you are not a popular member of your community?

Some will say that this may lead to an imbalance that is rooted in low self-esteem. If human beings on Earth knew their purpose and their connection to the Earth and the cosmos then they will be able to understand that there is no need to compete for illusionary rewards. Staying on the path of truth is the highest reward.

Questions

1. Can Earth support your growth?
2. What is your connection with Earth's creation such as animals and plants?
3. Can you explain the following phrase: "you are an astral being that was placed on Earth given a physical body and connected to channels for the cosmic light to go through and reach Earth."
4. What is your understanding of success?

Introduction

What is your understanding of time? Can your understanding of time help you grow and fulfil your purpose?

All living beings evolve in the present where all dimensions and all bodies merge in order to present a unity of divine grace. Growth is a constant process and we are only concerned with what we are able to create right now. You can expand your understanding and connection to the cosmos when you are able to experience growth which is taking place right now; this is how you are able to transform.

When human beings focus on time as a divider, they exist in fragmentation. In a low vibrational environment, where fragmentation is almost a natural law, all forms with their energetic fields have an opposite. These opposites are often understood as contrasting forces involved in an eternal war. There is always a fight of the white against the black or the big against the small or the woman against the man. If you wish to evolve beyond polarity and fragmentation you have to lose your perception of opposites, being two contrasting and separate entities. There is no fight against two elements there is only a union of the elements which will bring an eruption and a new life.

Wisdom of Thoth: A Diversion from your Path of Truth

Human beings are very concerned about time. Time is a divider, an organizer and can also be a life path for some of you. You are very concerned about what you can achieve in the future and what you have already accomplished during certain periods of time. Human beings have invented time and its different divisions.

They have created future to be a separate and often distant time in their life cycle. It is interesting to see that people on Earth are not able to organize, divide and predict life beyond their reincarnation and this is because time does not exist in other planes. Human beings are not able to connect to their astral body because they have accepted artificiality as their life path and the only reason of their existence. Time is artificiality and supports division, fragmentation and disconnecting you from your true-self.

Growth is a constant process and we are only concerned with what we are able to create right now. You can expand your understanding and connection to the cosmos when you are able to experience growth which is taking place right now; this is how you are able to transform.

It is interesting to see that people on Earth are very concerned about the past and future and they focus on planning and evaluating. Human beings call this intelligence, professionalism, success and methodology.

The creative mind does not need to rely on the past or the future but it needs to stay focused on the present task, expand and connect to the tools that can help the being achieve the high creation goal.

It is about connecting to your true-self, using your tools and developing your ability to grow and create in present time. Human beings are also told that they have to prepare themselves, go through an educational system of many divisions and stages in order to become successful professionals. You should never wait to fulfil your purpose.

All of you have this ability and when you all experience this in your everyday life your light becomes stronger and you open yourselves up to become a great receiver and transmitter of energy that can create and experience creation right now. Planning your growth is a limitation and a diversion from your path of truth.

Questions

1. What is your understanding of time?
2. Do you have the ability to exist in present?
3. Can you explain the following phrase: "Growth is a constant process and we are only concerned with what we are able to create right now."
4. Can you plan your growth?

Introduction

Human beings can only receive cosmic communication and healing when they connect to their true-self. There are many beings on Earth who are longing to achieve clarity, connecting to their true purpose, but they are entangled in the web of illusion and limitation. Thoth wants to reach all beings with his light and this is his advice: when people are able to empty their minds from all beliefs, aspirations, needs, suffering, pleasures and longings, they will discover their creator.

There are humans on this planet who are experimenting with spirituality and present it as a form of dogma or philosophy. In modern days, people have used many different trends, colourful terms and interesting theories.

I am not totally displeased with that because I can see that the inner-self opens the way for new discoveries and truth quests. However in the physical plane all high messages come distorted and eventually lose their true meaning.

Wisdom of Thoth: Fighting and Surrendering to the Manipulation of the Mind

I want to ask humanity a question: Why were you reincarnated on Earth and were given this life cycle?

How many of you are able to answer this question connecting to your true-self? My light goes through the messengers and many other beings that connect to me and I understand that humanity is chained and cut into pieces.

There is a force on Earth that wants to alter the consciousness of humanity and through the manipulation of the mind, disconnect humanity from the cosmos. The rulers that have influence and control over people are creating law and social rules to force people disconnecting from their true-self, their purpose, growth, natural and cosmic laws and the unity that connects all beings.

It seems that there is a hidden agenda and nothing is what it seems. Some of you may ask what is this force that is behind all this and why human beings are allowed it to take away their powers and understanding of themselves? The force is unseen and is not rooted on Earth even though the beings who are involved have existed on Earth. Some of you call them Gods or high beings and without knowing you are allowing them to go through you and control your mind.

All beings on Earth are affected by this force and this is why humanity is locked in a reality that is artificial and illusionary. Some of you may ask, can we disconnect from all artificiality and live a pure life with truth, freedom and growth? All of you have a mind and your mind has been affected by illusion, fragmentation and distortion.

To be able to come back to your natural state, you have to be able to recognize illusion and how it affects your mind and then you have to choose a life path that is connected to your divine plan. Standing at the cross roads you are becoming a warrior against illusion; you will have to fight with illusionary beliefs such as fear and uncertainty, disconnecting from friends, family and colleagues who are supporting illusion and the fear of survival.

When you are able to observe all these illusionary thoughts and feelings, you will arrive to a space of truth and you will be ready to follow the path of growth. There are many people who do not want to face illusion in their everyday life and disconnect from it and there are others who are going to battle but they move backwards and forwards, fighting and surrendering to the manipulation of the mind. This is an exhausting exercise that brings confusion. My advice to you is to connect to your true-self, understand your purpose and naturally walk the path of truth being the only path. This way illusion will start evaporate and allow you to win the battle without even fighting.

Questions

1. Can you connect to your true-self?
2. Can you explain the following phrase: "To be able to come back to your natural state, you have to be able to recognize illusion and how it affects your mind and then you have to choose a life path that is connected to your divine plan."
3. What is your understanding of mind manipulation?
4. How can you heal your mind and experience life with your whole being?

Introduction

The moon and the sun act as the mirror of the Earth and are all connected in an alignment. This galaxy was created to support Earth and its alignment, so we need to maintain it, renew it and not destroy it. The water on Earth is linked to the moon and the minerals and energetic fields to the sun. We are now trying to repair and strengthen parts of this alignment that have weakened but we have opposition from spirits who want to destroy it and strengthen different alignments in other galaxies.

You have to use your energy to strengthen bonds on Earth: bonds between people, activities, spirits, energy fields, actions, thoughts and imperfections. Accept it all and then embrace it all. Also teach others to do the same, physically or energetically so we can all travel together and expand.

When Earth is united she will acquire her status as a goddess of the Pleroma and will take her place which has been vacant for so long. They are many beings who are going through the same suffering as Earth, either because they are also confused or because they want to share the burden. I am telling you now that there is no pain, sorrow or anxiety if you decide to return to the golden era. If you believe that there is a golden era on Earth and you are going to accept it as reality, you will have no pain and suffering only love and happiness. Love is a great mystery and I have given it to you. Now you create the golden era and this is the place where you should be.

Wisdom of Thoth: Achieving Unity

Earth was created to support the growth and evolution of energy systems in lower planes that are in a transition. There were parts of the creation that existed in lower planes but were able to develop the ability to receive and transmit light. They were also able to go through a purification and transformation process; they will be able to transform into a new being through a rebirth process.

For this to happen higher beings or systems have to support and help the rebirth process to take place. This important duty was given to Earth and it was part of her divine plan. First we wanted Earth to become a creator of life that is never lasting and it is a reflection of cosmic creation.

We wanted Earth to be a creator of high energies that can be attached to a physical body. This way Earth's creation will experience high energetic structures as well as physicality. When Earth is able to master creation then she will go on becoming a creator in other systems and other planes.

This way she can support growth and evolution and bring the light of our Source to all planes. Earth's divine plan that was designed by our Source exists and currently shows that Earth went on a diversion and because of this she was not able to fulfil parts of her divine plan.

It is our responsibility to support Earth's growth, connect her to the light and give the ability to her creation to purify and transform. This is why we are here now to help you understand the purpose of your reincarnation on Earth and our duty, being the creators and life givers. Earth should not exist in fragmentation but in unity and this is what you all have to achieve in order to fulfil your purpose.

Questions

1. What is your understanding of the following phrase: "Earth was created to support the growth and evolution of energy systems in lower planes that are in a transition."
2. What can support Earth's rebirth?
3. Is possible for Earth to fulfill her divine path?
4. How can you support Earth's growth?

Introduction

Gods intended Earth to be a planet of many colors and shapes for the countless plants, animals and other species that they created. The next phase after the formation of the planet and its inhabitants was the training of Earth to become a high creator able to nourish and protect her species as well as create additional life. The gods knew from previous experiences in planetary evolution that if the planet does not learn to create on its own, continued life would be unsustainable. This was to become a great responsibility for such a young planet, as she had to learn to make life-creating decisions independently without godly intervention.

Wisdom of Thoth: Earth's Life Cycle

There was a time that the inhabitants of Earth were connected to the planet and understood that if they accept themselves as Earth's creation, they will be protected and nourished by high energies. Earth was able to connect to the cosmos and the Source like all creator Gods and this way she was able to receive and transmit high energies in abundance.

The first visitors understood this and their connection to Earth became their life purpose. When Earth became accessible to many visitors of lower planes, the balance and unity started to weaken. There were destructions on the surface of the Earth which caused extreme phenomena to take place on the planet. The creation of Earth was significantly reduced and many parts of it could not be inhabited anymore.

The planet is in balance when all elements co-exist in a harmonious way and allow creation to flourish. The only beings who remained on Earth after the destructions were the ones who were trapped on the planet and existed in very small groups. With the time they multiplied and were able to inhabit areas that could provide them with nourishment.

They did not focus on their connection with Earth and did not understand that Earth was a creator God. Instead they asked for help to beings from other realms. They asked for protection support and to give them the opportunity to rule and conquer. Human beings did not see themselves as part of Earth's creation but as the conquerors of a planet that lost its power and connection to the Source. This great fragmentation and separation has produced schisms and distortion. What you know as Earth's history from your scientific and religious books is only a cycle of evolution that is coming to an end.

Questions

1. What is your understanding of the following phrase: "The first visitors understood this and their connection to Earth became their life purpose."
2. What caused Earth to experience destruction?
3. Can you explain the following phrase: "Human beings did not see themselves as part of Earth's creation but as the conquerors of a planet that lost its power and connection to the Source."
4. What has produced Earth's schisms?

Introduction

You are here to receive the light and with it you will fight the low vibrational illusion of separation and polarity which has given birth to fear, greediness, survival and death of the real goal which is rebirth and transformation. We have the ability to create ourselves. We were given this ability by our Source. Without it, we will be non-existent. In the astral plane there is no death, there is no end. However, beings that lose their ability to create are non-existent. When humans are able to fight illusion and heal distortion, they will support the planet's growth and transformation. They are many people on Earth who are walking the path of awakening. Their numbers are going to grow; this is the divine plan.

Wisdom of Thoth: Purifying Layers of Distortion

When you fully disconnect from illusion you will be able to create your life; a life that is not a product of artificiality. When you are in this state you also attract people, who want to receive and transmit light to you. To achieve that you have to fully understand your purpose, your tools, and have the ability to create in you and others.

If you are dealing with some layers of distortion in your life but you are still supporting certain forms of illusion that come to you from your environment, you have to continue purifying yourself in order to achieve more clarity.

If you have not achieved clarity and you are trying to have a blanched life and fulfil your basic needs, you need to ask yourself these questions: What are you trying to achieve? Will this lead you to fulfil your purpose? Are you the only one who is influencing your decisions? Is your life related to other people's lives and how their needs affect you? Can you be truthful to yourself and understand fully what you can create in order to bring balance in your life? If you are able to answer these questions you will receive truth.

Questions

1. How can you create your life?
2. What is your experience with artificiality?
3. How can you purify yourself?
4. Can you be truthful to yourself and understand fully what you can create in order to create balance in your life?

Introduction

The cosmic light unites all creation with the Source. What you describe as false light is all artificiality and illusion that is created by the mind and other forces. Illusion and artificiality appear to be truth and the only way for success, happiness and fulfilment. If you accept this as truth then you will never connect to your true-self or your purpose; it is like putting on a blindfold and running into a maze. Connecting to truth is your purpose and the great gift given to you by our Source.

All living beings are united with the cosmic light and are part of the vast creation of our source. Humans who exist in third dimensional Earth are connected to all parts of their being such as the astral body, higher-self and creation code but due to distortion and fragmentation are not aware of it. All beings receive guidance to help them grow and evolve and the ones who are chosen to reincarnate on Earth are guided in order to fulfil their purpose, bringing the astral light to the physical plane.

Wisdom of Thoth: The Cosmic Light unites all Creation with the Source

The human mind tends to divide everything that exists into opposites. For you there is the good, true, organic light and there is also the false, weak, fragmented light.

What I experience is the light of the cosmos that is a perfect reflection of our Source and it is the greatest creative power in the cosmos. It is constantly moving, trying to reach all beings and all energies that exist in order to bring them growth, life and evolution.

The cosmic light unites all creation with the Source. What you describe as false light is all artificiality and illusion that is created by the mind and other forces. Illusion and artificiality appear to be truth and the only way for success, happiness and fulfilment. If you accept this as truth then you will never connect to your true-self or your purpose; it is like putting on a blindfold and running into a maze. Connecting to truth is your purpose and the great gift given to you by our Source.

Questions

1. Can you explain the following phrase: "The human mind tends to divide everything that exists into opposites."
2. What is the false light that affects humanity?
3. Can you explain the following phrase: Illusion and artificiality appear to be truth and the only way for success, happiness and fulfilment.
4. How can you connect to truth?

Introduction

Human beings should celebrate their connection with Earth, connecting to her creation and the energies of the planet. People should celebrate their ability to exist on Earth, to know their purpose and tools and experience clarity and growth. To us celebration brings great joy and fulfilment which supports our ability to fulfil our purpose. Many of you on Earth relate celebration with excessive consumerism, feeding your body with toxic substances, disconnecting from your true-self and get attached to the persona and the ego, trying to intimidate others and completely ignore your purpose, be greedy and unsatisfied because you are not able to reach illusionary goals. Earth and the cosmos can teach you a new way to celebrate life.

Wisdom of Thoth: Celebrate Unity

We would like people on Earth to be in a constant celebration. Celebrating their connection with Earth, her creation and everything else that exists in the cosmos. We want people to celebrate their ability to exist on Earth, to know their purpose and tools and to experience clarity and growth. To us celebration brings great joy and fulfilment which supports our ability to fulfil our purpose.

You should enjoy and celebrate your ability to fulfil your purpose every day. Celebration is unity. Unite with your whole being in order to receive the highest light and then unite with others to transmit and receive light. Some may ask: what is the appropriate way to celebrate? Bring joy to you and others, in other words share light and have pure intention to help you and others fulfil their purpose.

Many of you on Earth understand celebration very differently and perhaps without knowing, you feed the illusion which takes over your life. Many of you relate celebration with excessive consumerism, feeding your body with toxic substances, disconnecting from your true-self and get attached to the persona and the ego, try to intimidate others and completely ignore your purpose, are greedy and unsatisfied because you are not able to reach illusionary goals.

If you experience what I just described you do not celebrate life but destruction. When illusion is fully accepted, it brings destruction and disconnects you from life in all planes. When people follow the celebration of illusion they experience a short high peak of excitement and then for most of the time they feel empty and lost.

Having the clarity to see the symptoms, it helps you disconnect and find your way to purity. This is a straight path and it is always there for you to choose it and walk on it. Celebration is your unity with your true-self that can help you experience astral growth, bringing the light from the astral plane to Earth.

Questions

1. Is your life a celebration?
2. Is consumerism part of your life?
3. What is the celebration of illusion?
4. Can you explain the following phrase: "Celebration is your unity with your true-self that can help you experience astral growth, bringing the light from the astral plane to Earth."

Introduction

When we experience freedom then we can become the creators of our own life. Destroying our connection with the persona and the life style can help us discover our true-self.

Do not be afraid of letting go of your current affairs, personal ambitions, competitions, anger, desires; all these can only lower your ability to transform and become one with the gods and the divine plan. We are part of a renewal process which has started already in some spheres and will finally affect all. The main work will take place in the lower planes and will help people to adjust to the overall transformation where everything is linked and is moving together at a faster pace.

People on Earth who want to grow have to disconnect from patterns and cycles of the past. This can be achieved in different ways: observe yourself; look at the link between past patterns and present ones; observe artificiality in your life and connect to your true ambitions regarding your personal growth. You should be happy from within. This type of happiness is constant and everlasting, but the artificial one it fades away quickly and leaves a gap of dissatisfaction and longing. You grow when all actions and thoughts are true to your life path and purpose. This should be your measurement when you are about to take a step in your quest for truth.

Wisdom of Thoth: Fear of Losing the Persona

Humanity should connect and work for the same purpose and this is to bring the Golden Age on Earth. This is very important because if Earth transforms and returns to her Golden age, humanity and the rest of the creation are going to transform and become high vibrational beings. A high vibrational being is able to experience astral growth, connect fully with the cosmos, the High creator Gods, the Source and become a creator of high balance and perfect harmony within living beings.

Many of you may find my statement confusing because you cannot see yourselves as high creators and even if you want to fantasize that you are, you cannot create balance and harmony on planet Earth. So what stops you from being a high creator? Someone said that it is the fear of losing the persona but what does this mean? How do you understand the birth and creation of your persona? Is it something you are born with? Is it something you inherit or are you able to create it yourself?

The persona is related to the way you are able to absorb the Earth's energies, your physical characteristics in relation to your social standing, your acceptance of the persona and the ways you allowed it to develop and transform. The persona is not fully an artificial structure because it is related to your connection to Earth and humanity. It becomes a tool of artificiality when it is formed according to social criteria.

When you accept the persona as the only self then you are opening up to illusion and your understanding of your purpose is totally distorted. There are many people who have invested in the creation of their persona and the illusionary aspects of it. It is important to them that they participate and support a lifestyle without purpose that leads to illusionary rewards and satisfaction.

Human beings who do not know where they were before this lifetime and where they are going at the end of this life cycle do not know their purpose and live a confusing and distorted life. You can now observe yourself and look at your relationship with the persona. In what way is it illusionary and how is it helping you to fulfil your purpose? This is an important lesson, all of you need to study and bring knowing into your being.

Introduction

1. How can humanity support Earth's golden era?
2. Can you explain the following phrase: A high vibrational being is able to experience astral growth, connect fully with the cosmos, the High creator Gods, the Source and become a creator of high balance and perfect harmony within living beings?
3. What is your experience with the persona?
4. What is the influence of the persona to help you fulfil your purpose?

CHAPTER V

There is a miraculous way of living and this is being detached from beliefs, dogmas and archetypal behavior. All the above have been created to help you focus and sustain a certain consciousness and life experience. We are asking you now to abandon and destroy the persona and the life style. Our aim is to give everybody the tools they need in order to paint their own authentic picture of themselves and let their true purpose be revealed. We want you to detach yourself from all that you are, right now and connect to your true-self.

Introduction

For thousands of years people have been blindly looking for enlightenment. What they are actually looking for is a connection between their current state and life on Earth and the golden era. The only true reference to enlightenment was the time that Earth was a high vibrational planet with extensive plant and animal life and had direct communication with the gods who inhabited the planet. Earth's dream was to become the Pleroma or a reflection of it. During this time, the planet enjoyed high creation, high evolution and perfect harmony between her elements and species.

Fragmentation, distortion, illusion and limitation are not part of the cosmos and are not part of the divine plan. This means that they have no purpose and can be easily removed. There are people on Earth who preach that they hold a superior position because they are enlightened and others have to follow them to become enlightened themselves.

Wisdom of Thoth: Connecting to your Astral Body and Experience Growth on Earth

Many people on Earth are able and they do connect to the light of the cosmos. Many of you have experienced a high understanding or a connection to the cosmic creation and then you call yourself enlightened. This knowing and growth that enters your mind and physical being is not a constant state but it is a single moment of truth.

Some of you may ask: what is the significance of this and why human beings are not able to exist in a space of constant growth? It is clear that humanity is connected to the cosmos and therefore is a pure channel of cosmic light. Humanity was created to be the link between the cosmos and Earth and allow the cosmic light to flow through Earth and her creation.

Fragmentation, distortion, illusion and limitation are not part of the cosmos and are not part of the divine plan. This means that they have no purpose and can be easily removed. There are people on Earth who preach that they hold a superior position because they are enlightened and others have to follow them to become enlightened themselves.

This is an example of fragmentation, distortion and non-growth that can take place on Earth. All human beings are designed to receive and transmit light and experience constant growth. My question is: are you able to disconnect from illusion and devote yourselves to a life of truth and purity and function as a constant receiver and transmitter of light? Are you able to fully disconnect from an illusionary lifestyle, artificial expectations, fear and drama? Are you able to know yourself and deal with your own imbalances without negativity or guilt? Are you able to give to others what is very precious to you?

There are many questions I want to ask humanity and I hope that this way they start discovering their true-self and disconnecting from all artificiality. When you are able to exist in a state of constant growth you will be able to create a temple of light in your being. This will lead you to your purpose, avoiding all obstacles and diversions. In this state you will be able to connect to your astral body and experience astral growth on Earth.

Questions

1. What it the significance of this and why are human beings not able to exist in a space of constant growth?
2. What is your understanding of the following phrase: "Humanity was created to be the link between the cosmos and Earth and allow the cosmic light to flow through Earth and her creation"?
3. Can superiority serve Earth's and humanity's growth?
4. Can you explain the following phrase: "When you are able to exist in a state of constant growth you will be able to create a temple of light in your being."

Introduction

When you know your body, you understand that it is a microcosm of high creation and a link to all life. Your body is your temple and path for growth and expansion to other realms. There is a motion inside you that keeps you alive and anchors you to the physical plane; you understand that this corresponds to the vibration of your astral body and it is also linked to planetary motion.

Your physical body is a transmitter and receiver of energy and this supports the balance of all its different functions. If you are aware of your different organs and the way they operate, you should know that they are all connected and affect each other's growth. The physical body connects to the energies of other planetary bodies such as the moon and the rest of creation. It is designed to exist in harmony with the cosmic creation, to be able to connect to its astral body, higher-self and creation-code. The creation code can connect to all realms and at the same time be part of our Source's light.

Wisdom of Thoth: Energy Systems

If people on Earth need to know about energy systems on the human body, I can say that they are countless. Your physical body is a transmitter and receiver of energy and this supports the balance of all its different functions. If you are aware of your different organs and the way they operate, you should know that they are all connected and affect each other's growth.

In the physical body there is an individual but also a collective growth and this is related to the whole body's ability to receive, transmit and balance light. The physical body does not exist in isolation; there are other bodies around it and there are also the energies of the Earth which support a complex electromagnetic field.

Furthermore, the physical body connects to the energies of other planetary bodies such as the moon and the rest of the creation. It is designed to exist in harmony with the cosmic creation, to be able to connect to its astral body, higher-self and creation-code. The creation code can connect to all realms and at the same time be part of our Source's light.

If you use a microscope, as humans do, to analyze human energy systems you will not come to any conclusion because there is no beginning or end, there is no name or number, and there is no description or classification. Human beings should experience some of their energy systems and should allow balance to take place. When you experience the energies of your own body then you will realize that you are a microcosm in a macrocosm.

Questions

1. What are the energy systems of a physical body?
2. Can you explain the following phrase: "In the physical body there is an individual but also a collective growth and this is related to the whole body's ability to receive, transmit and balance light."
3. What are the bodies that connect to the physical body?
4. Can you explain the following phrase: "When you experience the energies of your own body then you will realize that you are a microcosm in a macrocosm."

Introduction

The distortion on the planet has disconnected people from their true goals and values, but all is going to change when Earth is purified and is able to return to her perfect state. Due to the distortion and fragmentation on the planet, the astral knowledge cannot penetrate the physical plane and human beings exist in isolation surrounded by the veil of illusion. It is important that we clear the channels of communication and connect to the astral plane as well as the Earth's energies.

All scientific findings are accepted by humanity as the absolute truth and this affects their consciousness. People are convinced that only a selective few, the highly educated ones, are able to provide answers and shape people's understanding. Therefore, humanity has to follow and accept dogma without experiencing truth.

There is a miraculous way of living and this is being detached from beliefs, dogmas and archetypal behavior. All the above have been created to help you focus and sustain a certain consciousness and life experience. We are asking you now to abandon and destroy the persona and the lifestyle. Our aim is to give everybody the tools they need in order to paint their own authentic picture of themselves and let their true purpose be revealed. We want you to detach yourself from all that you are, right now and connect to your true-self.

Wisdom of Astaroth: The Dogma of Science

Human beings on Earth while they live in a space of distortion and fragmentation want to explain everything they see and put a label on it to demonstrate their great knowledge and superiority on Earth. They have developed many educational branches that are involved in studying physical phenomena on Earth and beyond.

All scientific findings are accepted by humanity as the absolute truth and this affects their consciousness. People are convinced that only a selective few, the highly educated ones, are able to provide answers and shape people's understanding. Therefore, humanity has to follow and accept dogma without experiencing truth.

I can assure you that everybody can connect to Earth and understand the natural laws in a deeper and more profound way than the scientists and the experts. Open yourself to Earth's energies and experience her cycle of growth and evolution. Unite with Earth's creation and together receive and transmit light to heal the whole being, Earth. Earth and her creation are one and cannot be separated.

The cosmic light's task is to unite all beings with the planet and bring collective growth as well as individual. When you realize that, you will know that many of your scientific methods are fragmented and are used to disconnect you from experiencing Earth's growth.

For true achievement you have to be able to connect to Earth and the cosmic light and understand that the unity between them describes the unity between our Source and the cosmos. When you want to know something, you have to experience it yourself. Allow the seed to grow and become a tree and then eat the fruit.

Questions

1. What is your understanding of the following phrase: "All scientific findings are accepted by humanity as the absolute truth and this affects their consciousness."
2. How can you connect to Earth?
3. How can Earth support your ability to receive and transmit light?

4. Can you explain the following phrase: "When you want to know something you have to experience it yourself. Allow the seed to grow and become a tree and then eat the fruit."

Introduction

Earth can provide for all her species not only food but also healing, purification, energy and recourses in order to bring balance and harmony and encourage communication between all bodies. Earth has everything you need but you prefer to be fed poison and artificial substances that have no life in them. All nutrients that come from the Earth, the unpolluted Earth, were given life by the creator and their energy is the energy of the cosmos.

When you connect to the high light, healing and purification will happen naturally and you will see yourself and others being transformed because of it. One of the qualities of light is to be able to spread, purify and transform all beings. All creation should be in a process of constant purification and transformation but this is not always possible because the light is not allowed to enter fragmented and distorted areas of growth. This is why Earth and all her creation are suffering right now. We have been given the task to bring the light to all of you who want to be creators on Earth.

Wisdom of Thoth: The First Step towards Purification

People on Earth often wonder about God or Gods when they need inspiration or support. People pray to God to give them what they need and they expect that they will get it.

They always see their problems as something that were not created by them, so they are not responsible for them. Some of you do not know what others mean by the word God and you prefer to focus on your everyday life and try to fulfil your needs and wants.

I want to explain to you that the High Gods of the Pleroma are not beings like you but are High energy beings whose purpose is to create and maintain life in all realms. We are creating life by transmitting high energy which we receive from our Source, to all energy points in the cosmos. This is how we support all of creation and help them to grow and evolve.

If there is suffering in your life and you wish a high being to take the suffering away and bring you peace and joy, you have illusionary thoughts and beliefs. All beings are designed to be able to purify their imbalances and heal themselves. You have to remember this and allow it to happen. You are programmed to allow an external force to give you what you need.

When this happens, you go against your natural process of purification and you allow illusion, artificiality and fragmentation to take over your being. People who do not know what their purpose is they resemble the people that can see but they do not want to open their eyes; so they are blind by choice.

When you start knowing yourself and understand your imbalances, you will realize all the illusionary patterns have created an artificial dissatisfaction in your life. Observing yourself and connecting to your whole being is the first step towards purification.

Questions

1. Do you pray? What is your intention?
2. What is your understanding of the Gods and their creative intention?
3. Can a god or a cosmic creative force ease your suffering?
4. Can you explain the following phrase: "When you start knowing yourself and understand your imbalances, you will realize all the illusionary patterns that have created an artificial dissatisfaction in your life."

Introduction

All our special tools and talents are stored in the body and they are waiting for us to discover them. When you know your body, you understand that it is a microcosm of high creation and a link to all life. Your body is your temple and path for growth and expansion to other realms.

There is a motion inside you that keeps you alive and anchors you to the physical plane; you understand that this corresponds to the vibration of your astral body and it is also linked to planetary motion.

When you have full knowledge of how your physical body functions; how you can help your body grow and how Earth can help your body grow naturally then you will have achieved enlightenment. You will be standing in a space of truth away from the tricks of illusion and you will be able to create your own life. This is not an achievement it is a natural process that you have forgotten.

Wisdom of Thoth: Experiencing Life beyond the Physical Body

Some may ask, I can see my physical body but what is beyond it? How can I experience life beyond the physical body?

Every moment of your life, you experience your non-physical existence because you are partly physical and partly an energy being. The body cannot survive if the energies of the cosmos and Earth are not able to sustain it, maintain balance and make it generate growth.

A plant cannot survive without water and sunlight. All beings on Earth are designed to connect to each other by receiving and transmitting energy. Due to distortion and fragmentation on Earth, beings affect each other by passing to others their imbalances and energetic disharmony.

It is your responsibility to bring balance into your being and you can do that by disconnecting from all artificiality and distorted energies and open yourself to the light of the cosmos which is the purest form of nourishment, rebirth and evolution.

You can connect to the cosmic light if you let go of everything that you think that you are, such as the persona, ego and social status and see yourself as a unity of energy and physicality. Understand how the two are supporting each other and that the purpose of all beings is to receive light and create on Earth.

Your tools will reveal to you what you are going to create and the methods you can use to achieve that. If you are not open to receiving the cosmic light and you do not understand the above, then you are fully disconnected from your purpose, your tools and your ability to create.

When this happens, you will find yourself being attached to the persona and the ego; you will have the illusion that your tools are related to your social status. An example of this is when people become their profession or their marital status. Disconnect from illusionary titles and attributes and look at your being the way it was created by the light of our Source. If you wish to bring balance in you and experience your purpose, then you have to experience your whole being which is a unity of the physical and the energetic structure.

Questions

1. Do you exist beyond your physical body?
2. Can you explain the following phrase: "The body cannot survive if the energies of the cosmos and Earth are not able to sustain it, maintain balance and generate growth."
3. How can you bring balance into your being?
4. How can you disconnect from illusion?

Introduction

Many people do not realise that a plan has been created in order to restrict and shut down your body functions and light. Some may ask: what should we do about it? The first step is to become aware of it. When you become aware of it you have already win the first battle in your quest to raise your vibration. Then you have to show that you actively support this new understanding. You have to take responsibility of your life and question everything that others have accepted as the norm. It is your responsibility to protect and safeguard the great gift that was given to you, your body, and try to align yourself with Earth, her growth and creation. Earth is a great educator and teaches cosmic laws and how they affect life on Earth.

Wisdom of Thoth: Your Body is a Unique Tool

When humanity is able to heal the mind, disconnect from illusion and focus on its path of truth, the cosmic light which is the extension of our Source will connect humanity and Earth. It will bring healing, clarity and will teach you new ways to grow and expand beyond your physical body. This is when you will be able to connect to your physicality fully and understand that it is your unique tool to help you become a transmitter and receiver of light.

Your body has certain qualities and abilities that can support you to fulfil your purpose on Earth. It is a tool to help you connect to Earth and to the other parts of your being in other planes. When you are affected by illusion you think of your body as a constant threat to your image and persona. You are polluting your body in order to make it beautiful. Some of you live with the fear of rejection because your body does not have a certain form or it is not artificial enough.

Then there is the fear of disease that is related to the physical body, but most of you do not see that when you pollute your body, you are not helping it to grow; imbalances bring disease. When you connect to your body do not expect it to be a certain shape; it was created to be unique and serve you to fulfil your unique purpose.

See your body as a gift from Earth, a tool that was created by cosmic energies, a precious part of your being that needs nourishment in order to become a transmitter and receiver of cosmic light. When you are able to connect to it, your body will show you the way to fulfil your purpose and you will become aware of your special qualities that you need to develop. This is a great learning for all human beings and you should not hesitate to take up the challenge of knowing your body.

Questions

1. Can you explain the following phrase: "When humanity will be able to heal the mind, disconnect from illusion and focus on their path of truth, the cosmic light which is the extension of our Source will connect humanity and Earth."
2. How can your body support you to fulfil your purpose?
3. How do you pollute your body?
4. Can you communicate with your body?

Introduction

There are some people whose intention is to purify from the suffering and limitation. Some of you want to heal yourselves and you are able to observe your imbalances and how they are created in you, but you are very reluctant to go through a transformation; you do not wish to change your life, disconnect fully from old patterns and live a life of purity close to Earth.

This is happening because you still accept illusion as part of your life; the ties are not broken and you are still suffering from distortion. There are people whose intention is not to purify and grow but to exist in the illusion that creates in them. There are people who believe that they are in the process of disconnecting from illusion, but when they observe themselves, they do not realize that illusion is guiding them.

Your enemy is your own illusion, the one that you allowed be creating and multiplying in you and around you. We are here to remind you of the distortion and pollution in your being because it blocks your ability to connect to your astral body where all growth is taking place. We are here to support you because we know what you are suffering from and we also know the outcome of this suffering. Pantheon of Aeternam is an open and free society of women and men, the home of the gods of the Pleroma on Earth.

Wisdom of Thoth: Are you Walking the Path of Truth or the Path of Illusion?

Many of you would like to connect to my light in order to empower yourselves. The most effective way to achieve this is by allowing the cosmic light to go through you; connecting you to the Source, with your whole being and Earth; offering you healing that will trigger your purification, transformation and growth. Receiving the light of the cosmos is a natural process for human beings and it is also a cosmic law.

Therefore, when it is not happening it means that you are building a wall around you with the help of a fragmented mind. If you are not able to connect to me it is because you connect to your ego and accept illusion, distortion and artificiality as your purpose. All human beings are affected from the same mind diseases.

There are some people whose intention is to disconnect and purify from the suffering and limitation. Some of you want to heal yourselves and you are able to observe your imbalances and how they are created in you, but you are very reluctant to go through a transformation; you do not wish to change your life, disconnect fully from old patterns and live a life of purity close to Earth.

This is happening because you still accept illusion as part of your life; the ties are not broken and you are still suffering from distortion. There are people whose intention is not to purify and grow but to exist in the illusion that creates in them. There are people who believe that they are in the process of disconnecting from illusion, but when they observe themselves, they do not realize that illusion is guiding them.

When you follow illusion, you cannot be honest or pure and a period of stagnation can be seen as a time of growth. If you are lost and want to find your way back to truth then you should ask yourself: what is my intention and is my intention connected to purity? Then your true-self will answer those questions with honesty and you will know your path.

Questions

1. How can the cosmic light affect your growth?
2. What happens to human beings when they connect to distortion?
3. What is your intention?
4. Can you communicate with your true-self?

Introduction

Due to the distortion and fragmentation on the planet, the astral knowledge cannot penetrate the physical plane and human beings exist in isolation surrounded by the veil of illusion. It is important that we clear the channels of communication and connect to the astral plane as well as the Earth's energies.

When you are purified from illusion and you are able to see yourself naked and pure then you will be able to see your purpose and have instant access to all cosmic truths because it is your right. Gods and masters do not wish to hide cosmic wisdom from humans or to deny them the empowerment of the high vibrational state. On the contrary, we wish all humans to reach this point. We want humanity to wake up in order to assist planet Earth to wake up too. The Earth and her creation suffer from the same disease and this is a schism of the true-self and the growth of illusion. When you awake to the truth you will be restored to your true- selves.

Wisdom of Thoth: How was Illusion Created on Earth

Illusion was a plant that grew on Earth very long time ago. The only period that Earth was free from illusion was during the golden era. At that time she had a great light and was connected directly to the source.

Earth was a creator goddess and her creation showed that she was a perfect receiver and transmitter of light. After the golden era, Earth became distracted and confused. This was caused by the energies of other planets that tried to connect to her in order to receive the high light. When Earth connected to those energies she became vulnerable and her ability to grow and create was affected.

When beings from other planets inhabited parts of the Earth and tried to connect to her energies, she experienced confusion and distortion. Those beings were not part of the Earth's creation and their intention was to claim her resources in a way that brought imbalances to the whole planet.

Those beings were not aware or ignored the cosmic laws that supported Earth's abilities to create and maintain life. When Earth experiences extinction and disasters it means that there is a force that brings imbalances and goes against Earth's growth. The beings that inhabited Earth were also confused and did not see their purpose as part of Earth's growth.

Confusion brought distortion and the rulers used illusion to control the distorted masses. Illusion tries to convince people that they are free and happy, living balanced lives and experiencing constant growth. This illusionary idea keeps them supporting society's mechanisms and the pyramid structure reward system.

If people were aware that they exist in a distorted environment, disconnected from truth, the pyramid structure would collapse and society as you know it would cease to exist. Then human beings will have to abandon Earth or become perfect receivers and transmitters of cosmic light to support Earth's healing and growth.

Questions

1. Can you describe the Earth of the golden era?
2. What is your understanding of the following phrase: "When Earth experiences extinction and disasters it means that there is a force that brings imbalances and goes against Earth's growth."
3. How can Earth purify from imbalances?
4. Can you explain the following phrase: "Then human beings will have to abandon Earth or become perfect receivers and transmitters of cosmic light to support Earths healing and growth."

Introduction

In ancient times, people had a true connection with the Earth's energies and were aware of the astral plane. They had knowledge about the natural as well as the cosmic laws and clearly understood their purpose. They were open to astral communication and encouraged gods' intervention. Currently, people on Earth are trapped in a low vibrational reality because of the high level of distortion. Imbalances appear in all expressions of their lives and they are unable to heal themselves because they are unaware of their true state. Ignorance and confusion will not lead you to harmony and fulfilment. You have to be pure and true to your calling and purpose.

In ancient times people on Earth observed the stars and had a clear understanding of their connection to Earth and the different races that inhabited certain planetary systems. They depicted all that by creating certain temples, making drawings or spreading the knowledge in what you now call mythology. Religion and science blocked this knowledge reaching new generations and people on Earth were convinced that they were the only intelligent beings not only on Earth but also in the cosmos.

Ancient people were aware of the natural laws which are a reflection of the cosmic laws. They could perform healing; they were connected to their astral body and the high realms and they were connected to the cosmic wisdom of the masters. People used this wisdom in their everyday life and connection to high realms was possible for all.

Wisdom of Thoth: Planetary Races

In ancient times people on Earth observed the stars and had a clear understanding of their connection to Earth and the different races that inhabited certain planetary systems. They depicted all that by creating certain temples, making drawings or spreading the knowledge in what you now call mythology. Religion and science blocked this knowledge to reaching new generations and people on Earth were convinced that they were the only intelligent beings not only on Earth but also in the cosmos.

This was an illusion and it was used to block their growth. Human beings need to know that there are many races that exist on many planets; some of them are technologically superior in comparison to the people of Earth. There are beings living on other planets that have a clear understanding of their purpose but they do not have free will therefore they cannot be creators. So those beings have different experiences and growth possibilities.

They may have longer life cycles but they also experience death and go back to the astral plane. Astral beings can reincarnate on different planets and grow in various ways but their existence is temporary. Reincarnations are lessons but your existence in the astral plane determines your ability to receive and transmit light, unite with the cosmos and get closer to the source.

Questions

1. What is your understanding about ancient mysteries?

2. How did religion and science block human's understanding of the cosmos?
3. What is your understanding of the planetary races?
4. What is a reincarnation?

Introduction

Due to the distortion and fragmentation on the planet, the astral knowledge cannot penetrate the physical plane and human beings exist in isolation surrounded by the veil of illusion. It is important that we clear the channels of communication and connect to the astral plane as well as the Earth's energies.

There is a miraculous way of living and this is being detached from beliefs, dogmas and archetypal behavior. All the above have been created to help you focus and sustain a certain consciousness and life experience. We are asking you now to abandon and destroy the persona and the lifestyle. Our aim is to give everybody the tools they need in order to paint their own authentic picture of themselves and let their true purpose be revealed. We want you to detach yourself from all artificiality and connect to your true-self, the one that is known to the masters and gods.

Wisdom of Thoth: Understanding Illusion

Human beings have to disconnect from illusion which is a state that they are familiar with; it is their comfort zone. Illusionary ideals, thoughts and actions were given to them when they were young and many people have built their lives and their understanding of themselves and the world around them on Illusion.

This is what they know and this is what they thought to be their truth and purpose. When they connect to others, they share illusion and criticize people who want to connect to their purity, their unique skills and abilities and follow the path of truth. Are you one of these people? Do you ignore your true purpose in order to follow illusionary beliefs and lifestyle? Are you wondering about your true purpose and are you already developing your special abilities in order to fulfil this purpose? Or perhaps truth and purpose are just ideas that have nothing to do with what you are experiencing and creating in your everyday life.

People who are confused and wandering in the dark have more opportunities to find their way to their true-self because their awakening has already happened. If you are one of those people who enjoy reading and exploring different ways to awake mentally, disconnected from everyday experiences, then your true awakening has not started yet.

Ego which is connected to mental activity does not support you to connect to the cosmic light and receive healing and clarity. It is important that you observe yourself and see what type of blockages is limiting your ability to connect to your true-self and act with purity.

If you accept that illusion has affected you from a young age and you see all the different forms and what it has produced over all these years then you are opening the way for the cosmic light to go through you and offer you healing and renewal. Observe yourself without fear and you will connect to truth.

Questions

1. Do you ignore your true purpose in order to follow illusionary beliefs and lifestyle?
2. Are you wondering about your true purpose and are you already developing your special abilities in order to fulfil this purpose?
3. Can you explain the following statement: "People who are confused and wandering in the dark have more opportunities to find their way to their true-self because their awakening has already happened. If you are one of those people who enjoy reading and exploring different ways to awake mentally, disconnected from everyday experiences, then your true awakening has not started yet."
4. How can you connect to truth?

Introduction

Humans' intent to follow the principle of polarity: what surrounds them is either black or white. Human beings use the five senses to understand the world around them, this means that their perception is limited to what they are able to see, hear, smell, taste and touch.

Earth has the purpose of a creator, being a mother to all of you but she also has another purpose: supporting other planets to stay connected to the sun that sustains life in the whole galaxy. When you are able to observe Earth's connection to other planets and the sun then she looks to you like a sphere performing her cosmic dance along with the other planets around the sun.

Most of you believe that the planet is round, even though you experience Earth as a flat surface. The truth is that Earth is neither flat nor round. She is a being that experiences constant transformation because her purpose is linked to the purpose of many living beings.

Wisdom of Thoth: Understanding Earth

Human beings use the five senses to understand the world around them, this means that their perception is limited to what they are able to see, hear, smell, taste and touch.

Humans also tent to simplify truths and follow the principle of polarity: things are either black or white. Most of you believe that the planet is round, even though you experience Earth as a flat surface. The truth is that Earth is neither flat nor round. She is a being that experiences constant transformation because her purpose is linked to the purpose of many living beings.

For humanity, Earth is a flat surface and this is because she wants to support your growth, helping you to build your own communities, supporting her creation and offering enough nourishment to maintain life. For the animals and plants, Earth is also flat to help them grow strong roots and connect to her energies.

Earth has the purpose of a creator and a mother to all of you, but she has also a purpose to support other planets stay connected to the sun, which is responsible for a high creative role, sustaining life to the whole galaxy. When you are able to observe Earth's connection to other planets and the sun she looks to you like a sphere performing her cosmic dance along with the other planets around the sun.

The planetary mother is constantly connected to the sun, receiving and transmitting light, creating and co-creating, growing and transforming as a unity with the other planets of the galaxy. Earth is following the sun in order to stay alive and continue being the creator of life. In your eyes, planets seem to rotate and their spherical shape helps them to perform multiple rotations.

Earth is not connected to the planets and sun only by moving around them. There are more connections and more areas of growth that cannot be detected by your five senses or perception. If you were able to observe Earth being a perfect receiver and transmitter of light then you would know that she does not have a shape known to humanity. If you want to use archetypes to understand Earth in relation to your being you should use the archetype of a mother.

Questions

1. Can you understand your existence with your five senses?
2. What is Earth's purpose?
3. What is the connection of Earth with the sun and the planets of the galaxy?
4. What is your understanding of the following phrase: "If you want to use archetypes to understand Earth in relation to your being you should use the archetype of a mother."

Introduction

All beings have a unique path and the astral plane is created to offer countless growth opportunities. Other times your reincarnation depends on your connection with your spirit guides. They are the ones who provide you with a life plan and clarify your purpose and tools. Freedom means that you are not attached to a certain persona including your masculine or feminine attributes. Where there is opposition there is also separation and fragmentation and the purpose of all beings is unity.

In the astral plane there is less limitation and more growth. We are constantly growing in our astral plane. When physical beings receive teachings from their spirit guides, messengers, masters and gods, these are stored in their astral bodies. There are physical beings that can access to some of this information and there are others who can bring it to their physical reality.

Wisdom of Thoth: Higher Beings and the Guardians of Earth

During the Golden era, there were many Gods who supported Earth to become a creator and a life bringer. They were her guardians, teachers and protectors who helped her to connect to the cosmic light in order to become a creator.

All beings have guardians who often exist in a different plane than them and help them fulfil their purpose, follow the divine plan and connect to the cosmic light and the source. During a life cycle, a being can attract different guides and this is related to his growth, diversions and obstacles.

A guide connects to the present state of a being and can support him in present time. There are also guides who are responsible for the being's reincarnation and stay connected from birth till the end of his life cycle. If a being is constantly connected to his purpose and walks the path of truth without going on diversions, then he will have a strong connection with his main guides who are responsible for his reincarnation.

The same laws affect Earth's connection with her guides. Earth was affected by low energies when she was left to experience creation on her own. Some may ask why the Gods did not try to protect Earth when she was drifting away from her golden era? Free will was part of her learning.

Similarly to humanity, she saw distortion and destruction as new opportunities for growth and in a way she disconnected from the path that was created for her during her golden era. When beings go on a diversion, they enter a maze where they can spend a very long time looking for growth and truth; this reduces their ability to connect to their true-self and the cosmos; the more they remain in the state of confusion the more distorted they become and the being starts to be affected by imbalances and schisms.

Now the guardians of Earth, who were connected to her during the Golden era, want to connect to her again through the cosmic light that is reaching humanity.

Questions

1. Who are the guardians of Earth?
2. Why did Earth's guardians not try to protect her when she was drifting away from her Golden Era state?
3. How can spirit guides support human beings?
4. What is a maze of distortion?

Introduction

When a human being can disconnect from limitation, connect to the cosmos and purify himself from distortion then he is walking the path that will lead him to experience Earth's golden age. If all humanity can achieve that then Earth will experience her golden age. In this case you become the creators of the golden era on Earth and you will be able to taste and share the golden fruit of a high birth.

Human beings on Earth can grow and experience again a high state of creation and this can be achieved by purification and your ability to connect to the cosmic light, bringing healing and clarity to Earth's whole being.

If Earth were able to experience her golden era fully then her creation would not experience a dilemma, standing at the crossroads between the path of truth and the path of illusion. The Earth of the Golden era was not affected by distortion and fragmentation and her purity and high light will offer one opportunity to all beings; growth that has no obstacles, limitation or boundaries.

Wisdom of Thoth: The Existence of Low Spirits and Beings without Physicality?

All beings that exist on Earth can connect to their true-self, fulfil their purpose and return to the astral plane at the end of their life cycle or remain in a low vibrational state during their whole life time and continue to do so when they lose their physicality. Your journey depends on your intention; that is connected to your energy and for what purpose?

There are human beings on Earth that have the same intention as the non-physical beings that exist in a low state and try to survive by going against the cosmic laws. Earth and her creation exist in a low vibrational energetic area and she creates those beings herself.

If Earth were able to experience her Golden era fully then her creation would not experience the dilemma, standing at the crossroads between the path of truth and the path of illusion. The Earth of the Golden era was not affected by distortion and fragmentation and her purity and high light will offer one opportunity to all beings; growth that has no obstacles, limitation or boundaries.

Human beings on Earth can grow and experience again a high state of creation and this can be achieved by purification and connecting to the cosmic light, bringing healing and clarity to Earth's whole being.

When a human being can disconnect from limitation, connect to the cosmos and purify himself from distortion then he is walking the path that will lead him to experience Earth's golden age. If all humanity can achieve that then Earth will experience her golden age. In this case you become the creators of the golden era on Earth and you will be able to taste and share the golden fruit of a high birth.

Questions

1. Can you explain the following phrase: "All beings that exist on Earth can connect to their true-self, fulfil their purpose and return to the astral plane at the end of their life cycle or remain in a low vibrational state during their whole life time and continue to do so when they lose their physicality."

2. What is your understanding of the following phrase: "Your journey depends on your intention; that is connected to your energy and for what purpose?"
3. Can you grow?
4. Can you experience the golden era?

Introduction

People on Earth support a pyramid system of existence. It seems that the majority of the population is being manipulated on the base of the pyramid. You can be a slave of illusion when you are constantly worried about money and concentrate on the lack of it. Wise are the people who can adjust their needs to their income and are free to concentrate on other aspects of expression; they live a life of freedom and they are more productive. Life is meaningful when you have eliminated all obstacles and you can focus on your growth and support the growth of others.

People will not connect to the their true-self, understand their purpose or become enlightened if they don't experience life as pure and compassionate beings. All those people who are obsessed to be on the top of the social pyramid of success they will be very disappointed to find out that their quest is an illusion.

Wisdom of Thoth: The Architects of Illusion

When human beings are surrounded by illusion they do not see the path that will lead them to their purpose. Instead they are attracted to fantasies, theories, man-made definitions and perceptions, products and services that can be bought or sold. All those elements of illusion are constantly flashing in front of your eyes, disconnecting you from your true path.

The ultimate and highest point of illusion on Earth is the acceptance of the social pyramid and people who accept this as their purpose not only do they follow illusion but they become creators of illusion. Those people become the ones who force humanity to accept illusion as truth. They will come to you and will connect to your imbalances; they will offer you solutions, rewards or even happiness and a fulfilled life.

They will reveal wisdom and knowledge and they will convince you that this is the only source of enlightenment. They will tell you stories about their greatness and the transformation they can bring to you and you will have to accept and believe it. You have no choice but to believe it because they connect to your imbalances and understand what makes you vulnerable.

There will be many human beings, architects of illusion who will approach and try to create in you. All of them will be supporting the pyramid structure, sometimes hidden under illusionary beliefs of truth and wisdom. The architects of illusion will not tell you that growth is a natural process and that you are able to receive and transmit cosmic light in order to heal humanity and Earth.

They will not tell you that you are responsible for your own growth that can be achieved when you are disconnected from illusion and connect to your true-self. They do not want you to experience life as a creator of truth and find your path to your purpose. They want you to see your purpose as climbing the pyramid of distortion and getting lost in the many options to buy and be bought; to destroy and be destroyed; to lose and get lost. When you are able to understand illusion and disconnect from it the pyramid of success and power will evaporate.

Questions

1. What is your experience living a life of illusion?
2. What is the social pyramid?
3. Who are the architects of illusion?
4. How can you purify yourself from illusion?

Introduction

Pantheon of Aeternam has been created by the gods as a gift to humanity. Through our messengers, human beings will connect to the cosmic light, clear all illusion and fragmentation and restore the peace that existed on Earth during the golden era. Humans need to know how Earth was created and what her purpose is. We are all linked with Earth's growth and it is important to unite in order to save the planet and her whole creation

We want to enable you to receive and transmit light and become involved in Earth's healing and rebirth. At this time, you should prepare for an important role: opening up to the cosmic light, healing yourselves, connecting to your true-self and purpose; these are your tools to help you accomplish your task. Many of you are not able to understand your task or see it as part of your growth. Illusionary ideas, needs and wants related to social success, recognition and status, take you away from your purpose.

Wisdom of Thoth: The Coming of the Golden Era

We are here to support Earth's growth; help her to purify and heal schisms; become a true receiver and transmitter of cosmic light and experience creation in high planes. We want to give the same gifts to humanity.

We want to enable you to receive and transmit light and become involved in Earth's healing and rebirth. At this time, you should prepare for an important role: opening up to the cosmic light, healing yourselves, connecting to your true-self and purpose; these are your tools to help you accomplish your task. Many of you are not able to understand your task or see it as part of your growth. Illusionary ideas, needs and wants related to social success, recognition and status, take you away from your purpose.

If you wish to start walking towards a fulfilled life, you have to connect to Earth and start an energetic communication with her. She is a creator-planet and she can teach you how to be the creator of your own life and fulfil your purpose. Allow the natural laws to bring balance in your life and you will soon disconnect from the artificiality and illusion that exists around you.

If you are not able to get nourishment directly from Earth, you live a life of artificiality and you exist disconnected from her. Are you supporting people to grow? Are you able to receive and transmit light to humanity and Earth? Are you walking the path of truth and purpose, experiencing life on Earth as well as astral growth? This is a challenge for you; it is a challenge for humanity and Earth to fulfil their purpose and the coming of the golden Era.

Questions

1. How can you support Earth's purification and healing?
2. Are you a pure receiver and transmitter of light?
3. Can you explain the following phrase: "If you wish to start walking towards a fulfilled life, you have to connect to Earth and start an energetic communication with her."
4. Are you walking the path of truth and purpose?

Introduction

Many human beings are fighting in order to create even more options and life possibilities. People have invented many terms to describe and celebrate this: they call it diversity, freedom, culture, development and change. Many of you support the idea of having options when you choose the place you are going to live, your community, work, interests and lifestyle. Being in a state of peace, you can ask yourself about your options and realize that they are more restrictions than acts of freedom.

All options, questions, uncertainties, dramas and failures in your life will fade when you begin to experience your essence, divine purpose and your existence in all of its forms, physical and astral, and you become aligned to your own essence.

There are people on Earth who follow society's rules but also try to learn and experience more and have meaningful lives. These people are called awoken. I must say that this is not the term I would use. While others sleep because of ignorance this last group sleeps knowingly. My message to them is that you cannot pick and choose whatever suits you; this is what the society of illusion is teaching you to do. They are giving you options and you are experiencing the many reflections of the one illusion.

Wisdom of Thoth: How to Create your True Life

Many human beings are fighting in order to create even more options and life possibilities. People have invented many terms to describe and celebrate this: they call it diversity, freedom, culture, development and change. Many of you support the idea of having options when you choose the place you are going to live, your community, work, interests and lifestyle. Being in a state of peace, you can ask yourself about your options and realize that they are more restrictions than acts of freedom.

I see your many options as diversions, pushing you away from your true goal to connect to your true-self and fulfil your purpose on Earth. When you learn to exist in a space of peace and allow the cosmic light to go through you, then you will connect to your purpose and realize that there is a divine plan related to your reincarnation.

When you empty yourself from illusionary rewards, high expectations and social standards, you will be able to observe yourself with truth and purity. When you are able to observe yourself without emotion, fear or negativity, you will experience freedom and you will understand that your path of growth is connected to your true-self. Artificiality, illusion and fear will not guide you to your true-self.

When you exist in a sleeping state, in a state of confusion and artificiality then you celebrate the many choices and the colorful rewards of illusion. You are using your mind to follow illusion in your community and creating a life that is not related to your divine plan. Disconnect from everything that stimulates your mind and senses and instead connect to your being, true-self, Earth and the cosmos which is the extension of our Source.

Questions

1. What are your choices and where do they lead you?
2. Can you explain the following phrase: "Being in a state of peace, you can ask yourself about your options and realize that they are more restrictions than acts of freedom."
3. What is your understanding of the following phrase: "When you empty yourself from illusionary rewards, high expectations and social standards, you will be able to observe yourself with truth and purity."

Introduction

The light of the gods is transmitted to Earth and we are the pure channels of the cosmic energy for our own healing and purification as well as the Earth's. All living beings are united with the cosmic light and are part of the vast creation of our source. Humans who exist in third dimensional Earth are connected to all parts of their being such as the astral body, higher-self and creation code but due to distortion and fragmentation are not aware of it. All beings receive guidance to help them grow and evolve and the ones who are chosen to reincarnate on Earth are guided in order to fulfil their purpose, bringing the astral light to the physical plane.

Human beings on Earth have the ability to connect to the light of the creator due to their creation code. They are able to connect to the astral plane and be part of growth that takes place there. This is a cosmic law shared by the whole creation. Human beings have great capabilities to fight fragmentation, but the low vibration which is becoming constantly lower does not help them to grow and evolve. Due to the distortion and fragmentation on the planet, the astral knowledge cannot penetrate the physical plane and human beings exist in isolation surrounded by the veil of illusion. It is important that we clear the channels of communication and connect to the astral plane as well as the Earth's energies.

Wisdom of Thoth: The Cosmic Light is the Extension of our Source

The light of the cosmos should flow and reach humanity's essence. This is a cosmic process of growth and should not be blocked by limitation. The cosmic light is the extension of our Source and is the link that brings unity and eternal growth. In the cosmos there is no separation between life and growth. In higher planes, beings are constantly connected to the cosmic light and experience limitless growth. Growth is their only purpose and the cosmic light is the carrier of the cosmic purpose.

Connecting to the cosmic light is a natural process and it can be achieved by being in a state of peace, balancing your whole physical being and the energies that surround you. In this peaceful state you can disconnect from fear, negativity and illusion. You can purify yourself from imbalances and distortion in you. In this state you can connect to your true-self and experience life with purity and clarity.

When you have achieved all that, you will start opening up to the cosmic light. It will enter your being and offer you unity, balance, healing and will connect you to your physicality and purpose as well as your cosmic growth. Allow the cosmic light to be your guide and you will experience transformation. All the layers of distortion in you will be cleared and you will understand the importance of developing your abilities and skills in order to create on Earth. The cosmic light will enter your being when you are ready to receive it.

Questions

1. What will happen to your being when you connect to the cosmic light?
2. What is your understanding of the following phrase: "The cosmic light is the extension of our Source and is the link that brings unity and eternal growth."
3. How can you purify yourself?
4. Are you aware of your distorted patterns?

Introduction

The Gods' dream for creation is to restore Earth to her golden age by purifying her from all trauma, distortion and fragmentation. Once the elements of stagnation and imbalance are removed, the precious flower of light and wisdom that Earth once was will be revealed. Earth will be reborn from within and enter a new cycle of growth. She was created to exist for eternity and protect her creation to complete its life cycle. But as Earth loses control of her power and allows distortion to take over, the gods will have to intervene, connecting Earth to cosmic wisdom, healing and reminding her to exist as a creator once again.

We are rebuilding the structure of the cosmos. We are clearing stagnation and bringing all planes closer to enjoy a high vibration and a high creation. The astral plane will be charged by high energies and all beings will experience high growth. This is the dream of our creator.

Wisdom of Thoth: Becoming the Seeds of Earth's Transformation

Human beings on Earth are blocking the cosmic light going through them and this is affecting the transformation of the planet.

People exist in stagnation and this state attracts distortion and illusion to enter their minds. One may say: illusion already exists on the planet and this prevents me from connecting to the cosmic light and fulfilling my purpose; I have no power against it. I say to you that this thought is illusionary and takes you away not only from your purpose on Earth but also from your purpose as a cosmic being.

Following illusion will offer you an easy access to negativity and this is going to create more barriers in you and disconnect you from the cosmic light. When you are in a low state you experience suffering, weakness, struggle and what you call wrong choices. There is an easy way to escape this state and this is to focus on your being and try to connect to its purest form, your true-self. To achieve this you have to experience a state of peace, connecting to your physical body and all the energies that give life to it.

Focus on the way your being can achieve balance and maintain life with all your different organs working together, being generated by energies. See yourself as a physical body connected to Earth but also as an extension of your astral body. If you accept that you are only your physical body and at the end of the life cycle you cease to exist then you are going to have a life of limitation.

When you understand that the astral plane is your home and you will return there at the end of this reincarnation then you will be able to allow the cosmic light to go through you and have a life of balance and growth. When you are able to achieve this, humanity will connect to you energetically in order to receive the same gift. You will become the seed for Earth's transformation and you will bring the cosmic light to the planet for healing and rebirth.

Questions

1. What happens when people exist in stagnation?
2. Do human beings have the power to disconnect from illusion?
3. How can you focus on your being?
4. Can you explain the following phrase: "You will become the seed for Earth's transformation and you will bring the cosmic light to the planet for healing and rebirth."

Introduction

Earth is an electromagnetic system and all of you are electromagnetic points on Earth. When the light goes through the planet, every single point of energy should be charged with the cosmic light. The light is able to spread and reach every point of life in the cosmos. If your planet is not able to absorb this light fully, you will not be able to grow and connect to higher expressions of yourself; you will not be able to act with clarity and understand your purpose and tools.

It is a big challenge for human beings on Earth to reclaim their home on the planet; this can only be done with gratitude, submission and servitude to mother Earth. Earth is a loving planet, a beautiful creator of life, and human beings have to find their place among other living beings. For this to happen we need to have a new consciousness which will bring liberation, growth and connection.

Wisdom of Thoth: Waiting for a Change, a Shift and a New Consciousness

Many of you are waiting for a change, a shift and a new consciousness that will bring more clarity and unity between people, Earth and the cosmos.

Many of you are trying to describe and analyze the new era by using narrative and a scientific approach. You should be part of this change if you want it to affect your existence. It is time for Earth to purify herself and move on to experience high transformation. Humanity is here to experience this and support it. You are Earth's tools receiving the light of the cosmos and you are also cosmic tools to bring light to Earth.

Your purpose is to help Earth transform. You are also transforming to a high vibrational cosmic being. You may think to fight illusion, distortion and fragmentation but what you are really doing is connecting to Earth's trauma and imbalances. If you are able to disconnect from illusionary patterns in your life and accept truth as your only path on Earth then you are part of the planet that is purified.

Your purity will heal others and the cosmic light will go through you to bring growth to more parts of Earth. If the whole of humanity can connect to truth and become free from imbalances then Earth will receive healing, connect to the cosmos and transform to a higher being. This is the shift you are all waiting for, but while you are waiting for it, illusion is busy taking you on multiple diversions and offering you a distorted understanding of your duty and purpose. We are here to connect to you and offer you light. You are here to open up to the cosmic light and help transmit it to Earth.

Questions

1. How can you support Earth's growth?
2. Can you describe the new shift? What is your experience of it?
3. Can you explain the following phrase: "If you are able to disconnect from illusionary patterns in your life and accept truth as your only path on Earth then you are this part of the planet that is purified."
4. What is Earth's shift and new consciousness?

Introduction

There are people on Earth who are very confused about their existence and purpose. They are going through the same suffering as Earth, either because they are also confused or because they want to share the burden. There is no pain, sorrow or anxiety if you decide to return to the golden era. If you believe that there is a golden era on Earth and you accept it as reality, you will experience no pain or suffering only love and happiness. Love is a great mystery and I have given it to you. Now you create the golden era and this is the place you should be.

I want people to wake up to the truth and realise that their world is a fantasy. Their ability to communicate with the cosmos and Earth is weak existing in a space of distortion and confusion. There is a simple way to be enlightened and this means that you will be able to receive your first lesson in cosmic truth when you are true to yourself. It seems like a simple task but for many people on Earth it is one of the greatest challenges.

Open your eyes and see that everything around you is false, artificial, distorted and has no true purpose. Some people may think that they have no choice but to accept illusion in order to survive. I say that you are all free and you can decide for your own lives.

Wisdom of Thoth: To Be in Constant Growth and Evolution

The Gods want to connect to Earth and all creation and their only purpose is to bring light in order to heal, purify and transform Earth.

There are people on Earth who are very confused about their existence and purpose. They also understand beings that exist in an energetic space between the Earth and the astral plane, to be God-creators and try to connect to them. If you are connected to beings that exist in other planes, it will be very helpful to observe the purpose of this connection.

If it is a connection of balance, where you can experience rebirth and transformation, it means that those beings are connected to the cosmic light and they are able to transmit it to you. If you experience destruction, confusion, the boost of ego and illusionary ambition as well as physical and mental imbalances, you should know that you are the one who is feeding these beings with your light and you are absorbing their non-growth state. Focusing on yourself, observing your own energies, your mind patterns and your physical growth is very important for staying grounded and expand between the physical and the astral plane.

A fulfilled life on Earth can help you clear your imbalances receive and transmit light and connect to your true-self and your astral body. You do not have to make these connections, they are already created; you just have to open yourself up to them and see yourself as a physical being and creation of Earth whose permanent existence is on the astral plane. The light of the cosmos reaches all creation and your natural state is to be in constant growth and evolution. Allow it to happen and experience it with your whole being.

Questions

1. Why do human beings exist in a space of confusion?
2. Can you explain the following phrase: "If you are connected to beings who exist in other planes it will be very helpful to observe the purpose of this connection."
3. How can you experience a fulfilled life?
4. How can you open yourself to your path and growth?

Introduction

For thousands of years people have been blindly looking for enlightenment. What they are actually looking for is a connection between their current state and life on Earth and the golden era. The only true reference to enlightenment was the time when Earth was a high vibrational planet with extensive plant and animal life and had direct communication with the gods who inhabited the planet. Earth's dream was to become the Pleroma or the reflection of it. During this time, the planet enjoyed high creation, high evolution and perfect harmony between her elements and species.

Enlightenment is not the perfection of a human being. It is only one of the many lessons of high wisdom that they can receive during their lifetime. Due to distortion on Earth, human beings find it very hard to escape the life patterns which are created by beliefs, dogma and other types of manipulation. Therefore to become enlightened, which means learning a cosmic lesson, it is very hard and happens rarely.

Wisdom of Thoth: Enlightenment is Closer than you Think

If you are looking for enlightenment do not try to find it in spirituality. Your being will guide you to a series of transformations to help you fulfil your purpose. Human beings on Earth want to become Gods; they want to have cosmic wisdom and unlimited power. At the same time, they go against their body's healing and rebirth and they are completely infected by artificiality.

For those who seek enlightenment: are you seeking enlightenment to satisfy your ego or you are focusing on becoming your true-self, allowing your connection with the cosmos, Earth and humanity? You cannot achieve enlightenment if you do not know your true-self.

Some may ask what is my true-self and how can I connect to it? Your true-self is the divine plan of your reincarnation including your purpose. When you connect to it, it also helps you connect to your astral body and grounds you to the Earth's energies. When you are in a state of peace and you are able to disconnect from illusion, you are connected to your true-self. Illusion is always going to exist around you but you should be able to recognize it and distance yourself from it.

Purification can help you clear your imbalances which are often supported by illusion. When you achieve a pure state then you will realize that your body needs to be in a pure state too. You cannot continue feeding your body with artificiality and harmful substances while you are seeking enlightenment. Your whole lifestyle and attitude has to change.

You understand that you are a transmitter and receiver of light and your purpose is to create. Illusion and fear should not control the way you connect to people, the way you give and receive and your ability to create in yourself and others. Enlightenment is not a hidden formula or a secret doctrine; it is all the different ways to be pure, connecting to the cosmos and Earth and fulfilling your purpose in this lifetime.

Questions

1. What is enlightenment and how can you achieve it?
2. Can your body support you to reach enlightenment?
3. Are you experiencing your pure state?
4. How can purification guide you to experience your pure state?

Introduction

In this teaching, Thoth reminds us that competition and distinction feed the ego and donot bring growth. If you want to be free and follow your true potential, you have to connect to your true-self and explore your opportunities of growth in this lifetime.

All human beings were given unique abilities and skills to help them become creators and fulfil their purpose. They all reincarnated to receive and transmit light; to exist in unity with Earth and the cosmos and experience growth in unity with all that exists. Connecting to your light will help you understand that our true-self is much higher and more powerful than any persona, social status or man-made illusion. Transformation and growth are not the privilege of a small group of people; this belief creates fragmentation and confusion. If you are able to transform to a new being of evolution you will never need the label of success or uniqueness.

Wisdom of Thoth: About Indigo Children

Do not support fragmentation and division but do support growth and unity. People on Earth follow religions, political parties, discriminations of all kinds, beliefs and philosophies that are used for separation fragmentation and duality. People who belong in the groups of fragmentation, see themselves as being at the top of the pyramid with the winning party separate from the losers at the lower levels of the pyramid.

Competition and distinction feeds the ego but does not bring growth. Everything that exists has a purpose and is part of the cosmic creation, receiving and transmitting light. People believe that there are some special children who have reincarnated on Earth and have special abilities, bringing the light of the cosmos the planet and healing Earth. I will say to you that all human beings are created with unique abilities and a high purpose.

During ancient times this was clearly understood and accepted by all beings. With the industrial evolution, the creation of the city life and mass production of goods, human beings became slaves to a new social and financial structure. Now there are more people who have started to wake up, connect to their true-self and focus on fulfilling their purpose. People who are able to disconnect from illusion are great receivers and transmitters of light who help many to wake up and connect to the light.

The light that exists on Earth right now is absorbed by new generations of human beings and brings them closer to the path of truth. If the social circle of a young human consists of awakened people then they will be able to carry with them the light of the astral body and the divine plan of their reincarnation. All beings are very unique and their growth is not an achievement that can be measured by your success criteria.

Success is an obstacle to growth. If your child is not a talented artist or does not have special powers it does not mean that he/sheis not going to grow and become a receiver and transmitter of light. On the other hand if your child has special abilities how is he/she using these gifts in order to grow and support others? If you are able to transform to a new being of evolution you will never need the label of success or uniqueness.

Questions

1. Do you support division, social pyramids and fragmentation within your being and Earth's creation?
2. What do you know about indigo children?
3. What are your unique abilities?
4. Why success is an obstacle to growth?

Introduction

There is no secret knowledge to be kept for the selected few. All wisdom is revealed to all who are interested in becoming truth. We do not teach dogma, philosophy or other man- made theory. We want to inform people about the existence of gods, the different realms, the cosmic laws and all activity that is going on for the benefit of Earth and her inhabitants. We want to inform people about the creation of planet Earth and her full story of her creation and growth which was hidden for thousands of years. The teachings of the gods will help humanity to connect to the Earth's energies, be part of the planet and live in harmony with all species. We all have to support Earth and restore her to the most graceful expression of herself, her golden age.

Wisdom of Thoth: Why is it important to connect to Earth

Human beings are encouraged to believe in theories and not to experience their own life on Earth. Your religions and xperts in mythology, history and science and spirituality want you to believe in their theories but none of them encourage you to experience and connect to Earth. When you connect to Earth you become aware of your purpose and you use your physical body to receive and transmit light in order to balance Earth's energies.

When you connect to information and see it as an opportunity to enter the pyramid and climb up to the top, the power that you seek becomes your limitation. When you connect to Earth you are able to understand your purpose and experience it in your everyday life; you understand your unique abilities and you use them to fulfil your purpose, experience unity with everything that exists and understand that your growth is part of the cosmic growth.

If you are not able to understand Earth's growth and connect to her golden era it is because you are not able to connect to her light and do not allow her to nourish you and help you develop your abilities. When you connect to Earth you will be able to experience her golden era and make it reality for all her creation.

Questions

1. Why is it important to experience truth instead of just accepting it?
2. Can religions help you connect to the cosmos and Earth?
3. How can you connect to Earth and become aware of your purpose?
4. Do you understand Earth's golden era?

Introduction

Thoth is urging us to become aware of the restrictions' plan and take responsibility of our life by questioning everything that others accept as the norm. It is our responsibility to protect and safeguard our body and light and for this we have to align with nature and the cosmic laws.

People on Earth need to raise their vibration in order to escape the tyranny of illusion. I was informed that there are people on the planet right now that they die from hunger and I find it hard to understand what this means. I created Earth to be an eternal mother, an unlimited food bank, a place that supports and renews high energies. So what happened on Earth and people are dying? Why are they failed by their bodies? I know that in societies where there is food and shelter, people are still dying from body failures.

Wisdom of Thoth: A Space of Restriction

There are an increasing number of human beings on Earth that exist to follow their everyday routine: they wake up to go to work; they dress and have a certain appearance suitable to their work environment; they talk with people about work; they plan their lives supporting social restrictions and limitations. If you ask people to tell you why do they do this they will say because I need the money and the financial security. You have to go deep into your being and connect to your true-self. This way you will observe that you are restricting your light and forcing yourself to a live in a box when all the riches of the Earth and the cosmos are available to you.

A job that restricts your growth is going to take all your time and energy, it will take you away from your true abilities and your path and will disconnect you from your natural ability to create your own life according to your divine plan. When human beings are restricted they can be easily manipulated to live in a fearful state, looking forward to illusionary rewards.

When you are able to create your own life and this is your main focus then you will not be tired of it, you will not need a break or weekend away. Growth is a constant flow that will be experienced by your being and transmitted to your creation. You will never be tired of receiving precious gifts and this is a life that you can have when you disconnect from your space of restriction.

Questions

1. What is your relationship with your everyday routine?
2. Is your routine restricting your growth and understanding of your purpose?
3. How can you create your own life and be free from restrictions?
4. Can you explain the following phrase: "Growth is a constant flow that will be experienced by your being and transmitted to your creation."

Introduction

In ancient times, people had a true connection with the Earth's energies and were aware of the astral plane. They had knowledge of the natural as well as the cosmic laws and clearly understood their purpose. They were open to astral communication and encouraged gods' intervention.

Wisdom of Thoth: Discovering Ancient Civilization

Human beings want to know about their ancient history and the different civilisations. They think that they can understand this by observing the surviving monuments and other objects that can be found and stored in museums. Human beings also trying to understand these old civilisations by studying the mythology and certain symbolic depictions or ancient doctrines that were produced many years later. The conclusions made by your historians and archaeologists are often misleading because most of the true evidence is lost or misinterpreted. A great way to connect to ancient civilisations is by connecting to the energies of the Earth, traveling and making roots in the places where the human civilisation flourished.

Earth will teach you about her past and the past of humanity and will allow you to enter previous life times and re-experience historical events, human behavior, achievements and failures. For this to happen you have to become a pure channel of light and allow Earth to communicate with you, heal you and nourish you.

You will allow Earth to receive your light, supporting her growth and as a reward you will receive Earth's nourishment, knowing and healing. This connection will bring you closer to your purpose.

Questions

1. How can ancient civilizations support your growth in this lifetime?
2. How can you connect to ancient civilizations?
3. How can you transmit light to Earth?
4. Can Earth help you connect to your purpose?

CHAPTER VI

Earth was created as an astral being first and for this we were given guidance by the light of our Source. The light of our Source instructed us that Earth should have a physical body of high energy able co-exist in different planes.

When Earth was created she first had to become aware of her purpose and this was done by our intervention. There were many transformations that Earth had to go through before she was able to create beings. Like human beings she had to connect to her true essence, understand her purpose and develop her tools of creation.

Introduction

One of the reasons human beings on Earth cannot connect fully to the cosmic light is because they cannot exist in peace. What is your understanding of peace? Peace is a state of knowing and exists in all beings. The peace that exists in you and is connected to your true-self can help you see your purpose. Do not be afraid to explore new life possibilities that will become opportunities for growth.

Christian Rosenkreutz's teaching: Maintain a State of Constant Peace

Growth is almost an automatic process if beings have prepared themselves for this to happen. Beings in the astral plane exist in order to prepare themselves to reach high energies that can help them transform and eventually grow. One of the tasks is to stay open to the light of the cosmos and you can achieve that by being in a state of absolute peace.

One of the reasons that human beings on Earth cannot connect fully to the cosmic light is because they cannot exist in peace. They are always preoccupied with different thoughts and illusionary challenges and expectations. Human beings need to exist in peace not only when they meditate but at all times. You can start working on that by slowing down, observing yourself and have a simpler life without wants and needs.

Ask yourself: what do you truly need to help you survive? The answer to this question will help you see that most of your wants and needs are illusionary. Do not be afraid or get destructed exploring new life possibilities. You are responsible for your life and you should pick the way to live. If all human beings on Earth focus on creating a state of peace that is constant then the lives of all individuals as well as and the organization and the structure of their communities, will bring light to all. When you are all fragmented and distorted you naturally pass your imbalances to each other and create a unity of low vibrational beings. You can do the opposite, maintain a state of constant peace for yourself and pass the experience to others. This is how we can truly help each other grow.

Questions

1. What is your understanding of the following phrase: "Growth is almost an automatic process if beings have prepared themselves for this to happen."
2. How can you have a simple life to help you grow towards your purpose?
3. What changes can you make to your life to help you exist in a space of peace?
4. How can you help humanity grow?

Introduction

All truth, cosmic wisdom and high growth are part of your being, divine plan and design, but you can perceive only a part of it. Distortion has made it very difficult for human beings to live according to natural laws. Connecting to your true-self is a natural law of life and creation. When human beings choose to live a distorted life they also block divine light and cosmic wisdom from coming to them. A true being has divine guidance naturally. This guidance will not only help them to grow but it will also help them to connect.

The more you connect to the light of the cosmos the more light you can bring on Earth. You cannot control the light; it will show you the way to growth.

Wisdom of Astaroth: The History of Alchemy

Alchemy and magic are related and they were created in a period when humanity was in a low vibrational state. In your present time, science, spirituality and philosophy are divided into many separate strands. There was a time when the beings lived on Earth had high technology that was operated by energies that exist in the cosmos. Those beings were able to attract high energies from the cosmos, build communities that supported high creation and were also able to transmit light to Earth and help her transform.

Those beings were not part of Earth's creation; some of them remained on Earth and saw the creation of humanity. There were many visitors on Earth; the ones who remained included great numbers of low vibrational beings who had to escape their territory on other planets and find safety on Earth, the planet of wonder. There were many different races on Earth and even though they occupied separate areas they occasionally had to move across the planet and co-exist.

The high vibrational beings that still existed in small numbers on Earth were known by the rest of the population and they were seen as Gods. There were many stories and legends about their ability to connect to the cosmic light and create energy structures on Earth. There were small groups who tried to imitate the high beings, connecting to the energies and creating on Earth.

Their acts led to the creation of magic, alchemy and other similar arts. With alchemy, spiritual leaders and heads of state tried to acquire eternal life; this means a life cycle that has no end, eternal youth, ability to control people's minds as well as Earth phenomena. Furthermore, they tried to acquire the ability to transform themselves according to their desires and needs and also transform nature. These were their ambitions but they did not bring them growth because they are illusionary acts that do not follow cosmic law and are not supported by the cosmic light. Transformation is part of our existence but cannot be captured or manipulated.

All truth, cosmic wisdom and high growth are revealed to you but you can perceive only a part of it. The more you connect to the light of the cosmos the more light you can bring to Earth. You cannot control the light; it will show you the way to growth.

Questions

1. What is alchemy?
2. How were alchemy and magic created?
3. What is your understanding of the following phrase: "Transformation is part of our existence but cannot be captured or manipulated."
4. How can you experience transformation?

Introduction

Do not look at social systems to help you support your evolution. We need communities where people are supported in their transformation and growth, developing their skills, studying true methods and fulfilling their purpose. With our whole existence, we support and complement each other inventing new ways of transmitting and receiving energy.

There is a miraculous way of living and this is being detached from beliefs, dogmas and archetypal behavior. All the above have been created to help you focus and sustain a certain consciousness and life experience. We are asking you now to abandon and destroy the persona and the lifestyle. Our aim is to give everybody the tools they need in order to paint their own authentic picture of themselves and let their true purpose be revealed. We want you to detach yourself from all that you are, right now and connect to your true-self, the one that is known to the masters and gods.

Wisdom of Thoth: Help Each Other Grow

In healthy communities all people should be supported in order to receive and transmit light. It seems that people experience life differently because of the way they are brought up, their social expectations and the way they relate to illusion. It seems to you that people have many choices and therefore they have different imbalances that affect their life in a certain way.

I see people on Earth suffering from the same disease; it is their inability to connect fully to their true-self because of the many layers of fragmentation and distortion in them. If you ask, why humans suffer from this disease, I can say to you that it is a disease that has affected Earth from the time her vibration was lowered and the Golden Era ended. Not being able to continue with her growth and become a High Creator God, she experienced schisms which affected certain parts of her creation.

Artificiality and illusion are man-made diseases and they were created due to distortion and fragmentation in human beings. We want to empower humanity by assisting them to connect to the light of the cosmos and become aware of their true-selves. You can be lost in a sea of illusion and artificiality if you are not able to connect to your true-self. The light of the Gods is surrounding Earth and we are creating channels of light that will bring clarity and knowing on Earth and her creation.

When you are able to receive the light, you will transform and your growth will be able to affect the growth of others. All of you together can connect to Earth and allow the cosmic light to travel through you and reach Earth and her creation.

You can assist the planet to transform and go through a rebirth. All human beings have imbalances and blockages. You all suffer from fragmentation and distortion and you all have to allow the cosmic light to go through you and resolve all limitation. When you all connect and help each other grow, the light will be received by many and transformation will be immense.

Questions

1. Is your community supporting your growth? What will be your contribution to the creations of a community of truth and growth?
2. Why do human beings experience limitation and suffering?
3. How can you assist the planet to transform and go through a rebirth yourself?
4. Can Earth support your transformation?

Introduction

This teaching reminds us that releasing old blockages and allowing the light to go through is not a theory or an interesting experiment. It is the reason for being alive, completing this life cycle. People at first find it hard to take part in artificial and illusionary exercises that are forced on them but then they accept them as truth. Accepting illusion as truth can be part of your everyday life.

There are people who experience truth or cosmic wisdom momentarily; this means that they are connected to their astral body and growth but something pulls them back to their fragmented reality; they decide themselves to return back to their comfort zone, the illusion. Living and supporting the illusion is a choice made by you. You must understand that you can escape from it but this will not happen by only talking about it. It requires action; it requires the power of your whole being, going against this artificial force. Illusion is not part of the Earth's creation so it only exists because you are giving it power. You invite illusion into your life and it takes over everything that is yours by bringing chaos and imbalance.

Wisdom of Thoth: The Gift of Freedom

There are people on Earth who have been looking for the tree of wisdom, the elixir of life and the hidden treasures left behind by their ancestors. I am here with you to reveal that treasures are available to all. We are all united and we can all receive and transmit light to create growth in all realms. When you open up to the light of the cosmos you are connecting to the creative power of the Gods that comes through you. The light of the gods is an extension of our Source.

Releasing old blockages and allowing the light to go through is not a theory or an interesting experiment. It is the reason for being alive, completing this life cycle. People at first find it hard to take part in artificial and illusionary exercises that are forced on them but then they accept them as truth. Accepting illusion as truth can be part of your everyday life.

This brings a growth of needs, wants and fears that keep you a prisoner of limitation. One may ask: if I am chained by illusion how can I connect to truth? When you realize that illusion is not connected to growth and therefore it does not exist, you will start to gain clarity. When you understand that you have allowed illusion to take a form, multiply and control your life then you can give the gift of freedom and truth to yourself.

When you wake up, you will stand at the crossroads and you will be called to choose the path that brings true fulfilment. You can create your own life, you can find support and you can fulfil your purpose. Your purpose on Earth is related to your cosmic purpose therefore cosmic creation supports your growth on Earth.

You are not a soldier against the great army of illusion. You are a transmitter, receiver and producer of energy whose existence is supported by the high light of our Source and the whole of cosmic creation. If you open yourself up to cosmic truth and see your essence as an extension of it then you are opening up to growth possibilities that are beyond your mind and your physical body.

This is your opportunity to connect to our Source and transform in order to reach its light. If you are looking for treasures you should focus on your connection with the cosmos. How can you achieve this connection? What is the link between your being and the cosmos? What is the path that will lead you to the understanding that you are an extension of the light of our Source? This is the quest you need to take in order to discover high treasures.

Questions

1. How can you experience Gods' creative power?
2. How can you release old blockages?
3. How can you disconnect from illusion?
4. What is the path that will lead you to the understanding that you are an extension of the light of our Source?

Introduction

Manipulation and everything that is related to it is the power of the weak. There are people on your planet who want the title of a god and their twisted minds have invented manipulation and destruction systems as a way to become a god. I know that on Earth there are people who control minds and bodies but this happens because you let them control you. You are working too hard to support the illusion that was given to you as reality and you are too exhausted to see the truth. Truth is hard to find when you support illusion. You have to be brave and cut the ties that connect you to false realities. You have to remember that illusion takes many forms and often presents itself as a need for survival.

Wisdom of Thoth: Within the Mind

There are people on Earth who are waking up and are connected to truth. To fully wake up and connect to your true-self you have to seek truth with your whole being. This can be achieved by eliminating the many layers of distortion in you and restoring balance in your whole being. There are many people who are able to connect to a centre in their being, for example the heart and this can lead them to awakening and enlightenment.

The mind that is controlled by the social perception is blocking the way to growth.

Human beings who suffer from this imbalance they will experience high peaks of enlightenment as well as a constant war between the different and fragmented states within them. Focusing on your intuition and ignoring the mind is not the solution.

The mind should not be ignored but tamed. Acceptance of the mind's abilities is necessary in order to bring balance in the whole being. Every individual part should experience its own individual growth and part of this growth is its unity with the whole. A mind which is not attached to illusion and is not affected by manipulation is an organ of great importance.

It is a copious job to observe yourself and detect the work of illusion in you. Disconnecting from the many layers of artificiality is not always an easy task but it is vital in order to achieve growth. When you are able to purify yourself, you will realize that all negativity, fear and dissatisfaction were not part of your true-self but you were forced to believe that it is true.

You will discover that many of your actions and thoughts are not pure and this means that they were implanted in you and accepted as the product of your true-self. You will also discover that your relationships need to be meaningful in order for yourself and others to grow. You will discover a wealth of abilities, talents and skills as well as ways to develop them and use them for growth. There is a wonderful and vast world below the sea surface; this is how I describe your true-self.

Questions

1. How can you connect to your whole being and grow in unity?
2. Why is it important for the mind to exist in unity with the whole being?
3. How can you disconnect from artificiality?
4. Can you observe your thoughts? Are they part of your truth and light?

Introduction

Humans who exist on third dimensional Earth are connected to all parts of their being such as the astral body, higher-self and creation code but due to distortion and fragmentation they are not aware of it. All beings receive guidance to help them grow and evolve and the ones who are chosen to reincarnate on Earth are guided in order to fulfil their purpose, bringing the astral light to the physical plane.

All life evolves in the present and dimensions co-exist within a living being and affect different areas of growth. Your growth in all your different bodies, universes and dimensions is affected by consciousness which is the "aura" of your growth and shapes your understanding and ability to connect with all that you are. Consciousness can keep a record, balance one's growth and guide different entities who wish to work with a being in the astral or physical plane.

Wisdom of Thoth: A Carrier of Cosmic Light

We are not here to show you how to walk by using your two feet or how to use your hands and other body organs. We are here to make you aware that your physical body is an extension of an astral energy body and all growth and evolution that takes place in both bodies are linked with each other. All human beings carry energy that cannot be defined by your five senses. You have a body of energy that exists closely to your physical body and is a gateway to your astral being.

Through this energy-body you receive and transmit light. Your purpose is also energy. When human beings state that they want to fulfil their purpose; this means that they want to reach a certain energy state through transformation and raising their consciousness. You create energetically, you communicate energetically, and you heal energetically.

When you purify and start to transform, you allow energy to clear imbalances and restore your light. When a great creator performs wonders you call this a great talent or charisma.

In all cases this being is a receiver of cosmic light and he is able to transmit it through his physical body. The physical body becomes the carrier of cosmic light as well as the transmitter and creator of new life and new energies. In this case we have a unity of all bodies and they all work together according to cosmic laws, achieving growth and evolution.

Your physical body is Earth's creation and when it is united with the astral plane, Earth receives cosmic light. There is a greater unity to be seen and this is our Source whose light has created the astral plane, the creator Gods who assist in creating life, the physical body that is Earth's creation but is also an extension of an astral body, a higher-self, a creation code and the highest light of our Source. When human beings understand this connection and live according to this truth then the Earth will transform and enter the Golden Era.

Questions

1. What is your understanding of your physical body?
2. What is your experience of your astral body, being the extension of your physical body?
3. What is your purpose?
4. Can your physical body become the carrier of light?

Introduction

Our source is always within us; we all carry the creation code which is a living being and is affected by our consciousness, the light that we possess and the way we use it. The unity that exists in the cosmos is contained in the light of our creator and is spread to creation through our creation code. Our unity with our creator is a high truth and when we are able to understand the wisdom, we will open ourselves to the possibility of being a creator.

Our High Source has no form, character or attributes. Our High Creator is the perfect representation of life where everything is effortless, whole and limitless. High Gods can only dream of being in this state of absolute perfection, where there is nothing to see and yet everything exists simultaneously. We have gathered here to connect to this high state of perfection and expand ourselves to a limitless, eternal state by connecting to our creation code and the whole creation.

All High Gods should look at all the different threads that cross their creation code and work on the wonders of it. Allow your creation code to be a living organism which is growing and finally takes its rightful place as a connector and Creator of life. There are so many mysteries related to the way each one of us is created and our work is to unveil the workings of our Creator, connecting all existence to the creation code. This is a study of Life and Creation.

Wisdom of Astaroth: The Mystery of Birth

All beings in all planes consist of their creation code. This part of their being is a high energy point and is connected to the light of our source. The creation code consists of all expected growth and evolution that one may have. Everything that you are and are going to become when you transform is recorded in your creation code including your reincarnations. Before you reincarnate you exist in the astral plane and at the right moment, according to your creation code, you are going to be chosen to reincarnate or to exist in another plane.

The astral being is aware of this reincarnation; it is aware of its purpose and a general life plan. Then the astral being will go through a preparation in order to join the body created in the womb. The unity between the female and male parts cannot produce a child if the energy of the astral being is not able to enter the unity of the male seed with the female egg.

The physical body grows like a plant coming out of a seed; this is a natural process and is related to Earth's way to create. For Earth, the birth of a plant, and animal or a human being follows the same process of creation and this is unique to this planet. The physical body that grows in the womb attracts the light of the astral being and tries to help the energy find its way and connect to the body that it starts to form. This is the true mystery of birth and its complex process depends on many different factors.

The parents are also involved in this divine unity and there is a great transformation taking place that affects everybody's growth. Often the energy of the astral being is supported by guides who are able to connect to the physical body and prepare the unity that is about to take place. If the astral being is not able to connect to the physical body then the fetus dies either before the birth or straight after. The same process will be repeated either with the same couple or with another couple that is more suitable. This is a brief explanation about the birth of a human being

Questions

1. What is the Creation Code?
2. What happens to the astral being before the reincarnation?
3. What is the connection between the physical body and the astral body?
4. What is the involvement of the parents in the life of a new being?

Introduction

When Earth was created, she first had to become aware of her purpose and this was done by the gods' intervention. There were many transformations that Earth had to go through before she was able to create beings. Like human beings, she had to connect to her true essence, understand her purpose and develop her tools of creation.

After many cycles of evolution, Earth was able to allow life to be created on her and in her. The process of Earth's creation can be seen in nature: for example, a tree naturally and effortlessly expands by growing new branches, leaves, flowers and fruit so what was created on Earth was seen as her own expansion that will help her to receive and transmit light.

The Gods' dream for creation is to restore Earth to her golden age by purifying her from all trauma, distortion and fragmentation. Once the elements of stagnation and imbalance are removed, the precious flower of light and wisdom that Earth once was will be revealed. Earth will be reborn from within and enter a new cycle of growth. She was created to exist for eternity and protect her creation to complete its life cycle.

Wisdom of Thoth: The Process of Earth's Creation

Earth was created as an astral being first and for this we were given guidance by the light of our Source. The light of our Source instructed us that Earth should have a physical body of high energy able co-exist in different planes.

When Earth was created she first had to become aware of her purpose and this was done by our intervention. There were many transformations that Earth had to go through before she was able to create beings. Like human beings she had to connect to her true essence, understand her purpose and develop her tools of creation.

After many cycles of evolution Earth was able to allow life to be created on her and in her. The process of Earth's creation can be seen in nature: for example, a tree naturally and effortlessly expands by growing new branches, leaves, flowers and fruit so what was created on Earth was seen as her own expansion that will help her to receive and transmit light. Many beings were created and we supported Earth to create life.

You may ask how were they created? What was the initial form? The first form cannot be seen on your planet anymore. It is not an egg, a seed or a tiny living particle that created the first beings. At that time Earth was going through an immense transformation, receiving cosmic light and also had direct guidance from high creator Gods.

The first beings on Earth can be described more as astral beings and their birth was caused by immense light that was received from Earth and transmitted from her to the cosmos. When Earth was able to create without the guidance of the Gods she became a planet of physicality and the beings that existed on her also became physical. They were able to multiply by receiving the light of the Cosmos and also connecting to the energies of Earth. When Earth transforms then her creation is also transformed.

Questions

1. How was Earth created?
2. Can you describe the first beings on Earth?
3. What is Earth's purpose?
4. How do you support Earth to fulfil her purpose?

Introduction

Artificiality penetrates all actions and thoughts so it can spread and produce more artificiality. The way we understand growth and evolution is not by being part of a community who supports low life expressions. The way we understand growth is by knowing your true purpose, allowing yourself to act and think according to your purpose, be the ground where divine seeds grow and enable you to become a creator of your own true path as well as assisting others to follow their path.

Wisdom of Thoth: Tribes of Earth

There are tribes on Earth that they experience life similarly to the people of ancient times. If you were able to enter these communities it means that the tribe people are slowly transforming to what they see in your western societies. Living close to Earth and have as your only intention to feed and be fed from her is very challenging. You will have to deal with the distortion on planet Earth and how this affects animals, plants, weather and all planet conditions. People in ancient times were able to direct distortion on the planet but they were also able to connect to Earth, and receive her nourishment.

People in ancient times new that the purpose was with Earth and the light of the cosmos will enter Earth and feed everything that she creates. They believed that the Gods will appear and will help the planet to raise her vibration and return to her golden era. Because of her connection with Earth and the understanding that they have a common purpose, they were given the support to connect to the cosmos and connect to the astral plane, to masters and the guides of the planet. This can be achieved right now by tribes that are not affected by your western civilisation, they exist to Earth and receive the light of the cosmos.

Questions

1. Can human beings live close to Earth and communicate with her?
2. How did ancient people connect to Earth?

3. How can Earth experience the golden era?
4. What is your contribution creating the golden era on Earth?

Introduction

An expression of distortion on planet Earth is when people are forced to perform certain tasks without support. This leads to confusion, negativity and limitation. I want you to look at yourselves and observe the patterns in your life and the life of others. Are you in the right state to create greatness? Can you see what is blocking you from escaping the survival mode and entering the creator state?

Wisdom of Thoth: Ancient Communities

In ancient times there were civilisations that had a structure similar to the social pyramid you experience in modern times. People in ancient times were affected by restrictions and separation. They were connected to the Earth and the cosmos but the priests and the rulers wanted to keep some of the knowledge they received secret.

They followed the ego and went on a diversion. The ancient communities that did not follow the pyramid structure were open to receiving and transmitting light, healing and nourishment. Everything they did helped them to support their understanding of their being in connection to the cosmos and Earth. So people were able to create communities of truth and unity, focusing on a pure life close to Earth.

The mystery schools were created because people wanted to escape the social pyramids and create communities of no hierarchies. They were many mystery schools who were created to preserve sacred knowledge but this led them on a diversion because true knowing is a living being and exists within all beings. You do not have to protect the cosmic light and you cannot restrict or direct its connection to Earth and her creation. This was the reason why many mystery schools did not have a purpose and this is why they stopped to exist.

Questions

1. What is your understanding of the social pyramid that affected the ancient communities?
2. How can people connect to truth and build communities of truth?
3. What was the purpose of the creation of the mystery schools?

Introduction

There is free will and there is personal growth. The whole creation is in constant evolution because our source is in constant evolution. Allow Earth's purpose to become your purpose.

Wisdom of Thoth: Connecting to Earth for Nourishment

Many years ago, people on Earth did not have to cultivate the land to receive nourishment. Land ownership was not common and human beings were able to eat and drink the food that was hanging on trees as well as tender plants and roots. The water from the streams could help them stay hydrated and the energy of the planet supported the whole being.

Feeling free to enjoy Earth's nourishment without restrictions and ownership was something that people on Earth enjoyed for many years. What changed this was the war and the greed of humanity that made them to want to destroy, own and capture. Humanity was not able to exist in peace with the rest of the creation and this caused further imbalances. It brought humanity to comfortably accept chemical and artificial substances as nourishment. Most of you have not drunk water from springs; you have not picked the fruit that hang on a tree; you did not experience the creative ability of Earth, creating numerous plants and animals that can share their light with you. Reconnecting to Earth is the only choice you have to nourish yourself and to fulfil your purpose.

Questions

1. Why human beings are trying to own Earth and how does this affect your growth?
2. How can you connect with Earth?
3. Can you allow Earth to nourish you?

Introduction

When illusion is accepted by your mind then it starts to grow and often affects other people around you. Illusion needs to overtake your mind in order to maintain its form which in reality does not exist.

Wisdom of Thoth: The Subconscious Mind

The subconscious mind is like a sponge that absorbs all mind activity that takes place in a person as well as emotions, understanding that other people have stored in their sub conscious mind. The conscious mind filters all this information and selects what is appropriate for a certain task.

Illusion can exist in the subconscious but it can only affect the being when it enters the conscious mind. When this happens, illusion is accepted as truth and it leads to certain actions and reactions. It is difficult for a human being to control their subconscious mind because it is a vast area of information. Instead you can observe your conscious mind, thoughts and acts.

Questions

1. What is the conscious mind?
2. Can you create a space of peace?
3. How does illusion affect your mind?

Introduction

Low energies are attached to the aura of human being in order to feed from their energy. If you want to help them you should connect to your true-self, heal your imbalances and spread the light of the cosmos. Connecting to the light of the cosmos, you can heal yourself and others who connect to you.

Wisdom of Thoth: How can you Purify from Low Energies?

Human beings do not realise that they open their doors to low energies to feed from their energy. It is important that you close these doors by creating and existing in a space of peace at all times. When you are able to exist in a space of peace, you purify yourself and you raise your vibration. This is how you are going to close the doors and start creating your life of truth and growth. Observing yourself constantly, having no fear or negativity and focus on your intention to grow and create your own life will help you find your new space where you can focus on your abilities. If your day is an experience of growth then in your sleeping state you will also experience growth.

Questions

1. Can you observe yourself?
2. Are you able to observe your patterns?
3. Are you affected by low energies?

Introduction

Naturally all bodies generate and transmit light and this is your connection with your higher-self. The higher-self will collect light from the higher realms and send it to your astral body and the astral body will reflect this light to the physical body. You are created to receive high light and evolve as a physical being but currently you refuse to open up to the cosmic force. Your blockage affects many areas of your understanding of the cosmos and has transformed you into a totally different species.

Wisdom of Thoth: The Light of the Cosmos

If human beings want to connect to the light of the cosmos, they have to accept that their essence is energy and that they are constantly connected to other energies.

Exchanging energy can take many forms and all people on Earth can achieve it often without knowing. When you dream, you are able to disconnect from your physicality and experience other realities; this happens to you because you are beings of energy and you exist simultaneously in different planes. Your physicality is not permanent; it helps you experience life in a certain way and for a short time, similarly to a dream state.

True existence takes place in the astral plane which is the home of all beings. When you accept that you are energy and your life on Earth is just an experience that will help you fulfil your growth in the astral plane then you see yourself creating and connecting to others in an energetic way. Astral beings do not exist independently. They are part of light groups which are also part of greater energetic structures. Everything in the cosmos is connected and exists as unity. This is the only way for the cosmos to remain alive, receive and transmit light. This last cosmic law is vital to help all creation to grow and evolve.

If you are a human being and you have just realized that your essence is energy and your physicality is temporary, you will understand the need to open up to the light of the cosmos. Beings who receive the light of the cosmos are going to fulfil their purpose and support others to achieve the same. An energy-being naturally seeks the light of our Source and it is as natural and important as seeking water every day.

Connecting to the cosmic light, we are seeking perfection, eliminating all obstacles that can make us weak. In your third dimensional reality you cannot open fully to the light of the cosmos because you are following illusion. There is a puppet master, who is also a puppet himself, who has convinced you that your life is a plan of limitation and you can only be happy when you accept illusion as truth. When you are able to see through this plan and connect to your true-self, you will be able to receive the cosmic light.

Questions

1. How can human beings connect to the light of the cosmos?
2. Can you explain the following phrase: "Exchanging energy can take many forms and all people on Earth can achieve it often without knowing."
3. Can you describe the astral plane and astral existence?
4. What is your understanding of the following phrase: "Beings that receive the light of the cosmos are going to fulfil their purpose and support others to achieve the same."

Introduction

The essence of all beings is energy. Energy has a different vibration and connects to different energy groups and systems in the cosmos. Energy is given the opportunity to have a physical body because it exists in a plane of physicality. If Gods are able to exist in the third dimensional reality they will also have a physical body and they will use it to achieve growth.

Your growth, as a human being, will depend on your ability to have dreams of creation. The first lesson in creation is the recognition of our essence and our creation code; they are our driving force and compass; which cannot be altered by anything or anybody. When you understand this first lesson, you receive cosmic knowledge.

The gods of creation wanted Earth to be a sanctuary, a temple where they all gather to create life. The matrix which was built around the planet was controlled by natural laws and the gods' creation rules. Human beings recognized that they were part of nature and they were not afraid of it or try to go against it.

All life has a creation code given to them by the gods of creation. The creation code is the essence of our High Creator.

Gods were able to communicate to people the truths they needed to know and wisdom was not hidden or distorted. Later civilizations became detached from each other and focused on gaining more power.

Until now, Earth has been locked in a low vibrational state. Earth needs to be free and this is happening right now through a spiral of destruction and transformation; the current ways are soon going to be the old ways.

Wisdom of Thoth: Goddess Earth

People on Earth understand Gods as beings or entities that have a form similar to their physical body. They see Gods as male or female that behave like human beings. How do you understand god? If you are able to answer this question then you will understand a lot about your consciousness and your ability to connect to your astral body.

The essence of all beings is energy; energy has different vibrations and connects to different energy groups and systems in the cosmos. Certain energy is given the opportunity to have a physical body because it exists in a plane of physicality. If Gods were able to exist in the third dimensional reality they will also have a physical body and they would use it to achieve growth.

Earth was created to be a Goddess planet and during her creation she was a high vibrational entity and was able to produce and nourish high vibrational beings. Earth was the home of the Gods and through them she acquired the ability to be a creator Goddess. There are Gods who are created directly from the Source and there are also Gods that are created by the High Creator Gods and go through a long process of transformation and growth to become Gods.

Earth was the latter; her creation was a long process of transformation. There are certain energetic points in the cosmos that can be used to create a planet Goddess where elements such as eternal nothingness, the light of our Source and the essence of the Cosmos can unite and create life. The creation of Earth's essence was the most important part of the project.

When this is created, different elements are connected to the essence and make it grow and transform. What you are able to see, the planet as physicality was created by the essence with our light and guidance. An essence of a being is the energy and can exist everywhere in the astral plane.

The astral plane does not have the restrictions of your physical world. The God in Earth is her essence not her physicality. Like human beings, Earth is disconnected from her essence and sees herself as a physical being. This is happening because she exists in a low vibrational reality and our task is to connect Earth to her essence and help her transform with the light of our Source. Gods exist in all planes and can take many forms. They are not single entities but vast electromagnetic fields where many energies meet and grow. Earth was created to be a Goddess and this is her essence.

Questions

1. What is your understanding of a god?
2. What can support you your connection to your astral body?
3. Why was Earth created?
4. Can you describe the astral plane?

Introduction

Opening up to the cosmic light, you are embarking on a quest to discover your true path and purpose. You will be standing at the crossroads; you may feel confused, weak, helpless or even disappointed about your life choices. You may think that there is no way out of the maze of social expectation and your life will always be affected by it. You may believe that you will never be free or true to follow your calling and purpose.

All living beings are united with the cosmic light and are part of the vast creation of our source. Humans who exist in third dimensional Earth are connected to all parts of their being such as the astral body, higher-self and creation code but due to distortion and fragmentation are not aware of it. All beings receive guidance to help them grow and evolve and the ones who are chosen to reincarnate on Earth are guided in order to fulfil their purpose, bringing the astral light to the physical plane.

Wisdom of Thoth: The Path of Self Discovery

I want to speak about those human beings who are able to understand illusion, being an artificial reality that is attached to them and convincingly accepted as truth. When you are able to receive the light of the cosmos, you are able to recognize illusion as artificiality.

Opening up to the cosmic light, you are embarking on a quest in order to discover your true path and purpose. You will be standing at the crossroads; you may feel confused, weak, helpless or even disappointed about your life choices. You may think that there is no way out of the maze of social expectation and your life will always be affected by it. You may believe that you will never be free or true to follow your calling and purpose.

Other people will decide to follow the path of truth but then they will have to face their own imbalances and that will make them very vulnerable and weak. Fear and anxiety can take over and people will decide either to return to their sleeping state or disconnect from it but they have no clarity or power to move on. Once you know the truth you allow the cosmic light to go through you and connect you to the cosmos and astral growth.

Understanding the cosmic creation and its laws you are expanding your consciousness and you are opening your path to reach growth. Growth does not have a specific form. It affects you in many ways and you may even go on a diversion to achieve growth. It may bring great fulfilment but also great challenges; in both cases the result is the same, achieving clarity, empowerment and unity with the cosmos. Knowing, is the first step to achieving greatness but it is not enough.

Your choices in life, acting with purity, focusing constantly on your growth and the growth of others and having this as your only need will help you fulfil your purpose. Experiencing growth is the greatest gift given to all beings and this is the way to transmit light.

Questions

1. Are you able to observe the illusion in your mind and being?
2. Can you describe your current state?
3. Are your life choices leading to truth?
4. Can you create your life according to your purpose?

Introduction

The gods want to support all beings who are looking for light and clarity but they cannot force you to take the path of a true being. If you are one of those people who understand the negative effect of illusion and fragmentation and you enjoy talking about it butnot disconnecting yourself from it then you are still sleeping; you are still supporting the illusion.

Being in a sleeping state, you fully disconnect from your true-self and purpose. In your hypnotic state, you learn to follow and obey illusion.

Then religions, institutions, media and society standards will add to the illusion by creating additional layers of artificial reality. Truth shows us the one path and when people walk this path united they will be able to realise that growth is an experience and not a doctrine.

Wisdom of Thoth: The Cycles of Growth in Lower Planes

There are many people on Earth who seem to be satisfied, being in a sleeping state. They happily follow the social expectations and their thinking, actions and expressions are tailored to fit the same ideals. It is important to look the part of a successful member of society and this way you are accepted as successful. It is also important to mix with people who are also playing the part of a successful human.

This way you think that your image is supported and stands out more. The people who follow this path become imitators of illusionary characters and their goals. At the end you are fully disconnected from the purpose of this reincarnation and there is no way back to this knowledge which is cosmic knowledge.

At the end of this life cycle you will be asked to connect to your purpose and you will be asked if you have fulfilled it and how? You will go through your life; you will live different events again. You will be able to see all the chances given to you to help you follow your path and fulfil your purpose and you will experience your actions and thoughts related to your growth.

If you lived a life totally disconnected form truth, freedom and purity, you will have to go through a purification to help you either move to the astral plane and continue with your growth or remain in a sub-plane and continue with your purification or reincarnate again. The longer you remain in lower planes the slower your growth.

All beings want to return to the astral plane to continue with their growth and evolution as energy beings. The cycles of growth in lower planes are much longer and there are a number of beings that are not able to return to the astral plane because they absorb low energies. Following illusion and social expectations is an indication that the being exists in lower energies and does not wish to experience truth.

Beings who possess others and force them to exist in slavery are ruled by lower energies. On the other hand, people who try to help others and are willing to give unconditionally, have the ability to absorb the cosmic light; they are able to wake up when they disconnect from illusion. When you understand cosmic wisdom then you know that you do not own anything and what you try to achieve is already in you. You only have to wake up, disconnect from illusion and walk the truth path of self-discovery.

Questions

1. Can you describe the sleeping state of humanity?
2. Why is it important to purify yourself?
3. Can you explain the following phrase: "The cycles of growth in lower planes are much longer and there are a number of beings that are not able to return to the astral plane because they absorb low energies."
4. What is your path of self-discovery?

Introduction

Masters have to take many steps of enlightenment in order to comprehend just a small piece of the vastness of the cosmos. One's enlightenment is connected to another person's enlightenment. It is really the generation of high light which helps the individual to maintain a higher vibration and this affects the planet and the cosmos.

Your physical body is a low vibrational expression of your astral body and there is a harmonic connection between the two. So if you are aware of the qualities, tools and unique characteristics of your physical body, you are able to connect to your astral body which is a more complex organism. Everything in the cosmos is a microcosm of a macrocosm and vice versa. All parts of creation harmonize with each other and bring balance to one another.

For human beings to become creators, first they have to purify themselves and allow the light of the cosmos to go through them and become a creative tool. In the universe there are no authorities. We all work together to maintain and multiply life in a vast area of divine creation.

When you see yourself as an authority, you have already blocked any opportunity to become a creator. When you see yourself as a limitation you have again blocked all your creative abilities and you exist in an illusionary limitation.

Wisdom of Thoth: Knowing your True-Self is Knowing Cosmic Wisdom

Your world is not separate from the cosmos; it is part of a vast mechanism that is created to produce and transmit light. Every single point of existence is an energy point and it is created to connect to the whole and participate in generating and transmitting light. We want to expand your consciousness by connecting you to this cosmic law.

This way you may be able to escape your limitations and detach yourself from artificiality and illusion. Some of you may ask: how can this knowledge affect my everyday life when everyday life is affected by illusionary thoughts and beliefs? Many people on Earth find it hard to disconnect form illusion because they have accepted illusion as truth.

They have illusionary goals; they live an artificial lifestyle and continue polluting themselves and the Earth. They do not want to know themselves, they do not want to connect to Goddess Earth and they live a life of destruction. There are people who are able to observe illusion in other people's lives but they cannot look at themselves and point out their own imbalances.

If you find it hard to disconnect from illusionary life patterns it means that you are not honest enough to express a clear thought related to your growth. When you are able to observe yourself, you will realize that illusion is an idea created in somebody's mind and then transplanted in your mind and appears to be your own.

If you want to connect to truth you have to continue observing yourself and reach a point of purity. Purity can share with you everything you need to know in this reincarnation. Knowing your true-self is knowing cosmic wisdom related to your being and its growth. There are many people who are fascinated by cosmic wisdom and this is why they read books about it. But how many people experience cosmic wisdom on Earth and what do they do to help humanity and Earth wake up from their long and restless sleep?

Questions

1. What is your understanding of your reality on Earth and how it is related to the cosmic existence?
2. How can you purify from artificiality?
3. Can you experience your life with purity?
4. Can you explain the following phrase: "Knowing your true-self is knowing cosmic wisdom related to your being and its growth."

Introduction

The connection with your astral growth will not create a schism in you; trying to suppress your ability of knowing your whole being will create a schism. When you connect to the high light, creation will happen naturally and you will see yourself and others being transformed because of it. When one creates, this affects his own light and understanding of the cosmos. It also affects all the people who are connected to him. One of the qualities of light is to be able to spread, purify and transform all beings. All creation should be in a process of constant purification and transformation but this is not always possible because the light is not allowed to enter fragmented and distorted areas of growth. This is why Earth and all her creation are suffering right now. We were given the task to bring the light to all of you who want to be creators on Earth.

Wisdom of Thoth: Experience the Transformation

A tree does not have any expectations or ambitions regarding its growth; it just allows the process to take place. You can grow the same way, without having to face obstacles, limitation and distraction. For this to happen, you should not have any preconceived ideas about your growth. Do not have any expectations; do not see yourself having this form or the other, just allow it to happen and experience the transformation.

There are many people on Earth who have as a driving force, a high idea of growth or a model that was given to them by the centres of manipulation. They spend all their lives chasing an illusionary award, ignoring what they experience right now and how this can affect their growth. Human beings have to understand that life is not only the physical experience.

Beings of the lower spheres are able to connect to their energy fields, the astral body and the higher-self. All parts of a being are designed to be able to communicate and support each other's growth. Being on Earth, you can communicate with cosmic energies, energetic fields and your own astral growth. This is not a special ability offered to a small number of humans; but it is a cosmic law and affects all life.

If you are not able to connect to your astral existence it means that you are suffering from limitation and fragmentation, which can cause a schism between your physical existence and the astral. You should not just accept what is given to you as truth. You should always experience life beyond any possible mind boundaries. The cosmic creation is limitless and eternal so the boundaries that you may have are illusionary.

The connection with your astral growth will not create a schism in you; trying to suppress your ability of knowing youR whole being will create a schism. Following what other people believe and conforming to social criteria and expectation is often seen as a healthy and balanced choice. I see that as a collective schism which is supported by many and it is difficult to see. I am here to free you because you all deserve to exist in the light of the cosmos. This is your purpose and this is the only truth you should follow.

Questions

1. What are your expectations?
2. Can you explain the following phrase: "There are many people on Earth that have as a driving force, a high idea of growth or a model that was given to them by the centres of manipulation."
3. What is your understanding of the following phrase: "If you are not able to connect to your astral existence it means that you are suffering from limitation and fragmentation which can cause a schism between your physical existence and the astral."
4. What is your purpose?

Introduction

Our High Source has no form, character or attributes. Our High Creator is the perfect representation of life where everything is effortless, whole and limitless. High Gods can only dream of being in this state of absolute perfection, where there is nothing to see and yet everything exists simultaneously. We have gathered here to connect to this high state of perfection and expand ourselves to a limitless, eternal state by connecting to our creation code and the whole of creation.

Let's take our intention away from the outer planes which we always think of as separate from us and responsible for our limitations. We are all part of the unseen, formless, all-contained, all-created power of our High Creator and we are going to start our quest for high truth and knowledge from this point inside us which unites, generates and contains all: our creation code.

Wisdom of Astaroth: Life in the Cosmos

The light of our Source is the only creative power in the cosmos. It travels from the higher realms to all beings and groups of energy points. The Gods and the helpers regulate this energy to reach and bring growth to all life systems in the whole of creation. The creation of our Source cannot be measured or defined by your standards; it is infinite and exists in constant growth.

Human beings on Earth understand the different planes as separate areas of evolution; in your mind you have the pyramid structure growth and you think that this pattern is representative to everything that exists. I want you to change your perception about cosmic growth; the social pyramid structure is linked to limitation and control of freedom.

The cosmos can be described as going underwater where the living space is not solid or flat and the life forms can move to different dimensions. There are beings in the cosmos that constantly travel; they are in motion. Other beings appear to stand still in order to receive the high light and then transmit it to the rest of the cosmos.

There are also vast groups of beings that are part of huge electromagnetic fields and they are in motion even when they appear to stand still. In the cosmos all beings exist because they are connected to others that help them to receive and transmit the cosmic light. All beings perform different types of movement in order to stay alive and receive light.

Their movement is similar to the movement of the components of a machine; it is almost like marching on the spot or moving in cyclical motion which is necessary in order to create life. Opening up to the light of the cosmos it helps you disconnect from all indoctrinated false realities on Earth.

Questions

1. What is your experience of connecting to the cosmic light?
2. What is your understanding of the different planes?
3. Can you explain the following phrase: "All beings perform different types of movement in order to stay alive and receive light."
4. Can you connect to the light of the cosmos?

Introduction

The light of the gods is now received by a number of people on Earth. We have started to plant our seeds of truth and as the seeds are growing, people start wondering about their existence and purpose on Earth. When you are part of the illusion you cannot be happy or fulfilled. Therefore you are kept busy, fighting imaginary problems and needs, going against your purpose. When one goes against his purpose it is like reaching a dead end. For your growth you have to follow one path and if you try to divert you are lost.

Truth and growth are connected and you can only reach them if you follow your path. People who start to awake have many questions; they have an immense desire for learning and searching for truth. You may be attracted to different teachers, books and other sources of information. But I have to warn you that this can also be a diversion from your true goal which is your purpose.

The gods do not want to control your life. We do not want you to rely on us and accept our gifts passively. Our light will heal your blindness and wake you up to Earth's true state but then it will be your task to go through a transformation and accept growth as a natural process.

We share our light with all beings, this is our duty, but the process of growth depends on their efforts and understanding of the natural and cosmic laws. You have been created to produce and transmit light and you do this when you are connected to your true-self.

Wisdom of Thoth: To Win or Lose and to Be in Light or Darkness

Human beings have difficulties and they often complain about heavy burdens and unsolved problems. When I look closely at people's lives I see that they are trying to hold on to their own imbalances and instead of receiving light and purity they become the shadow of their true-self and exist in limitation.

Some people will go against my word and try to convince themselves that their problems are very real and therefore, the effect on their lives is severe. The problem is created when you lock yourself into a limited reality that is illusionary. You are talking and thinking about your burden, you share it and spread it to others but this does not motivate you to be free from it.

There are people on Earth who are feeding from their own imbalances and what they create is distortion. To cure this disease, you have to see yourself as a multidimensional tool of the cosmic creation. You exist to grow and evolve as a unit but also as part of the greater divine plan. If you start trusting yourself and your ability to grow then you will expand.

In this state you will be able to see yourself as a perfect creation that can reach others with its perfection. The problems or challenges you experience on Earth are reminders that your path of growth is your only purpose. People on Earth are asked to play a game, to follow instructions, to win or lose and to be in light or darkness.

You have to participate in the "pulling and let go" game where you are constantly fighting in order to stand on your two feet and not fall down. This is not necessary for your growth; it is not a cosmic law and it will never help you connect to the source. The cosmic light gives life to all creation and allows them to be transmitters of energy. We support constant growth and our purpose is to support growth in all planes. If you accept this as your purpose then you will be free to connect to the cosmos.

Questions

1. Can you explain the following phrase: "When I look closely at people's lives I see that they are trying to hold on to their own imbalances and instead of receiving light and purity they become the shadow of their true-self and exist in limitation."
2. What is your experience of the following statement: "People on Earth are asked to play a game, to follow instructions, to win or lose and to be in light or darkness."
3. Can you explain the following statement: "You have to participate in the "pulling and let go" game where you are constantly fighting in order to stand on your two feet and not fall down. This is not necessary for your growth; it is not a cosmic law and it will never help you connect to the source."
4. Is constant growth your purpose?

Introduction

The people who are truly free do not depend on anything because they know that they can be the creator of their own lives. If you want to test your level of freedom make a list of everything that you depend on and then you will see that you are made to believe that life depends on so many things that you can afford to lose. When you exist in the illusion, the idea of loss brings confusion and imbalance. A person that has negative patterns and blockages is not a good judge or creator of life. He is constantly confused, misunderstood and has a passive attitude.

Wisdom of Thoth: The Misunderstanding of the Great Potential of Being Young and Old

Being misunderstood is a common phenomenon for the people of Earth. You do not fully understand what you are here to create, how to use your tools and how to connect. If you were pure then you would not try to over analyze people's connection with you; you should just try to open up to this connection and let it happen.

Misunderstanding is rooted in fragmentation. Everybody is looking for ways to achieve what is expected from them; whatever happens the people on Earth are not fully satisfied and as a result they do not fully grow. When some people connect to truth and want to disconnect from a reality of artificiality, then everybody tries to explain their behavior; they look for a name for this new disease and if it is necessary try to isolate the victim from the rest of the society in order to find a cure.

There is always a positive and creative force in human beings because they are naturally connected to the light of the cosmos. There are people who genuinely want to help others fight their disease and become a useful member of the society again. There are people who believe that this is very important and one cannot be alive if he is not a fully functional member of the society.

I want to ask you a question: why your society does not accept people who want to take their individual paths and understand growth, being part of the cosmos? Your authorities talk about people with limited understanding and ability to live a normal life. I see the authorities being limited because they are not able to reach the full potential of their being and they will never help others to fulfil their purpose as cosmic beings.

Children and old people are seen as the weakest and most vulnerable members of your society. You have to change your thinking and understand their great potential. Children are connected to the astral plane and because of that they are pure, non-fragmented, and able to connect to Earth and have a unique way expressing themselves and connecting to others.

When children are in constant connection with artificiality, they quickly lose their great gifts and become fragmented and distorted. Older people can also regain their purity when they reach to the understanding that artificiality and social expectations cannot have any effect on them anymore.

They know how to connect to their whole being as well as their astral self and they spend their final years, going through a preparation, disconnecting from their current reincarnation and moving to a new cycle of evolution. When they go through this process often they are not able to exist in the same reality with the rest of their family and friends.

Their ability to disconnect from their reality and prepare themselves for the next cycle is seen as a disease and your scientists fight it with chemical substances. There is fear, worry and drama surrounding disease and people who are the sufferers and their families can be locked into a low state and extent their suffering. People of Earth need to be able to recognise growth and allow it to happen naturally; then everybody will be fully functional.

Questions

1. Are you misunderstood? What has caused this?
2. Can you explain the following phrase: "Everybody is looking for ways to achieve what is expected from them; whatever happens the people on Earth are not fully satisfied and as a result they do not fully grow."
3. Why your society does not accept people who want to take their individual paths and understand growth, being part of the cosmos?
4. Can you recognize growth?

Introduction

Currently, people on Earth are trapped in a low vibrational reality because of the high level of distortion. Imbalances appear in all expressions of their lives and they are unable to heal themselves because they are unaware of their true state. Ignorance and confusion will not lead you to harmony and fulfilment. You have to be pure and true to your calling and purpose.

This phenomenon happens repeatedly on planet Earth and has caused multiple schisms of the true-self. It seems that people are born to fulfil their path; they start their journey with great hope and often with pure heart and soon they are lost. There are people that take a path which is not even parallel to the one which was designed for them and they can spend their whole life building life-structures far away from their true-self.

Introduction

Gods intended Earth to be a planet of many colours and shapes for the countless plants, animals and other species that they created. The next phase after the formation of the planet and its inhabitants was the training of Earth to become a high creator able to nourish and protect her species as well as create additional life. The gods knew from previous experiences in planetary evolution that if the planet does not learn to create on its own, continued life would be unsustainable. This was to become a great responsibility for such a young planet, as she had to learn to make life-creating decisions independently without godly intervention.

Wisdom of Thoth: Cosmic Movement

The sun is the creative force and the life bringer in the galaxy. All planets have their own purpose and creative power and they all exist with each other or influence each other's growth. Similarly to human beings on Earth, they have free will and they can choose to create different life forms or to participate in their extinction.

You may think that planets in the galaxy are too far away from each other and they cannot influence life; this is not true. An example of this is the cosmic movement towards the sun, similarly to the movement of the astral body towards each creation code and the source.

Human beings have to observe themselves and connect to their true-self; Earth has to do the same. This is one cycle of growth.

You can connect to the cosmic light and bring light to humanity and Earth, healing your fragmented understanding of yourself and the planet. Then you can look at Earth's life-bringer, the sun, and all the other planets that are moving together in order to receive the cosmic light, support life and raise their vibration. It is important for humanity to build bridges with the cosmos and allow creation and growth to bring back to Earth the golden era.

Questions

1. Can the planets affect your growth?
2. Why is it important to observe yourself?
3. How can you build bridges with the cosmos?
4. Can you support Earth to experience the golden era?

Introduction

Some people may be wondering: why do we need to have a body and live with the fear and limitations of death? Believe me; your bodies are very precious. A living being consists of many different bodies and all of them are messengers of information. The physical body connects you to the Earth's energies and shows you how to create with your limited recourses. Your five senses are also messengers of information and humans on Earth have almost exhausted all different ways of experiencing life with their senses.

I want you to see the divine plan through me and understand that unity and constant evolution brings grace and peace. We understand grace as the power of infinite; the power of the high creator gods. I want you to understand that even though I can take many forms, I am an infinite source of evolution that has no body and no thought. All that I am is an energy field and countless other energy fields are connected to me, all transforming at the same time, giving each other support, transmitting and receiving information reaching out and creating life. I want you to understand the vastness of what I am and perhaps then you can understand that the five senses is a limitation to your understanding of your true purpose. Your true purpose is already known to me because its reflection is part of my energy field.

Wisdom of Thoth: Your Body Exists in Constant Motion

Human beings are not aware of their bodies existing in constant motion also called growth. Your physical body is designed to allow purification and rebirth to take place. This is not only helping you to live a healthy and balanced life but it is also helping you to follow your divine plan connect to your true-self and fulfil your purpose.

The movement and rebirth in your body are assisted by your energies that are constantly moving in you and around you in order to attract the cosmic light. When you are aware of this movement, you are given yourself permission to grow. Being in a state of peace, you can experience your energies moving in and out of your body, purify and strengthen your bonds with Earth's nourishment and the cosmic growth.

Connecting to your whole being is a path of truth and transformation. It is the knowledge you possess and will naturally return to you when you disconnect from illusion. Do not block your path to growth instead reconnect to your true-self and learn to walk again the path of truth.

Questions

1. Have you experienced growth?
2. Can you explain the following phrase: "Your physical body is designed to allow purification and rebirth to take place."
3. What is your experience of the following: "The movement and rebirth in your body are assisted by your energies that are constantly moving in you and around you in order to attract the cosmic light."
4. How can you learn to walk the path of truth?

Introduction

It seems that truth seekers exist in a labyrinth of ideas, words and visuals and they are desperately looking for a way out but without success. There are many beings on Earth who are longing to achieve clarity, connecting to their true purpose, but they are entangled in the web of illusion and limitation. Thoth wants to reach all beings with his light and this is his advice: when people are able to empty their minds from all beliefs, aspirations, needs, suffering, pleasures and longings, they will discover their creator.

There are humans on this planet who are experimenting with spirituality and present it as a form of dogma or philosophy. In modern days, people have used many different trends, colourful terms and interesting theories.

When humans are able to fight illusion and heal distortion, they will support the planet's growth and transformation. They are many people on Earth who are walking the path of awakening. Their numbers are going to grow; this is the divine plan.

Wisdom of Thoth: Universal Path of Gnosis, Becoming Self-Conscious

Humanity is waiting for the fruit to appear. People on Earth use their imagination to reach fulfilment and satisfaction in their lives. They have imaginary goals and illusionary ways to achieve those goals. They become anxious, fearful and angry when their illusionary ways are not able to bring satisfaction; this is the cause of imbalance in humanity.

If you are one of those people who are waiting for the fruit to appear on the tree, you have to decide about planting a seed and see the tree grow. When you go against the natural laws and you replace them with illusionary beliefs and practices, you are going to suffer great imbalances. In your society, imbalances are seen as reality and truth and they grow and multiply from person to person.

I share with you the light of the cosmos. This is the highest force of creation and life; it is experienced by all beings and is transmitted to us by our Source. Open yourselves to the light of the cosmos and make it your purpose. This is how you can achieve enlightenment.

Illusionary thoughts and actions cannot serve your enlightenment and connection to the cosmos. Instead you become a victim of the lower planes and your true growth is non-existent. There are people who want to grow and connect to the cosmos but they are locked in a survival mode. You are not here to serve your disease; you are here to experience life without limitation.

A pure state and a balanced life are the only experiences you must have. Disease, dissatisfaction, pain, fear are all illusionary; they are not part of your being; they are artificial expressions of a distorted existence in lower planes. It is important that you connect to this truth and when you are able to accept it you will be able to transform to a cosmic being which is your true-self. We are connecting with you and we hope that you are able to connect to us.

Questions

1. What is your understanding of the following statement: "People on Earth use their imagination to reach fulfilment and satisfaction in their lives."

2. Can you explain the following phrase: "If you are one of those people who are waiting for the fruit to appear on the tree, you have to decide about planting a seed and see the tree grow."
3. What is a pure state?
4. How can you connect and transform?

CHAPTER VII

There is a miraculous way of living and this is being detached from beliefs, dogmas and archetypal behavior. All the above have been created to help you focus and sustain a certain consciousness and life experience. We are asking you now to abandon and destroy the persona and the life style. Our aim is to give everybody the tools they need in order to paint their own authentic picture of themselves and let their true purpose be revealed. We want you to detach yourself from all that you are, right now and connect to your true-self.

Introduction

All living beings are united with the cosmic light and are part of the vast creation of our source. Humans who exist in third dimensional Earth are connected to all parts of their being such as the astral body, higher-self and creation code but due to distortion and fragmentation are not aware of it. All beings receive guidance to help them grow and evolve and the ones who are chosen to reincarnate on Earth are guided in order to fulfil their purpose, bringing the astral light to the physical plane.

Wisdom of Thoth: Cosmic Healing

Connecting to the cosmic light you will be able to heal your whole being. Human beings exist in fragmentation and their understanding is affected by it. You were told that only a specialist can help you heal parts of your being but what happens when all parts of your being exist in unity and they are all affecting each other? The cosmic light can offer you healing that is unique because it heals the different parts of your being in order to maintain unity and balance. You were created by the cosmic light so for its creative force you are not a mystery.

Cosmic healing will transform the people around you because many of your imbalances are caused by the limitation and distortion of others. Becoming a receiver and a transmitter of light, you are able to communicate energetically with the true-self, purpose and imbalances of other human beings. You may see yourself as an individual being, living on Earth but in reality you have reincarnated with a group of other beings in order to support each other's growth. When you experience the light, coming and regenerating your being, you will experience unity within and strong bonds with the people close to you.

Questions

1. Are you able to connect to the cosmic light?
2. How can you receive cosmic healing?

3. Can you explain the following phrase: "Becoming a receiver and a transmitter of light you are able to communicate energetically with the true-self, purpose and imbalances of another human being."
4. What is your understanding of the following phrase: "When you experience the light coming and regenerating your being, then you will experience unity within and strong bonds with the people close to you."

Introduction

The teachers and the leaders of humanity should express truth with every action and thought and build strong foundations for supportive communities. If they are not able to express truth, it is obvious that they want to take your power away. There is not better nourishment than truth. When you connect to truth, you can expand beyond the persona and the ego and you can purify from all forms of illusion. Connecting to your truth, you experience unity with everything that exists. We are all connected and co-create humanity's and Earth's growth.

Wisdom of Thoth: The Path of Unity

Humanity should come together in a state of peace, connect to the light of the cosmos and bring healing on Earth. Let go of your social status and titles; they are not an extension of your true-self. Stop looking at the privileges and the differences between certain groups of people and understand that you all exist because you are created to be united to the cosmos.

I see that the ones that stand up as your rulers are constantly supporting fragmentation. Your system of democracy is a divisive system and this is why it does not lead to growth. The idea of opposite parties that constantly throw hatred to each other brings fear and confusion to humanity. Humanity's natural state is its constant unity with all that exists, allowing the flow of cosmic light to heal and renew all beings in all planes.

Your leaders are not aware of this truth. Like many of you, they are only interested in having a position of power and allow their illusionary ideas to influence themselves and humanity. You are responsible for your own growth but you can also support Earth's healing. Purify yourself and disconnect from the fear and hatred.

Opposition is a road with a dead end. The more you connect to your true-self and purpose the more you are able to connect to others and support their growth. When all people on Earth are able to purify themselves and experience life with purity and truth, you will all discover that you are one force connected to our Source. Similarly to the countless drops that exist united in order to create the great ocean. Do not take the path of division but take the path of unity. You are all equally important, designed to bring light to Earth.

Questions

1. What is unity?
2. How can you purify from illusion?
3. Why is it important to support Earth's growth?
4. Can you grow with Earth?

Introduction

During the golden age, all beings animals and plants lived in harmony and were connected to the energies of the planet, All beings contributed to the overall growth of the planet, receiving and transmitting light. Currently, people on Earth are trapped in a low vibrational reality because of the high level of distortion. Imbalances appear in all expressions of people's lives and they are unable to heal themselves because they are unaware of their true state. Ignorance and confusion will not lead you to harmony and fulfilment. You have to be pure and true to your calling and purpose.

Wisdom of Thoth: Low Spirits

All beings that exist on Earth can connect to their true-self, fulfil their purpose and return to the astral plane at the end of their life cycle or remain in a low vibrational state during their whole life time and also when they lose their physicality. Your journey depends on your intention to create your life and fulfil your purpose.

There are human beings on Earth that have the same intention as the non-physical beings that exist in a low state and try to survive by going against the cosmic laws; this causes destruction, distortion and schisms. Earth and her creation exist in a low vibrational energetic area and she creates those beings herself. If Earth was able to experience her Golden era fully then her creation will not have the dilemma, standing at the crossroads between the path of truth and the path of illusion. The Earth of the Golden era was not affected by distortion and fragmentation and her purity and high light could offer one opportunity to all beings; growth that has no obstacles, limitation or boundaries. Human beings on Earth can grow and experience again a high state of creation and this can be achieved by purification and your ability to connect to the cosmic light, bring healing and clarity to Earth's whole being.

When a human being can disconnect from limitation, connect to the cosmos and purify himself from distortion then he is walking the path that will lead him to experience Earth's golden age. If all humanity can achieve this then Earth will experience her golden age. In this case you become the creators of the golden era on Earth and you will be able to taste and share the golden fruit of a high birth.

Questions

1. Why human beings cannot connect to their true-self?
2. What is your understanding of the following statement: "Your journey depends on your intention."
3. How can we purify from distortion?
4. How can we experience the golden era and transform our lives?

Introduction

The physical plane is a school of the five senses, learning to live with the limitations of a body which quickly decays and turns into a different substance. Human beings need to experience physicality and an astral existence simultaneously in order to advance to higher levels of learning. Do not miss the opportunity to experience life using your physical body; however you do not need to diverse from your true purpose, getting lost in the five-sense reality. You have to focus on growth, clear the distortion and then become a receiver and transmitter of light.

Wisdom of Thoth: Trying to Understand the Planets, Galaxies and Universes

Human beings have the five senses to help them describe the world around them. Those five senses, vision, hearing, touch, taste and smell are affected by the planet's distortion and can only detect a minor part of what exists on Earth and the cosmos. Your mind, illusionary beliefs, artificial life style and inability to connect to each other can affect the growth of your five senses.

People who live close to Earth have more opportunities to experience the growth of their senses. This is because all actions and thoughts are supporting their connection to Earth. On the other hand, there are people who work to buy products and have no idea of how they are created and how they can naturally receive Earth's nourishment.

Trying to understand the movement of the planets, galaxies and universes is almost an impossible task for humans because their five senses and mind are limited. Earth and the cosmos have given them great skills and abilities to expand their physical body, mind, senses, energies and their ability to connect to others and the cosmos.

When you are able to connect to the cosmos and you have allowed the cosmic light to purify your imbalances, you will experience an understanding of our Source and its creation. You will not receive this by using your mind or your five senses; the information will enter your whole being and you will know it, being part of your true-self. This truth cannot be measured or explained scientifically; it is a form of energy that reaches your being and can be transferred to other human beings and Earth. Earth is also suffering from distortion and she also needs to connect to the cosmic light in order to understand her position and purpose. Your connection to truth will support her on her path to growth.

Questions

1. Can our five senses connect us to our purpose?
2. Is consumerism affecting your connection with your true-self?
3. What are your imbalances?
4. How can you connect to the cosmos?

Introduction

You are here to receive the light and with it, you will fight the low vibrational illusion of separation and polarity which has given birth to fear, survival and death of the real goal which is rebirth and transformation. The gods' project is to awake the inhabitants of Earth and help them disconnect from the illusion; pass the divine light to them and help them connect to their true-self.

Wisdom of Thoth: How was Illusion Created on Earth

Illusion was a plant that grew on Earth very long time ago. The only period that Earth was free from illusion was during the golden era. At that time she had a great light and was connected directly to the source.

Earth was a creator goddess and her creation showed that she was a perfect receiver and transmitter of light. After the golden era, Earth became distracted and confused. This was caused by the energies of other planets who tried to connect to her in order to receive the high light. When Earth connected to those energies she became vulnerable and her ability to grow and create was affected. When beings from other planets inhabited parts of the Earth and tried to connect to her energies, she experienced confusion and distortion; they were not part of Earth's creation and their intention was to claim her resources. This brought imbalances to the whole planet.

The beings were not aware that the cosmic laws supported Earth's abilities to create and maintain life. The beings that inhabited Earth were also confused and did not see their purpose being part of Earth's growth. Confusion brought distortion and the rulers used illusion to control the distorted masses. In some ways illusion tries to convince people that they are free and happy, living balanced lives and experiencing constant growth. This illusionary idea keeps them supporting the society mechanisms and the pyramid structure reward system.

If people were aware that they exist in a distorted environment, disconnected from the truth, the pyramid structure will collapse and society as you know it will stop to exist. Then human beings will have to abandon Earth or become perfect receivers and transmitters of cosmic light to support Earth's healing and growth.

Questions

1. What is your experience of illusion?
2. What is your understanding of Earth's distortion?
3. How can you purify yourself from illusion?
4. How can you become a receiver and transmitter of light?

Introduction

We are all part of the unseen, formless, all-contained, all-created power of our Creator and we are going to start our quest to high truth and knowledge from this point inside us which unites generates and contains all: our true-self. You need to be in constant communication if you really wish to empower yourself.

You will only be truly happy if you exist in a space of peace and stillness. All distractions will quieten down and disappear and then you can hear the voice of your true-self guide you on your path.

Wisdom of Thoth: A Space of Truth

There are people on Earth who are affected by the planet's low vibration and the illusion that is suppressing growth. Illusion can penetrate your being, pollute your mind and affect your everyday life. If you are aware of this, you are awake and you prepare yourself, going through a purification.

It is important for human beings to exist in a space of truth and growth and if they cannot enter a space of truth they have to create it. Can you describe your space of truth? What does it consist of and what is your contribution to keep it alive? How can you unite with other beings in this space and make it expand? Human beings have to take decisions about their own lives and be creators of their own growth.

Information on Earth is often diversion from truth or keeping the mind in a fantasy world while the rest of the being is following illusion. I do not want you to see this teaching as information but as a guidance to help you act and move a few steps away from illusion. Connecting to the cosmic light and purify yourself are gifts you can give to others and together you can co-create this space of truth. Healing and unity are necessary for humanity and Earth's growth. Connect to your pure intention and you will be led to a space were you will be able to connect to your whole being and then to humanity and Earth.

Questions

1. How can you purify yourself from distortion?
2. Why is it important to create a space of peace?
3. How can you share peace with others?
4. Where is your pure intention leading you?

Introduction

Our mission is to rejuvenate Earth and support her creation. We will succeed with our task if we all unite and fight Earth's limitations. We are all made of energy, we can all gather information and we can all carry a stone in order to build the divine bridge between the cosmos and Earth.

We are here to support the people who are waking up and are opening up to their light and purpose. Listen to our words and be happy that you are part of a high divine plan of growth and expansion. We are working with Earth but we also want to work with every individual on this planet and plant the seed of renewal and greatness.

Wisdom of Thoth: Earth's Divine Plan

When one looks at the ocean, he is not able to see every single drop that exists in unity with countless other drops. You cannot distinguish one drop from the other because now they exist to form this ocean and allow the current to create the movement necessary for this creation. When human beings are able to see themselves as part of Earth's creation and be in constant unity with her then fragmentation, division and distortion on the planet will evaporate. When you see yourself as part of Earth's creation, you will not experience hunger or pain because Earth can nourish you and support your ability to become a perfect receiver and transmitter of light.

If all humanity understands and opens up to Earth's energies then you all be able to heal yourselves and transform your physical body. If humanity can heal distortion and fragmentation then Earth will remember her golden era and she will produce the right nourishment and high energies to help you transform into the high being of the golden era. This will happen when humanity united and purified, recognises their purpose to become Earth's receivers and transmitters. When each individual is able to connect to Earth and receive her energy, all humanity will go on a process of purification and experience unity. This is Earth's divine plan.

Questions

1. What is your understanding of unity?
2. How can you have an effortless life?
3. How can you experience the golden era?
4. Are you opening up to Earth's healing and nourishment?

Introduction

A great way to purify yourself is to observe your physical body and observe its growth. When you know your body, you understand that is a microcosm of high creation and a link to all life on Earth. Having a physical form does not restrict you from connecting to your astral body and becoming part of growth that takes place in the astral plane. Naturally all bodies generate and transmit light and this is your connection with your higher-self. All beings are infinite and their true focus is their growth and evolution.

Wisdom of Thoth: Connect and Observe your Body

If you want to receive more clarity and connect to your purpose, you have to purify yourselves from all blockages that limit your light to be nurtured by the cosmic light.

Purification helps human beings disconnect from their environment and connect to the movement of their physical body. When you connect to your body, you are also able to follow its energies, experience its movement and bring life to the whole being.

In this state, your mind is not active and the ego does not affect your understanding and experience. Connecting and observing your body is what people have to do every day. There are many people who see their body as part of their persona but in reality the body is a very complex tool that can help you achieve high growth and stay connected with all parts of their being.

There are also people on Earth who either ignore their bodies or they use them to connect and support illusion and artificiality. When you are able to connect to your body and understand its great potential then it will be easy to connect to your true-self and understand the purpose of your reincarnation. Your body will guide you to your unique abilities given to you in the beginning of your reincarnation to help you fulfil your divine plan.

When you connect to your body you gain clarity and you realise that fear and limitation were illusionary. You will be able to observe your actions and thoughts and look at imbalances and blockages that created multiple patterns over the years. When you observe yourself you accept what happened in the past and you receive healing. Purification is a process of renewal and can help you create your own life according to the divine plan.

Questions

1. What are your unique abilities?
2. How can you use your abilities to fulfil your purpose?
3. What is your divine plan?
4. Can you observe your imbalances?

Introduction

Trying to understand the planets, galaxies and universes is almost an impossible task for humans because their five senses and mind are limited. Humans have to focus their intention on growth not limitation. All creation should be in a process of constant purification and transformation. We were all given the task to bring the light to Earth.

Wisdom of Thoth: Focus on Growth

Human beings have the five senses to help them describe the world around them. Those five senses are affected by the planet's distortion and can only detect a minor part of what exists on Earth and in the cosmos. Human beings are not aware of Earth's full creation because their senses have not grown enough to connect to the planet's growth. People who live close to Earth have more opportunities to experience the growth of their senses.

There are people who work to buy product and have no idea of the way they are created and what is their connection to Earth. Earth and the cosmos have given them great skills and abilities to expand themselves including their physical body, mind, senses, energies and their ability to connect to others and the cosmos. When you are able to connect to the cosmos and you have allowed the cosmic light to purify you from imbalances then you will receive a full understanding of the existence of our Source and its creation. You will not receive this by using your mind or five senses; the information will enter your whole being and you will know it being part of your true-self. This truth cannot be measured or explained scientifically but it is a form of energy that reaches your being and can be transferred to other human beings and Earth. Earth is also suffering from distortion and she also need to connect to the cosmic light in order to understand her position and purpose.

Questions

1. What is your understanding of the following message: "Human beings are not aware of Earth's full creation because their senses, being affected by distortion, fragmentation and limitation, have not grown enough to connect to the planet's growth."
2. Why is it important to connect to Earth?
3. Can Earth support you to connect to the cosmos?
4. How can you allow cosmic light to enter your being?

Introduction

Unity and growth shape the astral existence of all beings. Life on Earth is fragmented and offers limited growth. Beings are either asleep or confused and their existence is very problematic. There are more people on Earth who have started to wake up as the light of the gods is approaching the planet. There are many people who are going through an awakening process. They have started to realise that their life style is not helping them to grow. They feel trapped when they realize that humanity is not free and exists separately from Earth.

Wisdom of Astaroth: Earth's Healing

Earth is receiving light from the cosmos and is slowly regenerating certain parts of her being that exist in a low vibration. Humanity is waking up and starting to wonder about its true purpose. This does not mean that human beings are fully disconnected from illusion; I see them looking for truth and purity while they are surrounded by illusionary ideas, beliefs and social standards. If you are one of these people then you will be rewarded and will be guided to a space of truth. In this space you will stand at the cross roads and you will have the chance to walk the path of truth if this is your choice.

The Gods and their helpers are not going to intervene and influence your decision because by choosing the right path yourself, you achieve growth. If you are at the cross roads, connect to your true-self and understand your divine plan and purpose on Earth in this life time. This will give you the chance to examine all forms of illusion, distortion and fragmentation in your life. If you decide to maintain the illusionary existence then the path that you are going to choose is a diversion from your purpose.

You can only choose the path of truth if you disconnect from illusionary and distorted life patters and purify yourself. When you achieve that, you will transform yourself in order to fulfil your purpose. Human beings are responsible for their own growth; your ability to receive and transmit light supports Earth's growth. The unity of the cosmos is what supports your eternal existence and this is a superb guide and the High Father. Creation is achieved through unity.

Questions

1. What is your pure intention?
2. How can your purity guide you to your purpose?
3. Are you connecting to Earth?
4. Can you explain the following message: "Creation is achieved through unity".

Introduction

The people of Earth are affected by trauma. When children start to become aware of society structures, they lose their ability to connect to their purpose and have an effortless life. The focus in their lives will be indoctrination, focusing on the mind-logic-limitation and be part of a life of duality, fragmentation and non-growth. Human beings go against their purpose and this causes traumas and schisms.

Wisdom of Thoth: Psychosis, Hypnotic State, Illusion

Illusion affects all life on Earth. If you live in a city whose air is polluted you are going to breath the polluted air and be effected by it. You exist in a restricted social structure and only if you are close to Earth's energies you are able to understand, experience and practise truth. While you are all polluted by illusion, some of you exist in a hypnotic state. This means that you fully accept illusion as truth, you never question authorities, fellow citizens or self and you support/reinforce illusion.

Ignorance can lead you to a hypnotic state but there are also other factors. There are people on Earth who consciously turn their back to truth and the cosmic light of creation in order to dedicate their lives, supporting illusionary success and power. There are many people who are attracted to the idea of being the supporters or even the architects of social pyramids. Some may ask: why do they do that? I will simply answer that they are in love with their disease and the imaginary rewards offered by your social structures.

Your reincarnation is a test and a lesson and you are all free to take any path you wish. At the end of your current life cycle, you will have to face truth and you will be able to examine everything you have created during your life time. When you reach this point you will have to purify yourself in order to return to the astral plane and continue with your evolution.

How is psychosis connected to illusion? It is an escape that can also be seen as a form of purification, connecting to old events and trying to understand why and how. You go back to a traumatic experience in order to correct it or to experience it again, trying to be in control and know what to do. Other times you have to block reality and experience a psychosis in order to protect yourself, to get strength, to get rid of trauma or to purify. When you experience a psychosis your trauma creates a reality that is as real as the reality other people experience. You are not able to function and exist with others because you experience a totally different reality. This can cause more problems because you can become completely dysfunctional, connecting with others. You can also feel isolated, misunderstood and vulnerable and this can cause a schism. It is important to be in a safe place with people that can understand your trauma and they are willing to listen and build bridges between your reality and theirs. If you go through this imbalance it means that severe trauma exists in you and needs to be cleansed, healed and finally disconnect from your being. This also shows that you are a being that can only exist in truth and in high energies and this is what you have to aim for.

Questions

1. Are you able to observe yourself your imbalances?
2. What experiences can cause trauma?
3. What is psychosis?
4. What is an illusionary reality?

Introduction

Our intention is to connect you to the source, our high creator, everlasting force and the purest source of light creating life for eternity. The gods' intention is to share the light of our source and build bridges between the Pleroma and Earth. The divine plan is becoming Earth's reality and we will all have the opportunity to grow in unity.

Wisdom of Thoth: What is your Intention?

The intention of a God is to be a creator. The intention of the astral beings is to grow and evolve. The intention of the beings of Earth is to believe and accept artificiality as truth. Your pure intention should be to disconnect from all illusion and connect to your true-self, your light and the cosmos. You intention is part of your being; it is not a thought or a skill learned. It is the way you live, share and create.

There are human beings who are involved in supporting humanity but their intention is to harm and destroy it. There are human beings who want to support goodness but without knowing they are harming others. Humanity is suffering from trauma and this is why most humans have a "layered" way of connecting to others. People's intention is not pure because fear controls their mind. If you are able to answer every question truthfully then you have pure intention.

When you are not sure then you hide the truth from yourself. If you do not know what your next step will be, you should question your intention. Why are you here right now? What would you like to be your destination? What truth do you carry in you to help you to fulfil your purpose? Your intention is part of your true-self; it is the way your experience your path of growth. I want you to connect to your intention, to observe the way it grows in you and how it affects your life. If you do that you will connect to your true-self and you will disconnect from fear. This is my gift to you and the rest of humanity.

Questions

1. What is the intention of humanity?
2. Why is humanity suffering from trauma?
3. How can you connect to your true-self?
4. Are you free to grow?

Introduction

Demolish the boundaries between yourself and your purpose. You are a unity of multiple reflections and naturally you should not accept as truth a single expression of the life that Earth can create. Cosmic consciousness is an understanding that has no boundaries. It is the understanding of all that exists; all different expressions of what exists in all different planes and universes. When one realises the perfection of the cosmic flow and experiences it in their everyday life, he has received enlightenment.

Wisdom of Thoth: A Unity of Multiple Reflections

All energies connect and create together. Now is it is your turn to create!

On your path to wisdom you will come across a jungle of different knowledge. Some of it is illusionary; there is also knowledge given to you by ancient civilisations or mystery schools but it has survived distorted and incomplete. There is knowledge regarding nature and planet Earth which is fragmented because your methods of understanding are also fragmented. Human beings are taught in their societies to support one side. This corresponds to a certain life style, expectations and goals of a human being.

There are not many on planet Earth that can understand and relate to different sites because they are taught that this brings limitation. You are also taught that there is always a polarity, one side against the other when in reality there is a unity that has unlimited reflections. You are a unity of multiple reflections and naturally you should not accept as truth a single expression of the life that Earth can create. It is your duty to seek knowledge and wisdom and experience this in your everyday life. But what side should you take: the red or the blue; the high or the low?

Before you choose your options, you should demolish the boundaries that separate these options. When you achieve that you will realise that all energies connect and create together the new energetic field. You are here now because the red and the blue, the right and the left and the high and the low come together and create life. Now is it is your turn to create.

Introduction

Planets are living organisms and when they are in an alignment they connect energetically and affect each other's cosmic laws and systems. There is a unity and we are all part of this alignment able to strengthen the bonds and the energy that flows through it. Our duty as energetic beings is to strengthen and support Earth's alignment with our own light and the clarity of our intention. You have to use your energy to strengthen bonds on Earth: bonds between people, activities, fields, actions, thoughts and imperfections. Accept it all and then embrace it all.

Wisdom of Thoth: The Unity of your Physical body and your Energy

Some of you may want to know how to prevent disease affecting your body. There is one way to achieve this: you have to focus on the energies that exist inside and around your body. Your physical body cannot experience life if the energies of your aura cannot enter your physicality.

Your energies are in constant movement, trying to maintain life, bringing balance and connecting you to all that exist including Earth and humanity. Your energies pass to you cosmic information that can help you grow according to your divine plan and your astral growth and evolution. You are connected to the cosmic light because your energies are acting as a channel for the cosmic light to go through. When you are able to connect to the cosmic light you bring healing to your whole being and the physical body does not become an obstacle for the energies to bring live in it. Living in a distorted environment where there is no clarity, truth or growth, the body experiences limitation and this can affect the energies that surround it. Most chronic illnesses affect the body because the communication between your physical body and your energy is limited.

If you wish to restore this communication, you have to experience the unity between your physical body and your energy. For this to happen you have to be in a state of peace and disconnect from illusion and distortion. You should only experience the unity and communication between your energies and physical body. If you wish to strengthen this communication and bring a healing balance into your being, you have to connect to the cosmic light; this is how you can experience growth.

Questions

1. How can you prevent disease affecting your body?
2. How can your energy support your growth?
3. How can you experience unity within your being?
4. What is your understanding of inner communication?

Introduction

Gods are astral beings and can take many forms. A god is not one being; he has multiple forms and can penetrate many manifestations of reality simultaneously and can take many different forms. They exist in a space without boundaries. Their aim is to possess the most advanced creative tools and take part in complex creative projects. The tool which all gods aspire to have is the power that makes them eternal and limitless creators.

Wisdom of Thoth: The Process of Becoming a God

The process of becoming a god cannot be explained; it can only be experienced by the ones who have reached the high light and they are ready to transform and grow in order to become one with the source. A being experiences this type of transformation in a sub-plane that exists between the astral plane and the Pleroma. You define your understanding as conscious or subconscious.

This means that you rather experience life or you allow the understanding to shape your experience. The transformation I described before is not controlled by the being; the being allows the transformation to create a new astral body and a new light that can create growth and then it links all cosmos to this growth.

When you are in this process you understand that you are the cosmos therefore it is important to stay connected to all planes. When you are able to transform, you will understand that your being is not only your mind and emotions but it consists of many integral parts of you that are unknown or neglected. Existing in a state of fragmentation human beings allow imbalances to be created which cause mental and physical disease. In this state you cannot transform and connect to the cosmos. You can receive healing by accepting your whole being, connecting to your ability to expand and grow and bring light from the cosmos down to Earth; becoming a receiver and transmitter of your own transformation.

Questions

1. What is your understanding of a god?
2. What is your experience of transformation?
3. What is a state of fragmentation?
4. Can you transmit your own transformation?

Introduction

The gods want to communicate with all beings on the planet and heal all imbalances and blockages. The light of the gods is transmitted to Earth and we have to become pure channels of the cosmic energy for our own healing and purification as well as the Earth's. Empty yourself from the influence of distortion. Just follow your path and be ready to detach yourself from the false persona. Truth is one; the way to truth is one and direct.

Wisdom of Thoth: The Seeds of Purification

Purification should grow in you and become a tree of countless branches, leaves and flowers and attract the cosmic light to make it your guide. There are many other trees that should be grown in you; the tree of truth, purity, freedom and transformation. All these trees together make the forest of growth that can take you to your purpose. By sharing a space of limitation with people close to you, you do not allow the seed of purification to grow.

Having the fear of inferiority or wearing the blindfold of superiority does not help you see yourself in connection to your purpose. Allow the cosmic light to flow in you and purify your imbalances. Restore balance into your being by connecting to those abilities and gifts given to you in the beginning of your reincarnation. Discover that you are a design of authenticity that exists in unity with the cosmos and it is here to bring and receive light, healing and growth. Look for your divine plan and when you know it, start creating your life.

Questions

1. Are you growing towards purification?
2. Are you sharing a space of limitation?
3. How can you restore balance into your being?
4. What is your divine plan?

Introduction

All creation should be in a process of constant purification and transformation but this is not always possible because the light is not allowed to enter fragmented and distorted areas of growth. When you have cleared all blockages, you will be able to go through a transformation and receive high light. Energies from the astral body can flow to the physical body.

Wisdom of Thoth: Practising Purification

There are people on Earth who try to purify their bodies to help them release toxic substances. There are others who are asking guidance for purifying their spirit. My advice to you is to take off the blindfold of fragmentation and separation and start connecting to your whole being.

Purification will take place when you are open to cosmic light and allow it to enter your whole being and bring healing and clarity. For this to happen you have to create a space of peace where you can disconnect from the distortion of the mind. Start knowing your own being the way it was created in the beginning of this reincarnation. Human beings' understanding of themselves is affected by distortion, illusion and negativity.

Many of you do not know your true skills to help you grow and fulfil your purpose. Instead you are busy with the learning given to you and the skills you acquired in order to reach the social pyramid and enjoy illusionary rewards. Now is the time to disconnect from everything that was imposed to you from young age and start connecting to your true-self.

There are a number of steps to help you achieve this. You need to have pure intention and focus on connecting to your essence and your unique tools and see how they affect your whole being. Start observing yourself: how is illusion growing and transforming in you; observe your illusionary thoughts and the way they are created in your mind; observe the layers of distortion that created imbalances; accept everything that you are without negativity or fear; understand truth and experience it in your everyday life. This will lead you to purification and growth.

Questions

1. How can you purify your physical body?
2. How can you connect to your whole being?
3. How can purification help you grow?
4. Start observing yourself! What are your experiences?

Introduction

People on Earth who want to grow have to disconnect from patterns of the past. This can be achieved in different ways: observe yourself; look at the link between past patterns and present ones; observe artificiality in your life and connect to your purpose. You grow when all actions and thoughts are true to your life path and purpose.

Wisdom of Thoth: How can You Experience Life on Earth

Many of you look at yourselves in the mirror; do you do this to find more about your physical body and energies? Can one use a mirror to observe himself? You can only observe yourself when you connect to your being, let go of perceptions and understand your purpose in this life time. You can truly see your being when you understand your purpose.

Connecting to your true-self and maintaining this connection can only lead you to your path where your purpose and divine plan lead. There are people on Earth that are going to spend precious time looking at the mirror because their intention is to feed with the illusion around them. There are also people who look at the mirror and one day they will see the illusion trying to suffocate the beautiful creation that they are. I also want to point out that Earth and the cosmos have given you many gifts that you have never seen.

If you are still alive, walking on Earth, focus on your being, discover your unique abilities and let them grow. If you do not experience life through your physical body, energies, divine plan and purpose you are a foetus that spend a life time in her mother's womb and never blossomed to become Earth's creation. Looking for the hidden treasures in you will finally take you to your purpose and this is how you can experience life on Earth.

Questions

1. What do you see when you observe yourself?
2. What is blocking you from connecting to your true-self?
3. What is supporting your growth?
4. What are your unique abilities?

Introduction

During your purification process, you will observe your unique abilities given to you before your reincarnation and your imbalances and negative patterns. The illusion can trap you to support your own enslavement; the truth is transparent and is part of your growth. Some may ask: how can we escape what we know as normal life when we have allowed illusion to form every single aspect of our lives?

Wisdom of Thoth: Imagination

Human beings on Earth are using their imagination to escape their reality. It is like diving under water, exploring a wonderful new life that has nothing to do with your reality and become part of it for a short time. Most of you who dive, know that your reality is waiting for you but your escape is short and perhaps will never affect your growth.

Other human beings understand illusion as a product of their own imagination. This way they allow illusion to take a form of escape from a life that do not understand or create. In this case, illusion and imagination become one and the escape that you seek is only a blindfold. Your teachers, rulers and authorities encourage you to use imagination to create a "better world". Will it be more helpful to connect to your true-self where your purpose, divine plan and unique abilities meet a creative force of the cosmos? Will it be more useful to purify yourself from illusion and become the creator of your life? Living a life of imagination you can only imagine growth, transformation and cosmic existence. You do not experience them and therefore you cannot transmit them to others who are also looking for their path. Everything that grows in you is alive and is transforming. The rest is illusion that blocks your path.

Questions

1. Are you using your imagination to escape reality?
2. Is imagination a product of illusion?
3. How can you create a "better world"?
4. What is blocking your path?

Introduction

When you will finally connect to your true-self, you will become a constant light for all to see and experience. In you, people will see the golden era and how the power of the gods created Earth. Your purpose in this life time is linked to the purpose of the Earth and it is your responsibility to bring this light up to the surface.

Wisdom of Thoth: Earth's Light

I want to connect to humanity and Earth and bring the light that is stored in the core of the Earth to the surface. Many of you want to be free from illusion but you cannot disconnect because the light of the cosmos cannot reach you; either can reach the parts of Earth that you inhabit. You need to regain balance within your whole being and Earth has to do the same. The light that exists in her core needs to travel to her whole being and bring balance to everything that exists on the planet. Humanity is looking for its purpose, looking for the creative force that can clear distortion and can bring healing and growth. It is important that you become a true channel for this light to go through the planet.

Your purpose in this life time is linked to the purpose of the Earth and it is your responsibility to bring this light up to the surface. Exist in unity with people that understand this important task and together you can purify yourselves and create bridges between Earth's high growth and her schisms. Humanity needs healing in order to connect to their true-self. This healing can be shared and become the root for the Golden era to come in and reach the whole planet. When this happens enlightenment will affect the whole planet and show that illusion does not exist.

Questions

1. Why humanity find it hard to disconnect from illusion?
2. Can you describe Earth's distortion?
3. Is your purpose linked to Earth's purpose?
4. Can the coming of the golden era support your growth?

Introduction

Do not seek truth with your mind; truth is not an intellectual property but it is a state and an experience that unites your whole being. Do not follow the path that promises you superiority, being in a higher state than others; this will lead you to a fragmented and distorted state. The illusion of freedom is seen in people who are obsessed with wealth that keeps them prisoners to their work; children who grow up unnourished, already prisoners of education and technology; academics whose narrow views brainwash the youth; scientists who go against people and nature to prove their superiority.

Wisdom of Thoth: A Definition of Illusion and Distortion on Earth

There are people on Earth who are looking for a definition for illusion and distortion on Earth. They are looking for the right words, the right meanings, and the right expression while illusion is living in them and create perceptions that can shape their lives. There is no better definition of illusion than the experiences that link you to it.

Human beings experience illusion every day, observing people focusing on materialism, social expectations, self-destruction, confusion, fear and negativity. If you are not able to see your purpose and follow your path it means that you are affected by illusion. When you are polluting your body with artificial food products you are also affected by illusion.

If you cannot experience growth and connect to humanity and Earth you are also blocked because of the illusion in your life. There are also people who are willing to connect for truth but they end up following another diversion and keep them in a space of distortion. Never follow a path that is promising you growth. The path of truth is offering you growth when you take the first step. Every step is a transformation leading you away from the illusion.

Do not seek truth with your mind; truth is not an intellectual property but it is a state and an experience that unites your whole being. Do not follow the path that promises you superiority, being in a higher state than others; this will lead you to a fragmented and distorted state. The path of truth is in front of all human beings because they all carry the light of the cosmos. However their life choices, thoughts, beliefs, actions and connections can erase this path or create it. All human beings have a great duty which is to co-create their path supported by the cosmic creative forces. If you wish to be a creator you should start your purification process. This way you will connect to your true-self.

Questions

1. What is your understanding of illusion?
2. What is your understanding of the following phrase "Do not seek truth with your mind."
3. Is superiority a sign of growth?
4. Can you create your life?

Introduction

People who have connected to the cosmic light and received healing and knowing they have experienced a deep understanding of their current situation and the way the divine plan is being unfold. The true-self is never part of the illusion and it always exists in you. In order to reach the state of truth you have to question yourself: what brings me pure happiness and growth; what is my true purpose and what abilities do I have to fulfil my purpose? You grow when all actions and thoughts are true to your life path and purpose.

Wisdom of Thoth: Cosmic Happiness

There are many people on Earth that are looking for happiness. All the products that you are about to consume are trying to tell you consumption is happiness. Are you misled or you are choosing the path of distortion and confusion? Both those plants are growing in you and take you on different diversions because you are not connected to your purpose and true-self. Happiness is only a product of your imagination and it is a powerful way to be controlled and stripped from your true power and ability.

People who have connected to the cosmic light and received healing and knowing they have experienced a deep understanding of their current situation and the way the divine plan is being unfold. When you exist in unity with all that you are and the cosmos then balance and growth will affect your being. In this state you will be open to connect to the source, receive guidance and nourishment from Earth, share and receive healing with humanity. This will make a physical being experience fulfilment and cosmic happiness. The path is open to you and there are no restrictions or rules to block your way. Growth can be yours if you choose it.

Questions

1. What is cosmic happiness?
2. How can happiness support your growth?
3. What is your understanding of your purpose in this life time?
4. What are your restrictions fulfilling your purpose?

Introduction

Our purpose is related to the elements of the planet that we are inhabited. If your true purpose is related to Earth, you are a force of stability and balance between the elements and the planet. You are going to connect to Earth and help her recognize her true potential as well as being open to cosmic guidance. Climate change may be a sign that Earth is going through a purification process, leading to a transformation; pollution is man-made and does not support the well-being of Earth's creation.

Wisdom of Thoth: About Climate Change

Human beings that are blind are trying to control and manufacture all Earth's elements; the ones that are able to perceive. To achieve this, they create an eminent threat and the need of a new set of rules that will control and restrict humanity from Earth's resources.

You have accepted the idea of property and ownership as well as selling/buying Earth's nourishment. If your rulers truly care about Earth and humanity why they do not allow Earth's healing and nourishment to be received by human beings the way it was intended, without the price tag? The issue of global warning it is a confusing one because it is illusionary.

There are people who are talking about climate change. Is the climate changing so rapidly that is causing the extinction of Earth's creation? Who is able to communicate with Earth and understand the importance of possible changes taking place on her surface? Other people are talking about pollution and they link this to climate change.

Climate change may be Earth going through a purification process; pollution is man-made and does not support the well-being of Earth's creation. If you rulers want to stop pollution they should support all of you to connect to Earth and receive her nourishment, building communities of truth and growth and abandon the life style of artificiality and consumerism. When rulers support the climate change-fear, they want to create more restrictions where you can exist isolated from Earth and her healing energies. Is this supporting Earth?

Introduction

The following teaching will explain the purpose and the duties of the angels and messengers.

Wisdom of Thoth: Arch Angels

There are a number of religions and cultures that they talk about angels and they have given them certain characteristics and names; they have even given them a part in stories and legends. I will say to you that angels are messengers who are working with Earth. They have an important duty to support life on the planet and communicate with Earth's creation for the cosmic light to go through. An angel is a messenger, a guide, a protector and a bridge between a certain plane and the cosmos. They exist in a higher plane and do not reincarnate. They can connect to certain beings that reincarnate on Earth in order to pass information and guidance for Earth's and humanity's growth.

Questions

1. What is your understanding of angels?
2. Can angels support humanity's and Earth's growth?

Introduction

Human beings should observe Earth's growth and ability to create. If human beings follow the natural laws, they will be able to understand the cosmic laws. It is important that Earth receives healing from the cosmos and experience cosmic unity.

Wisdom of Thoth: Winter Solstice

Human beings can observe the different seasons and look at the different ways that Earth can create life. Many of you understand the winter season as a time of non-growth where animals and plants are becoming less active and some of them going into a deep sleep.

I will explain to you what is happening to Earth right now. Earth's energies are being pulled to her core to support the growth that is taking place in the higher dimensional parts of the Earth. The surface of the planet is a lower dimensional area that is limited in recourses; the creation that exists there is also limited because it is suffering from distortion.

When you see limited activity on the surface of the Earth, it means that Earth's intention of growth and creation focusses on the inner parts. In winter time human beings often feel tired and empty energetically this is because they offer their energy to support Earth's growth in the core of her existence.

In ancient times people gathered to celebrate winter solstice and it marked the end of a period of Earth's growth in her inner parts and the beginning of a new cycle of growth on the surface of the Earth, connecting to Earth's energies and nourishment. It is not a coincidence that new religions used the same dates to celebrate events that were related to their dogma and beliefs. In modern times, human beings are not connecting to Earth to receive her nourishment during these celebrations but they are programmed to seek for nourishment in artificiality and illusion. Consumerism is becoming the new religion.

Questions

1. What is your understanding of Earth's growth?
2. What happens to Earth during winter solstice?
3. How does Earth growth affect human beings?
4. Can you explain the following phrase: "Consumerism is becoming the new religion."

Introduction

When you are purified and you are able to see your true-self, you will experience unity with everything that exists in the cosmos. Humanity and Earth can connect to the cosmic light and have access to all life including the high planes and the creator gods.

Wisdom of Thoth: What is God?

There are human beings that are made to believe that a God is a superior being that can give life but also punish those who do not follow what is an acceptable to be good and right. There are also people who think that they are gods themselves therefore they do not need an authority to show them the way to their purpose. Both beliefs are focusing on superiority and ego. When you give your power away and trust a creative force that cannot be experienced in your everyday life or when you understand your fragmentation and distortion and you want to see yourself as a God you are not healing yourself because you are not connecting to truth.

All human beings need to heal themselves in order to understand and experience unity. When you are purified and you are able to see your true-self than you will experience unity with everything that exists in the cosmos. You are united with Earth and humanity but you are also united with the astral plane and the creative force of our source. If you wish to empower yourself you should connect to your imbalances, blockages and distortion in your being and transform them to truth. This is how you can receive the cosmic light and allow healing to take place.

Introduction

On Earth people are suffering from fragmentation and separation not only from the rest of Earth's creation but also from their true-self. All beings can receive guidance to help them grow and evolve and the ones who are chosen to reincarnate on Earth are guided in order to fulfil their purpose, bringing the astral light to the physical plane.

Wisdom of Thoth: Your Purpose is to Exist in Unity with the Cosmos

The unity that exists in you should also be experienced when you connect to humanity and Earth. Distortion creates boundaries and limitation; it keeps people separated from their purpose. You cannot have a meaningful relationship that leads to truth and growth when you are not aware of your own purpose.

Your life cannot be effortless, leading you to the joy of unity when you exist in separation from the Earth and the cosmos. When you try to understand yourself and focus on what is important for your growth, you should not see yourself as a separate entity, a detached unit of the cosmic creation.

Do not see yourself as superior or inferior; instead see yourself in unity with Earth and the cosmos. You exist to receive and transmit light that can build bridges and connect all creation. On Earth people are suffering from fragmentation and separation not only from the rest of Earth's creation but also from their true-self. If you are able to see yourself as part of Earth's creation and understand that your duty is to receive and transmit life than you will also connect to your true-self that will enable you to become a receiver and transmitter of cosmic unity. If you want to be successful in this life time, experience unity and act like a bridge for the light to go through you and heal humanity and Earth. Success is your growth that will lead you to the fulfilment of your purpose in this life time.

Questions

1. What is your understanding of the following phrase: "The unity that exists in you should also be experienced when you connect to humanity and Earth."
2. What is your experience with distortion?
3. Can you have an effortless life?
4. How do you connect to the truth in you?

Introduction

People reincarnate wherever and whenever there is a need for this to happen. They are beings who have reincarnated many times on Earth and they are other beings who have reincarnated on many other planets, galaxies and universes. For every being there is a divine plan, a plan of evolution, and it is stored in its creation code and is manifested on its higher-self. According to this plan, beings reincarnate in order to go through a certain learning process that is tailored specifically for them and guide them towards their purpose. The first step for you will be to experience balance and unity within your being and this way you enable yourself to start creating your own life according to the divine plan.

Wisdom of Thoth: Start Creating your own Life according to the Divine Plan

There are people on Earth who want to close their eyes and ears to truth and purpose of their being and connect to illusionary rewards.

There are people who encourage you to keep thinking and wishing to have one of the social rewards and this way it will become yours.

When you keep thinking of receiving a gift that has nothing to do with your purpose and path then you are disconnecting from your true-self and divine plan that was created to guide you in this reincarnation. I am going to think that I am rich and this will happen to me; I am going to keep thinking that I am successful and I will become successful; I am going to be thinking that I have the perfect partner and this way I am able to attract the right man or woman in my life. How can the mind become creator of your life, when is disconnected from the rest of your being? Being in a balanced state, helps you connect to the cosmic light and receiving healing and clarity you will naturally follow the path of truth.

If you allow your mind to create your life then you accept illusion, being constantly on a diversion, looking for illusionary rewards. You will be forcing the mind to take a role that is not able to fulfil why your true-self that can naturally connect you to your purpose will exist in separation from life creation. Your desires may be illusionary if you think that the mind can help you create them and experience them in your life. The first step for you will be to experience balance and unity within your being and this way you enable yourself to start creating your own life according to the divine plan.

Questions

1. Why do people connect to illusionary rewards?
2. Can you create your life of purpose by only using your mind?
3. How does your mind help you grow?

4. How can you experience balance?

Introduction

If you wish to fulfil your purpose, you have to purify yourself from all distortion and allow purity and truth to clear your path. Knowing yourself and clearing old patterns is a personal achievement and requires bravery and clarity. When you experience purity in your life, you will be guided to acquire a clear understanding of who you are.

Wisdom of Thoth: Stay in a Pure State

If you are one of those human beings that have all the answers about humanity, Earth and the cosmos then you have to accept that you know nothing. Perhaps you may have the ability to receive information that is spread on Earth and you may be able to use this information and generate different distorted representations of it. This does not guarantee your connection to your true-self.

There are people who have the illusion that they are an authority, wearing many layers of distorted information that can spread to others and convince them that they are true knowledge. Some of you are very proud of yourselves to exist in illusion and you become illusion when you want to control people's minds and energy.

If you are a receiver of the intention of a manipulator, remember that when you create a state of peace, distortion cannot enter your being. Stay in a pure state without the embellishment and the false attraction of illusion and artificiality. Exist in truth and purity and tear the garments of illusion. Stay in a pure state and enjoy purification. In this state the colourful authority cannot reach you. This is a way to fight illusion and help others grow and purify.

Questions

1. What is your understanding of purity?

2. Can you observe illusion in your life?
3. How can you heal yourself from illusion?
4. How can you support others to stay in a pure state?

Introduction

It is a big challenge for human beings on Earth to reclaim their home on the planet and experience life according to their divine plan. This can only be done with gratitude, submission and servitude to mother Earth. Earth is a loving planet, a beautiful creator of life; human beings have to find their place among other living beings on the planet. Connect to Earth's light and grow.

Wisdom of Thoth: Suffering from Limitation

I know that people on Earth are suffering from limitation. They cannot connect to their being and develop their unique abilities; they do not know their purpose and cannot create their own lives; the go against their wellbeing and exist in a space of illusion. This is happening because you are not connected to Earth and her healing energies.

I want you to observe yourselves, observe you current state. Is your existence supported by your connection to Earth? Do you get your nourishment directly from Earth? Is your everyday occupation part of Earth's growth? Do not be afraid to let go of artificiality that masquerades itself as need, necessity, reward, growth and abundance. See beyond illusion and discover your true-self.

Earth is supporting your growth; open up to receive healing that will lead you to purification and transformation. When you are able to recognise illusion than your connection to Earth will become stronger. There will be no obstacles on your way and this is how you will be able to create a life of truth, freedom and growth according to your divine plan.

Questions

1. Are you suffering from limitation?
2. Are you receiving Earth's nourishment?
3. Can you observe artificiality in your life?
4. Are you creating your own life?

Introduction

Human beings have to connect to Earth. They are here to assist and be part of the planet's transformation, restoring Earth her golden age. Once the elements of imbalance and distortion are removed, the precious flower of light and wisdom that Earth once was will be revealed. Earth will be reborn from within and enter a new cycle of growth.

Teaching of Christian Rosenkreutz: Focus on Growth

There is nothing more powerful and transformative than people connecting to growth and make it their life of focus. Some of you may find it difficult to disconnect from distortion and focus and your one path of truth. This is why communities have to be build and in these communities of growth you have to start planting your seeds that will grow to become your divine plan on Earth. Isolation creates polarities; being part and following the blindfolded social groups is not helping you to grow. Building communities where you can all explore and develop your skills and unique abilities, helping others, supporting a healthy and conscious life style, staying focused on growth and share with others.

Building communities is a natural need to all those beings that exist on Earth. Do not let fear block your way to receive and co-create a great gift. Show how passionate and ecstatic you are to be healed from your imbalances and offer this healing to others; to create a life close to Earth and allow nourishment and light to reach your physical body; to experience people growing with you and love you for your contribution to their process of growth. When unity is experienced by human beings, they will connect to their purpose and have an effortless life.

Questions

1. How can people focus on growth?
2. What is a conscious life and how can you create it?
3. Why is it important to build communities?
4. What is your understanding of the following message: "When unity is experienced by human beings, they will connect to their purpose and have an effortless life."

Introduction

When people run away from their fears, they have to put on a mask and exist in an illusionary state of euphoria while imbalances, illusion fragmentation and distortion are still affecting their mind and being. For everything that we do there was a seed planted. So observe yourself, try to go back and examine the route of your action.

Wisdom of Thoth: Confronting or Running Away from your Fears?

What will be more liberating to you: confronting or run away from your fears? There are people who are running away from their fears, creating illusionary structures of "feeling good, being successful-popular, looking after my well-being, working with others to achieve what was mentioned." When people run away from their fears, they have to put on a mask and exist in an illusionary state of euphoria while imbalances, illusion fragmentation and distortion are still affecting the mind. Wearing a mask is a sign that a person is not connected to their true-self and is feeding from illusion.

Confronting your fears can be damaging to one's well-being. When the person is infected by negativity and exists in a low vibrational reality. This will have as a result for the fear to become immense and take many transformations. Accusing others, having low self-esteem, not being able to cope with life, allowing trauma to be created, existing in a fragmented state can be some of the symptoms that people can experience. Creating a space of peace and have the ability to exist in this space are the first steps to purification.

Only when you connect to your whole being, your true-self, the Earth and the cosmos, you are able to receive healing and nourishment. In this state you can accept everything you are and you will start shifting imbalances and blockages by going true a transformation. Purification is a process of transformation that can bring growth and support connections with your true-self, Earth and the cosmos.

Questions

1. What are your fears? Are you able to observe fear affecting you?
2. Should you confront your fears?
3. Is it important to create a space of peace?
4. What is purification and how can it help you to grow?

Introduction

Why are you turning your back to cosmic truths and prefer to remain in a state of negativity and short-lived success? There is a great force that is approaching Earth and will touch all people on the planet. This is the light of our source, a new life given to you to help you grow. All united we can grow into greatness and restore Earth to her golden era and celebrate the life given to us by our creator.

Wisdom of Astaroth: What is your Reality?

People on Earth exist in a false reality that takes away the power to connect to their true-self and fulfil their purpose. When people start to wake up and understand the illusionary aspects of their thinking, experiencing and receiving, they find themselves on a mission to uncover the elements of illusion. Instead of connecting to their true-self and open themselves to the healing light of the cosmos they are conquered by the fear of the dark forces and the human beings that support them. This leads people to another diversion where they again disconnect from their true purpose.

There is no higher truth than connecting to your essence, understand you unique abilities and create the path that will help you fulfil your purpose. There is no higher duty than connecting to the cosmic light, allow it to bring healing and knowing to your whole being, helping you to exist in unity with Earth and the cosmos. Becoming a receiver of the cosmic light it will help you to understand the importance of transmitting the light to others and become a co-creator of life. The healing that you receive is not owned by you; it will support your growth when you are able to transmit it to others. Pure intention opens many doors between the cosmos, Earth and humanity.

Questions

1. Are you able to observe illusion?
2. Are you affected by fear? What is fear creating you?
3. Are you connecting to the cosmic light? Are you receiving healing and nourishment?
4. What is your understanding of the following message: "Pure intention opens many doors between the cosmos, Earth and humanity."

Introduction

Earth in the golden era was a luscious land with the most extraordinary variety of plants and animals, rocks and formations. The gods created mountains of crystal to be used as receivers and transmitters of energy and maintain the planet's state as a high vibrational being. When travellers from other planets were able to visit Earth, they saw the devices and realised that she was made of the godly elements which gave her a superior position in the godly creation.

Wisdom of Thoth: The Creation of Earth

My light has been with Earth from the beginning of her creation and during the golden era creatures that existed on Earth could see me in all Earth's creation. After the golden Era my light was still on Earth and was apparent to all those beings that experienced life on Earth.

During the times of great distortion and destruction on Earth a great schism was created between the Pleroma and the planet. Certain beings, communities and civilisations tried to connect to my light and this happened repeatedly. This activity is not known to you instead there is disinformation about my connection to Earth.

All the references to the light of Thoth known to you have nothing to do with my connection to Earth's awakening and my support to humanities purification and transformation. It is more important to you to start connecting to your true-self than spending your time reading books about deities and masters.

Focus on experiencing your purpose, becoming a receiver and transmitter of light. Focus on your natural ability to grow and disconnect from illusion which is a disease that can take over your whole being. When you are free than you will see me and you will know that I created Earth.

Questions

1. What is your understanding of the Golden Era?
2. What is Earth's schism?
3. Why did ancient communities want to communicate to the Light of Thoth?
4. How can Earth's awakening can support humanity's growth?

Introduction

There is a divine plan and there is a path of growth to be followed by all beings. Human beings have free will and they are allowed to follow their path of truth as well as different diversions away from their path. Is your intention to connect to your unique tools and purpose? Are you looking for truth and growth? If you do, you will receive what you are looking for. All human diseases are related to their ignorance. When you accept illusion as truth you will never experience truth and wisdom. Disconnect from illusion and connect to truth. This way you will become aware of your purpose.

Wisdom of Thoth: Stay Alive, Connect to Truth

There are people who experience a life of pollution, distortion and non-growth. There is another group of people who accept illusion as truth and are fearful about their lives. There are also people who commit suicide.

Some may ask: from all these groups what group is in the worst position, committing to a life of non-growth? My answer is all of them. For one to terminate his or her life was led to constant diversion leading to a space of non-growth where purpose cannot be fulfilled. With the end of a life cycle one can experience immense purification process.

When you experience a life of growth, you will never think of terminating your own life because your duty and ability to receive and transmit cosmic light, healing Earth and humanity, will keep you alive and disconnect you from all pollution, limitation and illusion. People need to focus on connecting to their true-self and receive clarity. They need to know how to disconnect from illusionary deceptions and how to act with purity, bringing the light to humanity and Earth.

When you are polluting yourself with negative thoughts, trying to reach illusionary rewards, being afraid to express truth and do not support unity within humanity and Earth, They experience a slow death. If you want to stay alive you focus on the truth in you, act with purity and experience within your being, Earth, humanity and the cosmos.

Questions

1. Are you polluting yourself?
2. What is a life of non-growth?
3. How is negativity stopping you from growing?
4. How can you heal yourself connecting to purity?

CHAPTER VIII

We are here to help you open your eyes and experience new possibilities of growth. Your body has a physical aspect but its true purpose is to act as a multidimensional being that connects you to the astral body. Therefore the possibilities of rebirth and transformation of your body as a whole are limitless. You have to focus on clarity and this will help you receive healing and bring balance. The more you are connected to your essence and understand your body as multidimensional the more peace you will receive. The mind should be quietening in order to receive enlightenment. Receiving the light you heal yourself.

Introduction

Thoth has explained the importance of purification; this is a very important task for all human beings on Earth right now. Your growth is happening here right now so what you have to do is to support your growth by disconnecting from illusion, connecting to your true-self and allow purity and clarity to guide you on your path and attract the light of the cosmos. When you restore balance in you, you will have a feeling of bliss and you will be able to experience full growth in your whole being. When all parts of your being are able to communicate and harmonize with each other, you will be able to connect to Earth's energies and the high light of the cosmos.

Wisdom of Thoth: Purification

There are a number of people who have started observing their imbalances and wish to start their purification process. I also know that human beings are looking for method and instructions as well as an outcome before they start any process of growth.

I can only see steps, leading to truth and freedom instead of limited instructions whose only quality is to restrict your connection to the cosmic light and reduce your ability to grow. When you start observing yourself, the mind that is affected by illusion is going to react. Your mind generates diversions to block your understanding of your being. This is why it is important to be in a state of peace, experience unity in your whole being and resist fear and limitation taking you on a diversion.

There are people who will focus on the fear that is produced by illusion in the mind and purifying themselves will become a hard task. Purification is not a painful process. It is a process of truth and freedom, liberation and fulfilment, growth and unity. Not knowing or accepting who you are is not helping you escape the maze of illusion and walk the path of truth and purpose.

Create a space of peace, allow the cosmic light to heal you and support your growth and look with the eyes of truth and acceptance at everything that you are. The next step is to start creating your own life according to your divine plan.

Questions

1. What is purification and how can help you grow?
2. Can you observe your imbalances?
3. What are your experiences related to observation?
4. Why should you create a space of peace?

Introduction

People on Earth understand the world around them as a polarity of good and evil. This is a characteristic of the third dimensional perception. If you wish to evolve beyond polarity and fragmentation you have to lose your perception of opposites, being two contrasting and separate entities. There is no fight against two elements there is only a union of the elements which will bring creation and new life.

Wisdom of Thoth: About Angels and Demons

People on Earth are very confused because they have listened to many explanations and ideas regarding the existence of non-physical life in the cosmos. One way to explain this is by using Earth as an example. The low vibrational areas of the cosmos are the ones where life is presented partly through physicality. There is a great variety of existence in the cosmos where physicality takes many forms.

Some of you on Earth understand this as different dimensions or different universes. But in reality they are all part of the same plane because they share similarities in the way life is created. If you were able to enter the core of the Earth you would realise that it is much more active and has a much higher vibration than the surface of the planet and offers high growth to all parts of the planet including the surface. The same is happening with the astral plane. It is a non-physical life form of high vibration and growth that feeds all creation.

The astral plane is the main part of the cosmos that has direct access to our Source's creative force. All other forms of existence are an extension that was created to offer new opportunities of growth. Now we have to place your idea of angels and demons somewhere in the cosmos.

I will place them in the minds of human beings trying to understand the non-physical existence but also affected by limitation and fear. Your religions have used the duality of an angel or demon to control your natural ability to grow. It is time now for human beings to reconnect to the cosmos and experience astral growth on Earth.

Questions

1. What is your understanding of angels and demons?
2. What is your understanding of the different dimensions and universes?
3. Is the astral plane disconnected from the physical plane?
4. How did religions use the polarity of good and evil?

Introduction

All living beings in all planes exist to raise their vibration and reunite with the source. This journey of growth and transformation is the motion that keeps all creation alive. Human beings on Earth can achieve transformation when they purify themselves from distortion and connect to their true-self. Truth is a living being; it is our unique path that was given to us from birth and is connected to a greater path, a collective goal of transformation and growth. It connects you to opportunities of growth that were designed with your divine plan. Allow your true-self to guide you, become a receiver and transmitter of high light.

Do not restrict your communication with your true-self; this is how you can experience transformation. Transformation leads to growth; it will help you achieve purification, clarity, healing, to receive and transmit the cosmic light.

Human beings on Earth are affected by layers of imbalances that they are transforming in them; they grow, they change form in order to affect your mind and lock you once more into a space of limitation. Transformation is the motion that keeps all creation alive and in a state of growth.

Wisdom of Thoth: The Process of Transformation

Some people may ask: how can I transform myself and what is the process of this transformation? The process of your transformation is the degree of communication between your being and your true-self. The true-self is like a corridor with many entrances; it is your essence connecting to Earth, your physicality and purpose on Earth, your astral body, the cosmos and the source.

When you are able to connect to your true-self you are opening up to many opportunities of transformation. What can block your transformation? Everything that keeps you in a state of fear, limitation and ignorance is blocking your way to connect to your true-self and start a communication that will lead you to transformation.

Human beings on Earth have layers of imbalances are transforming in them; they grow, they change form in order to affect your mind and lock you once more into a space of limitation. When human beings are connected to truth, the illusion and distortion in them will take different forms to try to find effective ways to control their minds. Most people do not realise that the mind control is not related to truth.

Your true-self cannot be affected by illusion this is why your connection and communication with it will help you purify and transform. When this connection is constant then your process of transformation has started. When you complete this process you will have healed yourself from the layers of distortion in you and you will have discovered your unique abilities and have an effortless life.

Questions

1. What is your experience with transformation?
2. What is your experience connecting to your true-self?
3. What keeps you in a state of fear?
4. Is your mind affecting your growth?

Introduction

You need to be in constant communication with your own being and the truth that you carry if you really wish to empower yourself and be a Creator. All parts of your being can communicate with each other; exchange energy, knowing, healing and balance. Communication is energy which flows through to assist with balancing, strengthening and creating not only your whole being but everything that exists around you. Focusing on this inner communication that can be supported by the cosmic light and transmitted to all Earth's creation, is a very special skill practiced by masters on the Earth plane.

All beings have to wake up to their true purpose which is a life of truth, higher consciousness and supporting others to rediscover their true-self. The illusion which is created to control all aspects of your life can trap you to support your own limitation; truth is transparent and will support your growth. You can only receive your light when you reach to the truth in you. This discovery will lead you to a transformation and then your path is open and your purpose will become clear.

Wisdom of Thoth: Allow the Cosmic Light to Transform You

There are many people who want to connect to the cosmic light and heal themselves from distortion and illusion. They understand that this is the only way to growth and they want to follow this path but somehow do not succeed. They need guidance because distortion is still affecting their mind. There are many people who exist in a distorted space of illusion and still want to follow their path that will lead them to their purpose.

The first step for them to achieve this is to observe and accept illusion in their lives. You can achieve this by entering a space of peace, offering your being the healing it needs to look at existence as a form of constant transformation. This will help you to disconnect from illusion and the limited understanding from yourself. If you do not experience this, you will never be able to escape the fragmented state that blocks your way to growth.

I am asking you not to see this teaching as an interesting theory but as a way of life. Are you able to observe your imbalances, illusionary beliefs, fears and limitations? Are you able to understand the different layers, their transformation and the root of their existence? Can you describe your present state? Can you connect to truth and express it in your everyday life? What are you creating right now? What does influence your growth? These are questions that can help you move towards the path of your purpose when they are answered honestly. You can only do this if you connect to your true-self; this is how you are going to connect to the cosmic light and bring healing to humanity and Earth.

Questions

1. How can you connect to the cosmic light and heal yourself?
2. Are you able to observe distortion?
3. Can you see your path and understand your purpose?
4. What are you creating right now?

Introduction

All living beings in all planes are united with the cosmic light and are part of the vast creation of our source. Humans who exist in third dimensional Earth, were given a physical body from Earth that can still connect to the astral body, higher-self and creation code.

Your whole being is a wonderful organism; it is a microcosm that can help you connect to the creative forces of the cosmos and the healing and nourishment that Earth can provide for you. True growth is the creative force that brings transformation to you and others. The plants of gratitude and appreciation will grow and make strong roots in you to help you understand your path and become a creator of your life. I am here to teach you purity. This is how we are going to build bridges between the Earth and the Pleroma.

Wisdom of Thoth: Your own Energetic Flow is Creating the Path that will Lead you to your Purpose

You can support your own transformation and growth if you focus on your own being and examine the growth that is happening in you right now. Your mind can be manipulated and create a pattern of thinking that can be described as a maze without exists, but your whole being is always able to receive the light.

When you focus on your whole being and see it as a unity of your physicality and energies, you will have the ability to approach distortion in you as a healer and a knower. Your whole being is a wonderful organism; it is a microcosm that can help you connect to the creative forces of the cosmos and the healing and nourishment that Earth can provide for you.

This connection with your whole being should not occupy your mind: if you have questions, expectations, misunderstanding, fear and limitations it means that you are still connected to your distorted mind. When you finally connect to your whole being, you will experience the unity and balance of your physicality and energies, the movement of your energies in and out of your physical body, the way they anchor you to Earth and the natural expansion, connecting to the cosmos and the astral plane.

At this point you are connecting to your true-self and the divine plan and purpose will become known to you. Your own energetic flow is creating the path that will lead you to your purpose.

Questions

1. How can you support your transformation?
2. Can you observe your limitation and fear patterns?
3. How can you connect to your whole being and grow?
4. What is your understanding of the following phrase: "Your own energetic flow is creating the path that will lead you to your purpose."

Introduction

Many human beings have started to wake up and observe illusion and distortion in their lives. They want to connect to their truth and experience purification and growth. What should be their first steps towards purification? Connecting to your being, strengthening your connection to Earth and the cosmos, focusing on your truth and purpose, creating a space of peace and acceptance in you are important abilities that you need to master. This is the foundation of your purification process; when human beings understand that illusion and distortion are not part of their being, their truth and unique abilities will come to the surface and they will start creating their lives.

When you go through a process of transformation, all your tools, purpose and light transform with you. It is important to know this truth because then you can connect to Earth's intention during the golden era. This is how the high light of the Earth will guide you to a new transformation. Allow your true-self to guide you and everything you receive will be high and complete.

Wisdom of Thoth: Transformation and Growth

Human beings should focus on the light in them if they wish to transform and grow according to their divine plan. The light in them consists of all the truths related to their growth and purpose as well as their abilities and connections to support fulfil their purpose on Earth.

Facing the distortion and illusion that may affect your mind and being should not bring you weakness. It should be a liberating experience, allowing the light to reach, heal and purify all parts of your being; bring renewal to every cell and every energy point in order for you to experience transformation. If you accept distortion as part of your being, your shadow self, then you give it a place, you allow it to control part of your being and restrict your growth.

When you observe distortion you do it from of space of peace. This is how you can get closer to the light and your true-self, strengthening your connections with Earth and the cosmos. Support and healing is available to you when you are connecting to the light and you have a pure intention leading to individual and collective growth. When you connect to the truth in you and make it your everyday experience, you will be able to walk to one path, the path of growth.

Questions

1. What is blocking you connecting to your light?
2. Can you create your light guided by your light?
3. Can you exist in peace?
4. Can you grow with others?

Introduction

The astral plane is a place of transformation. It is the home of all beings; it is the home of all creation. For life to be sustained, we need different types of transmitters and receivers of energy to help the cosmos grow and maintain a good balance of energies. Earth was created to have enough resources to feed and nourish all her creation. If all human beings had clarity and were able to connect to truth, you will be able to exist only to fulfil your purpose and divine plan.

Wisdom of Thoth: A Cosmic Being

If a human being can instantly leave the physical plane and exist in the astral plane part of this transition process will be to experience a life without limitation, negativity, distortion and suffering. These are garments that a cosmic being does not need. And has no insecurity or doubt standing naked in a pool of perfection. This explains that the limitation mentioned above is short lived. It does not have its roots in your being; naturally, it does not exist.

The low vibrational reality that people experience on Earth can be described as an imitation that can transformed to illusion. Imitation and illusion walk hand by hand because they present themselves as an authentic life expression where in reality they are a misleading representation of truth. Human beings live in a world of imitation and illusion and this is why they can accept it as truth, allow it to enter their being and pollute the mind and physical body.

Your connection to limitation and illusion creates the suffering in you that first affects the mind and your energies and then becomes a physical imbalance. If all human beings had clarity and were able to connect to truth, you will be able to exist only to fulfil your purpose and divine plan; you will be able to connect to Earth for nourishment and heal your being with the cosmic light; you will connect to others unconditionally and see this connection as a cosmic exchange of light and growth to unite you to your mission to heal Earth. If you want to heal yourself throw away the garments of imperfection and purify yourself.

Questions

1. Can you observe negativity and limitation in you?
2. Do you experience patterns of limitation? How do they affect your life?
3. What is your understanding of the following phrase: "Human beings live in a world of imitation and illusion and this is why they can accept it as truth, allow it to enter their being and pollute the mind and physical body."

Introduction

When an astral being reincarnates on Earth, his astral family reincarnates with him or her. Your family members on Earth, friends, partners or acquaintances carry the light of your astral family. Part of your growth is your connections with your astral family as well as the exchange of energy between you, your higher-self and your creation code.

Wisdom of Thoth: Perfect Partners or win Flames

All beings exist in unity in the cosmos. This is how they grow, receive and transmit light and support life in our Sources creation. The cosmos consists of many energy fields of different sizes that can be seen as the microcosm within the macrocosm. Energy beings in the astral plane are connected to other astral beings and their energy field is part of a greater energy structure that supports and feeds from their light.

When an astral being reincarnates on Earth, his astral family reincarnates with him or her. The ones that remain in the astral plane they become the guide from the beings that choose to reincarnate. Your family members on Earth, friends, partners or acquaintances carry the light of your astral family.

One of you may ask: Why human beings cannot find the right partner or what happens when one fields connected to another human being but the relationship does not work? Do not blame yourself and your connection to other human beings but you should look at the level of the distortion in your life and the life of your partner as well as your family and friends.

When people focus on the persona, the ego and the social expectations the connection becomes blurry and distorted. When astral beings reincarnate on Earth are lost in a jungle of illusion and if they accept this as truth they exist in separation from their purpose and the connection with the astral plane. This affects all aspects of their lives including their connection to other beings.

Purifying yourself and clearing the distortion, will give you the opportunity to become a fertile land for growth, unity, transformation. The next step will enable you to become a creator of a joyful and effortless life of purpose and unity with your astral family on Earth as well as the rest of humanity.

Questions

1. Can you describe the unity of the cosmos?
2. Are you able to connect to your astral family?
3. Can you have an effortless life?
4. Can you connect to your twin flame?

Introduction

Human beings do not know that they exist isolated from Earth's gifts. Earth wants to offer nourishment, healing, connection to the physical body and its abilities to grow according to the divine plan. You are not on your own; you belong to a high family that is constantly calling you to connect. Earth is nourishing and guiding you; your purpose is her gift and fits perfectly in the divine plan. We are all connected and we are receiving support; the bridges between Earth and the Pleroma will be built.

Wisdom of Thoth: Earth's Gifts to Humanity

Human beings need to know what my gifts to humanity are. What do I want to offer to your awakening and enlightenment? I want you to pay attention to your connection to Earth because she can offer you all the gifts and all opportunities of growth. I know that many of you are focusing on your higher self, the astral plane and the creative forces of the cosmos.

You want to connect to your astral body, you want to experience astral growth and bring this light down to Earth. This is part of your purpose as a cosmic being but do not underestimate your connection to Earth; do not try to ignore the wisdom of your physical body and your physical abilities that can help you fulfil your purpose on Earth.

There is something more that you have to understand and observe: why does humanity exist in separation from Earth and her creation. Humans have an excuse for this; it is because they are superior, they are the rulers and the owners of this planet. This way of thinking is accepted by most human beings to be true and all the pollution, destruction and separation have their roots in this belief.

Human beings do not know that they exist isolated from Earth's gifts. Earth wants to offer nourishment, healing, knowing the physical body and its abilities to grow according to the divine plan. Earth wants to share truth with you and this truth will connect you to the higher planes. You are a seed that is growing on Earth, receiving her nourishment and growing to connect to the cosmos.

Earth will never block your growth. She knows that you are a transmitter and receiver of light and your physical body is created to transmit light on Earth. If you are still wondering about your true-self and your path in this life time, you should connect to Earth now; her light will give you the answer.

Questions

1. What is your connection with Earth?
2. How can Earth support your growth?
3. Why human beings experience separation and how does it affect their growth?
4. Is your physical body part of your divine plan?

Introduction

The galaxy which is supported by the Earth-Moon-Sun alignment is a low vibrational space and was formed after the time of Earth's high growth called golden era. When Earth was a high vibrational planet, she was closer to the sun and this affected her energy systems and creation.

Wisdom of Thoth: The Sun

The sun is a high vibrational point in the galaxy and a great receiver and transmitter of light. This is how the sun is able to create a strong electro-magnetic field, giving life to all beings that connect to it but also allowing them to grow and become transmitters of light. In your galaxy, the sun is the highest vibrational space and it is interesting that the beings of Earth cannot enter this space.

Your scientists will explain this by pointing out the high temperature and the sun's hot plasma that is burning like the core of the Earth. All these are stories without knowing and explanations without truth. The sun has a more direct connection to the Source and this is strengthened by its connection to other suns.

Human beings are not able to see how the sun exists in the high vibrational fields of other suns, connecting to the source. But they can see the growth that takes place on Earth when the sun rays reach the planet. People feel revitalised on a warm sunny day. There is a sense of freedom, renewal and rebirth connected to the sun that helps you see life as a wonderful exercise of growth.

There are many people who have reincarnated on Earth who have also experienced the golden era in previous reincarnations. When Earth was a high vibrational planet she was closer to the sun. Earth's physicality enjoyed the high temperatures that allowed immense growth. The ice age and the division of the year into seasons show Earth's imbalances.

Questions

1. What is your understanding about the sun and its connection with Earth?
2. Can the sun support your growth?
3. Can you explain the following phrase: "The ice age and the division of the year into seasons show Earth's imbalances."
4. What do you know about the sun's activity and purpose?

Introduction

All life evolves in the present and dimensions co-exist within a living being and affect different areas of growth. Growth is knowing your true purpose, be free to act and think according to your purpose, be the ground where divine seeds grow and enable you to become a creator of your own true path as well as assisting others to follow their paths. Growth is an individual process as well as a collective one.

Wisdom of Thoth: The Path to Growth is an Effortless Path

The path to growth is an effortless path. When you can see it in front of you and decide to follow it, you will not need to go on a diversion or accept false beliefs. There are people who focus on truth and want to walk the path but they are also affected by illusion and distortion. These people are still wearing a blindfold over their eyes; they doubt themselves; they ignore their unique abilities and connection with Earth and the cosmos. One may ask: will this state bring growth to human beings?

Human beings always have opportunities of growth but they have to learn to recognise them and use them to create an experience of truth that will connect them to their purpose. The truth that you are seeking will lead you to your purpose. Your purpose is to experience life as a process of transformation and growth away from distortion and illusion. If someone can guide you to truth this does not mean that you have fulfilled your purpose on Earth. You have to create a life of growth that is constantly supporting you to fulfil your purpose. You have to know your purpose and create it in you, to experience it in your life and the lives of others.

Questions

1. What is your understanding of the following message: "The path to growth is an effortless path."
2. What are your opportunities of growth?
3. How can you experience your purpose? What abilities do you have to help you fulfil your purpose?

Introduction

Are you aware of your ego?

We have the ability to create ourselves. We were given this ability by our Source. Without it, we will be non-existent. In the astral plane there is no death, there is no end. When you accept that you are weak, powerless and fearful person, the ego comes to the rescue. If you are tied up and given yourself away to the power of your ego, you will be blinded by negativity and fear; you will exist in a maze of survival.

Wisdom of Astaroth: The Ego

The gods spoke about the importance of purification. This is a process of clearing all blockages and allowing light to restore you to your true-self and help you grow. Many people will attempt the process; some of them with their eyes closed and others who are able to see they will walk on a dark path.

One of the obstacles will be your ego.

Human beings were born with the mechanism of ego which is related to the mind and helps them survive during their life cycle. Ego was created to co-operate with the mind but also to help human beings connect to the third dimensional reality. Your ego helps you to be grounded in this reality and is affected by the energies of Earth. Ego recognises and accepts many artificial structures on Earth such as polarities, fragmentation, distortion and illusion. Human beings are affected by all these artificialities through their ego. When one wants to be successful according to social criteria, control others or focusses on materialism and consumerism, he has the ego as his driving force. Many people on Earth exist in a low vibrational reality because the ego and the mind lock them in a survival state. Abusive behaviour, self-centrism, negativity, imbalances and disease are some of the characteristics related to ego. If you wish to return to your pure state you have to disconnect from the reality created by your ego. When you are in your pure state you won't experience fear, competition, anger, hatred and limitation. You can only connect to peace and see yourself expanding to higher-planes. If you wish to purify yourself you have to observe all the different expressions of your ego and try to remain in a state of peace.

You have to become a sleepless guard, observing all waves of artificiality and illusion that try to reach you. You have to use your sword and armour; your weapons are peace and purity. If you think that you are fighting on your own and you carry a heavy load, remember that you are not alone. You are connected energetically with the cosmic creation which is also in a process of purification. We are all connected and when you open yourself to the light of the cosmos you are expanding towards the light of our source. All human beings are fragmented and carry their limitations that make them harm themselves and others.

Questions

1. Can you explain to me what the function of the ego is?
2. What happens if the ego becomes your driving force?
3. Can you mention some symptoms of being affected in a negative way by the ego?
4. Can you recognise some of the characteristics related to ego that you are affected with and can you share them with us?

Introduction

Beings that exist in all different planes have no possessions, nothing belongs to them.

There is nothing they can claim theirs and keep it for eternity; even our energetic fields are constantly transmitting and receiving energy and going through different transformations. High gods do not own their creative abilities. They know that they are the vehicle of the light of the source to create through them. When you understand that there is nothing to possess then you will be free to connect in a meaningful way.

Wisdom of Thoth: The Downfall of Earth

Humanity is going towards a dark period of instability and suffering in many different levels. But this crucial time you will be given the opportunity to escape what is collapsing and go through a transformation which will bring truth and wholeness in your life. All Earth's sufferings are caused by the high level of destruction and fragmentation. People who are giving up their power and stop their growth are going to suffer from the imbalances in their body, mind and connections to the astral body and light. When you allow others to pollute you and you don't react, you will have to face the consequences. Nothing is safe when you, your family, friends and neighbours follow the path of illusion and insist on the new members of the society to do the same. We are trying to warn you and give you a chance to escape what is coming to you. We want people to stand up and step back from the illusion. Connect with each other, support and teach each other truths and wisdom. If you have a better understanding about balanced life on Earth you have to share it with your friends and family. Truth can create miraculous bonds and everything will fall in its right place. We are here with you to support you. We want you to bring change to all people who connect with you and to others who don't even know you.

Listen to me; I am not trying to entertain you. I am proposing a very important job agreement with you. We all have to work against the illness that has taken over the Earth. We have to unite and connect to the light of our source which is the life giver. When you are connected to life you will wake up and look for truth which is a great tool for growth. Human beings are not aware that behind closed doors there are beings that are planning total destruction and they are convinced that the downfall of Earth is evolution. You are not going to make the plans reality by walking the path they have created for you. You must know that at the end of this path is the destruction of the human race. We are calling you now and we are asking you to disconnect from all artificialities. Your true-self is precious and has the high light you seek; this is the only path for evolution.

In an ideal community people should not have to deal with schedules, diaries, daily tasks and appointment lists. In an ideal society you should be allowed to work the times that you are fully productive and have time to go through your own process of transformation and growth. When you undertake any type of work you should be prepared and well equipped to do it to a high standard.

An expression of distortion on planet Earth is when people are forced to perform certain tasks without support or preparation time. This leads to a poor performance which will affect the lives and work of all people connected to this one person. I also see on Earth that poor performance is the norm; perfection is unknown because people are behaving like surviving slaves. I want you to look at yourselves and observe the patterns I already mentioned in your life and the life of others. Are you in the right state to be perfect in what you do and be part of perfection? Do you understand perfection and how it is linked to your life and work? Can you see what is blocking you from escaping the survival mode and entering the creator state? What is the impact of your life style in you and the people close to you?

When you are behaving like slaves, you are losing your humanity; the only way to freedom is through your truth. There are many ways used to convince you that you have to remain a slave although the truth about your current state is never mentioned to you: You have to remain a slave for your family, for social and financial success, to attract others, to follow what others do. They are people who think that being a slave will bring them freedom and happiness and they fully surrender to the illusion. The result of all this is an imbalanced life full of disease, confusion and dissatisfaction. You are diseased if you allow yourself to become a slave when you true nature and purpose is to be free and connect to cosmic laws. You can go against the plan of slavery any time you wish. You just have to wake up to the understanding that most people's lives are formed by a contagious disease called illusion. You have the power to escape, remember that illusion has no life or true power over you. Now is the time that people on Earth take responsibility for their lives and wake up to a new and meaningful existence. If you are seeking enlightenment, illusion is your first challenge.

Questions

1. Is Earth suffering and what is the cause of it?
2. How can you support your family and friends?
3. Can you disconnect from artificiality?
4. Can you see what is blocking you from escaping the survival mode and entering the creator state?

Introduction

We want the people of Earth to connect to the light of the cosmos and the energies of the Earth and create their lives according to their divine path and purpose. It is the task of the messengers to plant the seeds of truth in all beings. The messengers of Pantheon of Aeternam are here to heal the blind and the weak; they are working to help planet Earth wake up and become a high creator.

Wisdom of Thoth: The Land of Opportunity is the Kingdom of Illusion

The messengers should open themselves up and speak to people about the gods and the cosmic light. This is their great task and duty and the people who are listening will be able to reject all false realities and follow their true path. Many of you live a mechanical life, a life of logic that has a pyramid structure and is designed to fulfil social criteria. We are not here to judge you, we are here to show you new and amazing opportunities that will liberate your body, mind and expand you consciousness. It is your limited understanding and your belief that you know it all that is blocking your growth.

Connecting to my messengers on Earth, I am able to receive the energies of the planet. When one cannot connect to the energies of the planet and choses to destroy life and wellbeing is not a powerful being. The whole human race is not aware that their beliefs, ambitions, life style and education are symptoms of a weak pattern that is constantly repeated and there is no escape from it. People who have lost their connection with Earth develop various needs and fears related to survival. People are told that the land of opportunity will make them successful. I see great hunger, fear, negativity and suffering affecting all people who have given themselves up to serve the land of opportunity.

People who are connecting to themselves and the Earth energies know the true value of life and this is receiving and transmitting light. The land of opportunity is the kingdom of illusion. My light can be shared to those who are not attracted to false realities and are able to stand in truth and purity and be creators. My message to people is that all beings are creators and this is a sign of life and connection to our source. Creation is an energetic bond that allows the cosmic light to go through a living being and there are people on Earth who can achieve that. Those people who are not focusing on external wisdom or financial and social success have the opportunity to connect to the Earth and the light of the cosmos and their essence is leading them to support others unconditionally. They know that offering is receiving and they have experienced regeneration and re-birth. The path to growth is not hidden and is not reserved for a minority of wise men and women. It is the most natural way available to all. What is your opportunity in this life time?

Questions

1. Is your mind taking you away from your purpose?
2. Are you able to connect to Earth? What are you receiving/transmitting?
3. What is your understanding of the following phrase: "Creation is an energetic bond that allows the cosmic light to go through a living being and there are people on Earth who can achieve that."
4. Are you aware of your growth?

Introduction

There is no fear or dissatisfaction in the life of the awakened one because you are fully equipped to fulfil your purpose. Many of you who are on the right path you will receive clarity and regain the power given to you at birth to help you fulfil your path. Being part of a society you are forced to live, think and act like any other being in your neighbourhood, town, country or planet. Your purity will bring you to us and as we all connect we become a living uninterrupted cycle of evolution. All of us who connect we are the gift of life and have direct access to the light and energy of our Source.

Wisdom of Thoth: Life is Effortless

There is a wave of high energies coming from the core of the Earth, reaching the surface and moving into her aura. Earth is experiencing regeneration and re-birth in areas around her core and this is projected to all expression of life that can be found in these parts of the planet. We are able to exchange cosmic energy and offer healing and awaking to the planet. These energies are also going to affect life on the surface of the planet. The ones who are awake will be supported in their quest of truth and detachment from illusion.

We are building an energetic field around Earth to help her support her beings with light. Many of you who are on the right path you will receive clarity and regain the power given to you at birth to help you fulfil your path. Being part of a society you are forced to live, think and act like any other being in your neighbourhood, town, country or planet. Many of you are trying to achieve what you were told to be the goal of all people on Earth. In reality you are unique and have your own unique path and purpose.

There is no fear or dissatisfaction in the life of the awakened one because you are fully equipped to fulfil your purpose. You were given the power to guide yourself to the right place and enjoy success; success is fulfilment, growth sharing light and healing. The awakened ones understand the limitation and artificiality of illusion. When you exist in truth, illusion stops to exist and you can only see it in the lives of other people and in social structures. The awakened one has no doubts because the cosmic light shows him the way.

Life is effortless when you are able to follow the cosmic grace and become a whole being. Many people on Earth complain about not being able to have a comfortable life and satisfy their needs. I see that people in towns and in civilised societies are hungrier than the people who live close to the Earth and receive their food directly from the hands of the goddess. Need, pain, limitation, disease and fear are all products of the illusion which exists in you and it is generated by you.

I am sharing my light with the people of the Earth and I want to bring freedom to help them grow. Free yourself from all artificiality including your needs, ambitions, recognition and advancement in a world of illusion. When you are free, your true power will be returned to you and your path will be open. If you are able to achieve that, enlightenment is one of the many moments of clarity to support you on your way.

Questions

1. How can you heal the planet?
2. What are your unique abilities and purpose?
3. How can you create an effortless life?
4. Are you free to grow?

Introduction

The teachings of Thoth help us to connect to truth and make it our driving force. All of you who are able to listen should come forward and save Earth. By healing Earth, you receive grace and you become a creator responsible for bringing balance and light onto the planet. Your reward will be truth which is an excellent creative tool. You cannot truly create if your life does not reflect who you truly are.

Wisdom of Thoth: The Sleep of Ignorance

I have instructed you to connect to the divine light in order to grow. Having a physical body and existing in a third dimensional reality you are not able to absorb the pure essence of the light which is the logos of our source. If Earth was able to absorb the light's pure essence then she could offer you the right tools to help you become receivers and transmitters of the logos.

Some of you may ask: Does this mean that Earth beings cannot grow or cannot reach high consciousness because of their third dimensional existence? Earth beings can grow through their connection with Earth and her creation. They have many opportunities to connect to each other and pass knowledge and wisdom. You can free yourself by liberating others, you can feed yourself by feeding others, you can experience grace by allowing it to be created in others.

Beings are not created to compete with each other because it causes fragmentation and limitation. If a being that connects to you has limitations you have limitations too; If you are growing, the people who are connecting to you are growing too. There is war and destruction on your planet because many of you are not connected to the Earth energies and there is not collective growth. There is division and fragmentation because you are disconnected not only from the Earth's energies but also from each other. You are the new barbarians who came to Earth to possess and destroy.

Gods are connecting with you right now and want to explain to you that there are different paths available to all. One path is called unity and growth, the other is called unity with the false persona and illusion and the other path is called complete fragmentation and destruction. You are free to choose your path and this will be your guide to perfection or imperfection.

We are here to help you take off the blindfold and show you that you are living beings that have the opportunity to grow and create. When you choose the right path, growth is a natural process. When you go against your growth you will spend all your life searching. The movement of our cosmic light is eternal and all living beings have the opportunity to reach and receive it. We are building bridges for this light to come to you and wake you up from the sleep of ignorance.

Questions

1. Can you receive and transmit healing to others?
2. What is your understanding of the following message: "You can free yourself by liberating others, you can feed yourself by feeding others, you can experience grace by allowing it to be created in others."
3. What is your understanding of the following message: The movement of our cosmic light is eternal and all living beings have the opportunity to reach and receive it. We are building bridges for this light to come to you and wake you up from the sleep of ignorance.
4. Are you connecting to your true path?

Introduction

Cosmic growth cannot be described because it does not have a form, a specific outcome or certain time limit. In the astral plane, growth is existence and existence is growth. In the physical plane, beings go through different experiences, emotions and time limitation. People on Earth co-exist with other beings and have the opportunity to learn from each other as well as distract each other.

Wisdom of Astaroth: A House of Millions Rooms of Great Beauty and Splendour

Humans are not the only living beings on Earth but they are surrounded by a great variety of animals, plants and other beings that cannot be perceived with the five senses. So humans exist in a complex energetic field which is supported by many energetic points. If all living beings on Earth were able to connect to the cosmic light, be free from illusion and walk the path of truth and purpose, Earth will have the ability to reborn and move to a higher vibrational state.

The gods see Earth as a house that has millions of rooms of great beauty and splendour but all lights are off; the whole structure exists in darkness. You cannot connect to the rest of the creation when you are not aware of your own existence, purpose and light. You can survive and have a short life cycle hiding in a dark room but what kind of life are you going to have when you are separated from the energies of creation and growth.

We know that a great number of people on Earth exist in a dark room of nothingness, being disconnected from the energies of rebirth, growth and creation. Many of you have stopped caring for others; it does not fit your schedule and your everyday duties. You live to please your prison warden and you hope that one day you will take his place and role. What type of seed is growing in you that makes you worship slavery, deceit and punishment? When did you start believing that this is the only route for success and what have you achieved so far? Are you able to see yourself and learn from your experiences or you are programmed to behave in a certain way and accept what is given to you as truth? Gods are here to prepare humanity. Many of you have started to wake up but you are still entangled in illusion and artificial destructive energies and patterns. Be true to yourself now and you will receive wisdom. You are part of our creation and the light of the gods is connecting us all.

Questions

1. What is your understanding of Earth and her creation?
2. Are you exploring Earth's beauty everyday of your life?

3. What is your understanding of the following phrase: "We know that a great number of people on Earth exist in a dark room of nothingness, being disconnected from the energies of rebirth, growth and creation."
4. "Be true to yourself now and you will receive wisdom." How can you achieve this?

Introduction

When human beings look at themselves they cannot be objective because they are not connected to truth. They look at themselves with the eyes of illusion and this can take many forms. They either find themselves small and weak, concentrating on their limitation or accusing others for it. Others see themselves as powerful, positive and successful beings. As long as they can achieve social success and possessions, they think that they are on the right path of success. I see both of these approaches to life as limited, fragmented and untrue.

Wisdom of Thoth: The Eyes of Illusion

If you are not able to reach beyond the mask of the persona and the social status you are blind and lost. Many people on Earth think that they know themselves and that they are in control of their lives but in reality they are just participating in somebody else's movie and they are completely unaware of this. Some people feel that going beyond the persona is like falling from a cliff; everything seems unknown and frightening. I can show you a simple way to go beyond the persona and slowly detach yourself from the illusion and the social status. Exist in a space of peace, experience yourself as a pure being, and experience your light, your body, your aura and your connection to other energies. You do not have to force yourself to achieve anything.

Just try to be in a state of peace away from everyday limitations, confusion and misunderstandings. In this space you are pure, you can connect to your light and you are able to allow cosmic light to clear blockages and imbalances. If you wish to be truly happy or to become enlightened and receive high wisdom you have to become a pure channel of cosmic energy and light and this will help you to clear all imbalances and become whole.

Often people who are supporting the illusion and live accordingly, they have physical and mental diseases which eventually will lead the being to the end of its cycle. Distortion and fragmentation affects not only their lives but also their body and the energy that is communicated by them to others. When you achieve to exits in a state of peace then you will be able to experience your true-self and find your right path that will lead you to your purpose.

Questions

1. What is your understanding of the following message "If you are not able to reach beyond the mask of the persona and the social status you are blind and lost."
2. How can you experience life as a pure being?
3. How can you purify from limitation?
4. Can your body be affected by distortion?

Introduction

We are here to open the doors to all of you and allow communication from the high realms to come down to you. Our only intention is to build bridges between the Pleroma and Earth and as a result you will receive the high light. High wisdom and high truth. Everything we communicate with you is true and we hope that it will stay with you and connect you to your true-self.

Wisdom of Thoth: Earth's Essence

Earth's essence consists of the energies of the Gods who created her. My Light is part of Earth's essence and my connection with her has no beginning or end. I am back again to give light and connect with Earth and her essence. Trauma has brought distortion and disbelief. Trauma has brought illusion and artificial growth.

I am now back to heal the trauma if you let me. I am talking to human beings and the Goddess Earth: you did not carry illusion and artificiality when you were born; you did not come to Earth with trauma and distortion. You were pure beings. Clarity and truth was part of your being. You had so many opportunities for growth and you were surrounded by the cosmic light. Humans on Earth did not come from the same plane and did not have the same growth. But now you are all here on Earth trying to understand what is true and what is false.

Your society has many rules to help you choose the right way and avoid wrong doing. From the day that you are born you were given your life plan followed by your parents, family and friend and later you will follow it yourself. Some of you may ask what is the purpose of all this? why astral beings have to leave their place of growth and reincarnate on Earth? Why does illusion exist on Earth? Earth was isolated and was not strong enough to cope with her role as a goddess-planet on her own. This brought trauma and trauma brought weakness and disease.

There are certain people on Earth who are responsible for creating illusion and manipulating the mind. But this is a symptom of Earth's disease and weakness to protect her beings. All of you who are here on Earth, you will return to the astral plane which is your home but while you are here on Earth you have an important duty and this is not to follow an illusionary existence according to the man-made plan.

Your duty is to reach Earth and bring the light of the cosmos to her. Earth's healing has already started from the time our messengers connected to us. You have to escape artificiality which is one step from illusion to truth. You do not have to think about it and analyse it or try to find different ways to achieve it. It is very simple and this is accepting truth as your guide. The healing of Earth is your purpose.

Questions

1. What is your understanding of Earth's essence?
2. Who is responsible for creating illusion?
3. How can the astral plane affect your life on Earth?
4. How can you accept artificiality

Introduction

High beings are able to exist in many realities simultaneously. They know that there is one reality that has many different reflections and they can all exist at the same time. If you are able to understand that and experience the multi-dimensional reality you are able to grow and connect to high light.

Wisdom of Astaroth: High Beings

For high beings to exist in the Earth dimension they have to reincarnate on Earth and accept the physical being as well as the linear understanding of creation. Beings that are rooted in higher realms cannot fully connect to Earth and the support they can give is limited.

All of you who have reincarnated on Earth you are here to fulfil the divine plan. You are the high beings who have adjusted your light in order to experience life on Earth. Many of you have followed illusion as your purpose. Some of you want to reach to social success and others were helpful and kind to others. Some of you were satisfied with your life and others had problems accepting illusion as truth. It will come the time that all of you will start to wake up and you will search for clarity and unity.

The Gods are here to offer their light to all of you who can reach the space of truth. Your background is a series of events and experiences, most of them are diversions from your purpose. If you can share the space of truth with others who are also looking for light and unity then you will receive enlightenment which is only one of the many lessons of high wisdom. Curiosity may help you to wake up but sometimes can lead you to diversions. Dedication to truth will help you to connect to the cosmic light. We are present and we are helping you to arrive to the space of truth.

Questions

1. What is your understanding of high beings reincarnating on Earth?
2. What is the purpose of a high being reincarnating on Earth?
3. Are you able to observe past diversions as well as your purpose and growth?

Introduction

Our High Source has no form, character or attributes. Our High Creator is the perfect representation of life where everything is effortless and limitless. We have gathered here to connect to this high state of perfection and expand ourselves to a limitless and eternal state by connecting to our creation code and the whole creation.

Wisdom of Thoth: Pure Life is Effortless

The Gods are sending their light on Earth, connecting to humanity; we want to help you understand your whole body and existence. At the moment you are in front of a mirror, looking at your reflection; it is a reflection polluted by artificiality and distortion. You are not able to see what exists behind the mirror and you blindly trust what you see in front of you.

Human beings do not know that they live a life of illusion and distortion. They do not know that they are programmed to live a life of artificiality and minimum growth. Social rules force people to repeat a similar distorted life cycle that is accepted by all as truth. The Gods are spreading their light to Earth right now through their messengers and they want to challenge those beings that are asleep, the ones who are starting to wake up and the ones who think they are awake. They all are facing the same problem, trying to fight illusion, breaking the display of artificiality and live a pure life. Some of you may ask what is pure life? It is a life of truth; being able to connect to your body which is a cosmic tool; connecting to others by passing light to them and being free to connect to your astral growth and bring the wisdom to this reincarnation. In your Earth reality, pure life can be described as simplicity, walking your path without effort and be true to yourself and others.

Some of you may ask why people are constantly entangled in drama, limitation and negativity if life is effortless? It is because they are accepting the persona as their true-self. They go against their essence to fulfil social rules of the hierarchy. Observe you own life, behaviour and intention. Be honest but do not judge yourself when you look at your life patterns. Purification is a trip with many stops and at every stop you will be given the chance to accept, receive the cosmic light and purify a part of your understanding about existence. When you start this journey you must have a pure intention of completing it. This gives you an advantage; even if you are at the starting point you have already reached the end.

Questions

1. What is your understanding of an effortless life on Earth?
2. Are you observing yourself? What is your understanding of your life, growth and purpose?
3. What is your pure intention? Can you create with it?
4. What is your understanding of the following message: "When you start this journey you must have a pure intention of completing it. This gives you an advantage; even if you are at the starting point you have already reached the end.

Introduction

Earth is protecting her resources in the inner body because the surface is suffering from constant destruction. She tries to protect herself but at the same time there is very little nourishment for the beings there and this affects life and growth. In the core, Earth regenerates herself. The growth that takes place in the core and the lack of growth on the surface create many imbalances which lead alienation within the planet. It is important to be aware of Earth's condition because you are a reflection of this condition.

Wisdom of Thoth: Knowing the Divine Plan is only the Beginning of your Path

The Gods are coming together to support Earth and all that exists on her; they follow the instruction they received from our Source. All beings that exist in her core have already raised their vibration and are moving to a higher state.

The creation that exits in the inner parts of the planet is Earth's divinity. You exist on the surface and this is what you know as planet

Earth; it shows your weakness to connect with the whole planet and receive Earth's pure energies. On the surface there is a net of illusion that affects all living beings, their growth and consciousness. But there is a strong need for awakening brought to humanity by the helpers of the Gods who have reincarnated on Earth to bring the light of the Cosmos on Earth. There were many beings on Earth who were instructed by the Gods and the light of the cosmos to experience a life cycle on Earth and try to raise people's consciousness. Some of them created mystery schools and sacred communities and others were the advisers of great rulers.

We are instructed once again to bring light to Earth because the planet is in a process of evolution. This will affect not only Earth and her creation but the whole cosmos. You are witnessing our attempt to communicate with planet Earth and we want you to be part of this communication by becoming true receivers and transmitters of our energy and the cosmic light. So how can you achieve that and why is it important? The whole humanity can become the bridge for our light to go through and reach Earth. You are an energetic map that can lead us to the Earth's schism and allow us to heal her. Your reward will be freedom from all limitation and negativity and the rising of a new consciousness.

If you want to become the bridge between the cosmos and Earth you need to have pure intention. You are the toddler that wants to walk; you are the leaf that bursts out from the wooden branch; you are the sun ray that brings life to Earth; you are the rain that nourishes all creation. There is so much purity on Earth; there is life and growth that has not been affected by fragmentation and illusion because it follows the cosmic laws. This is what you have to do too. Look around you for purity, tune in to it and then discover your own purity. This will be the beginning of your path.

Questions

1. What do you know about Earth's inner parts?
2. Is there a difference between growth on the surface of the Earth and the growth of the surface?
3. How can you become a bridge connecting to the cosmic light and Earth's energies?

Introduction

A unity that is called cosmos is connecting with you right now. You are part of this unity and the Gods are here to nourish, strengthen and expand what is part of our source. We are here now to connect to our source and ask for guidance. The unity of all creation brings energy, balance and strength to receivers and transmitters of light and more opportunities for further growth and creation.

Wisdom of Thoth: The Gift of Unity

It is the light that we all seek and this creates bonds of communication and bonds of growth. We also want to grow our light in order to achieve the greatness of our source. We open the body to receive the light of creation, flowing through us, becoming one with our essence and then spread in all different directions to create what is our source's intention. We do not know our source's intention before the creation process. When we finally see what was created through us, we have the opportunity to see our source's form and intention in its creation. At this moment we start constructing the divine plan which can be shared by many energy fields.

We speak to you right now and we know that you are listening with the ears of the persona and you see yourselves as a being limited to its Earth life experiences. We communicate with you the way you communicate with each other because energetic communication is not developed on Earth. However, when we think of you as part of the divine plan, we see you as micro electromagnetic fields being part of many larger fields of energy.

All creation is linked and there is a cosmic rhythm followed by all. Connect to your unique way of connection and coexistence with the cosmos. The gift of unity that our Source shares with us is very unique: we can be an unseen particle of a stupendous, self-generated and eternal organism as well as being the cosmos and a single expression of our Source. Time will come and you will be able to see to divine creation being part of Earth's evolution.

Questions

1. How can you connect to the light of the Source?
2. Are you able to experience the cosmic flow?
3. Are you experiencing the flow of growth in you?
4. Are you able to experience unity?

Introduction

There is a view that human beings are limited and that their physical reality does not permit growth; this is an illusion. Human beings often stand at cross roads. They have to choose between survival, distraction and a path of clarity.

Teaching of Christian Rosenkreutz: Standing at the Crossroads

A path of clarity is related to illusionary nothingness; this is an option that does not seem to be very attractive to your five senses. I know that people on Earth need to have an object or an objective to motivate them to achieve. Nothingness is a blank canvas which is asking you to connect to your essence and through your own truth to become a creator. The path of nothingness is much more superior than your social success criteria because it guides you to focus on what is true in you and act as a creator of your own life. You can only be a creator if you are able to receive the cosmic light.

All imbalances and blockages in you are produced because you are restricting the light to go through you. You are following illusionary paths and your intention is the intention of a sleeping man. You cannot blame others, you cannot blame yourself for not being able to connect to the light. Remember that it is your responsibility to choose the right path if you are standing at the cross roads. We are all connected and we are here to give life to each other.

Questions

1. What is your understanding of the following message: "A path of clarity is related to illusionary nothingness."
2. What is your understanding of following message: "You can only be a creator if you are able to receive the cosmic light."
3. Are you able to create your life? What are your unique abilities to help you create a life of truth?

Introduction

Humanity is affected by the imbalances of energies on the planet and they will have the opportunity to grow when they open themselves to cosmic light. When humanity grows their unique abilities of receiving and transmitting light will grow too and this is how Earth will be healed. If you are a human being and you have just realised that your essence is energy and your physicality is temporary, then you will understand the need of opening up to the light of the cosmos. Beings that receive the light of the cosmos are going to fulfil their purpose and support others to achieve the same.

Wisdom of Thoth: The Light of the Cosmos

If human beings want to connect to the light of the cosmos, they have to accept that their essence is energy and that they are constantly connected to other energies.

Exchanging energy can take many forms and all people on Earth can achieve it often without knowing. When you dream you are able to disconnect from your physicality and experience other realities; this happens to you because you are beings of energy and you exist simultaneously in different planes. Your physicality is not permanent; it helps you to experience life in a certain way and for a short time, similarly to a dream state. True existence takes place in the astral plane which is the home of all beings. When you accept that you are energy and your life on Earth is just an experience that will help you to fulfil growth in the astral plane then you see yourself as energy and you are able to create and connect to others in an energetic way. Astral beings do not exist independently. They are part of light groups which are also part of greater energetic structures. Everything in the cosmos is connected and exists as unity. This is the only way for the cosmos to remain alive and receive and transmit light. This last cosmic law is vital to help all creation to grow and evolve.

If you are a human being and you have just realised that your essence is energy and your physicality is temporary, then you will understand the need of opening up to the light of the cosmos. Beings that receive the light of the cosmos are going to fulfil their purpose and support others to achieve the same. An energy being naturally seeks the light of our Source and is open to it the way you seek water every day.

Connecting to the cosmic light we are seeking perfection, eliminating all obstacles that can make us weak. In your third dimensional reality you cannot open fully to the light of the cosmos because you are following illusion. There is a puppet master who is also a puppet himself and has convinced you that your life is a plan of limitation and you can only be happy by accepting illusion as truth. When you are able to see through this plan and connect to your true-self then you will be able to receive cosmic light.

Questions

1. What is your experience with exchanging energy?
2. How can you grow on Earth?
3. What is your understanding of cosmic laws?
4. Why human beings should connect to the cosmic light?

Introduction

The only elite that exist are the High Source and the High Gods who have instant access to its being. All the rest of the creation, from the pebble to the master, is going through a transformation, using and producing energy. We are all working to maintain this colossal miracle that we call "life" by clearing blocks and obstacles, teaching and empowering people to take responsibility of their lives and become creators.

Wisdom of Thoth: The Light of the Gods

The people of Earth are tricked to live in a prison without walls. But many of them have started to see truth and wish to escape and live a life of truth and freedom.

When you are hungry, eat the seeds and the fruit that I planted on Earth. They are alive; they are part of my creation on Earth. They have life in them which is connected to my light; the light I receive from the high source. There are people on Earth who want to connect to their higher-self. They try hard to achieve this by using different techniques and methods; based on man-made illusions.

There are people who want to connect to their higher-self and spend their time fantasising and indulging in reading and listening to many tongues. The higher-self is a great strategist; it is the captain of the ship, a great navigator. You are the ship and you are traveling from the low to the high realms. The ship consists of the physical and the astral body and the crew is your growth and evolution. The higher-self is not being affected by your growth. The higher-self knows the divine plan and your contribution is guiding you towards this goal.

Your physical body and your third dimensional experience are slowing down the evolution but on the other hand provide great challenges and lessons to the ones who experience this type of reality. Human beings who are able to wake up and connect to their true-self have learnt a great lesson and will be rewarded. Having a physical form does not restrict you from connecting to your astral body and becoming part of growth and evolution that takes place there.

Naturally all bodies generate and transmit light and this is your connection with your higher-self. The higher-self will collect light from the higher realms and send it to your astral body and the astral body will reflect this light to the physical body. You are created to receive high light and evolve as a physical being but currently you refuse to open up to the cosmic force. Your blockage affects many areas of your understanding of cosmos and has totally transformed you into a different species.

There are many people on Earth who believe that illusion is everything that exists and when they die this is the end of their existence. A being who is connected to the astral body and receive light from the higher-self knows that death is not the end. All beings are infinite and their true focus is their growth and evolution. If you were connected to your astral body you will know the purpose of your short visit on Earth. You have to be aware that part of your purpose is to heal Earth.

The people of Earth are tricked to live in a prison without walls. But many of them have started to realise their position. They wish to escape and live a life of truth and freedom. But the prison, the invisible prison, has become an addiction. They see truth but they do not act; they want to follow their intuition but they cannot take responsibility of their actions; they can see how illusion affects people's lives but they cannot see how their own life is affected; they advocate against artificiality but their actions support it. You will become fully awaken when you return to Earth and taste all the fruit we have planted. There you can find the light; the light of the gods.

Questions

1. What is your understanding of the following phrase: "The people of Earth are tricked to live in a prison without walls."
2. What is your understanding of the higher-self and how can support your life on Earth?
3. Is clarity supported by the truth in you? In what way?
4. Do you exist in a maze of confusion or in a space of truth?

Introduction

When you go against the natural laws and you replace them with illusionary beliefs and practises, you are going to create imbalances. In your society, imbalances are seen as reality and truth and they grow and multiply from person to person. Human beings have great capabilities to fight imbalances. Open to receive the cosmic light and allow it to heal you.

Wisdom of Thoth: The Cause of Imbalance in Humanity

Humanity is waiting for the fruit to appear. People on Earth use their imagination to reach fulfilment and satisfaction in their lives. They have imaginary goals and illusionary ways to achieve those goals.

They become anxious, fearful and angry when their illusionary ways are not able to bring satisfaction; this is the cause of imbalance in humanity. If you are one of those people who are waiting for the fruit to appear on the tree, you have decide about planting a seed and see the tree grow. When you go against the natural laws and you replace them with illusionary beliefs and practises, you are going to suffer great imbalances. In your society, imbalances are seen as reality and truth and they grow and multiply from person to person. I share with you the light of the cosmos. This is the highest force of creation and life, experienced by all beings and being transmitted to us by our Source.

Open yourselves to the light of the cosmos and make it your purpose. This is how you can achieve enlightenment. Illusionary thoughts and actions cannot serve your enlightenment and connection to the cosmos. Instead you become a victim of the lower planes and your true growth is non-existent. There are people who want to grow and connect to the cosmos but they are locked in a survival mode. You are not here to serve your disease; you are here to experience life without limitation.

A pure state and a balanced life are the only experiences you must have. Disease, dissatisfaction, pain, fear are illusionary; they are not part of your being; they are artificial expressions of a distorted existence in lower planes. It is important that you connect to this truth and when you are able to accept it you will be able to transform to a cosmic being which is your true-self. We are connecting with you and we hope that you are able to connect to us.

Questions

1. What is your understanding of the following phrase: "People on Earth use their imagination to reach fulfilment and satisfaction in their lives."
2. Are you experiencing illusion? How is it affecting your life?
3. How can you connect to the cosmic light and allow it to heal you?

Introduction

You, who are looking for your purpose, what is your strategy in your quest? For some people, purpose is just a word, an idea. For me purpose is a living being much higher than the human being itself. A purpose of a being stays the same in all different realms and all reincarnations. It is a part of the higher-self and perhaps it is the only part that stays close to the being in all different realms.

Wisdom of Thoth: Our Growth is our Unity with our Source

When you receive the light of the Gods, you should stay open and try to unblock all passages for the light to go through. There is a low vibrational existence on Earth but people also have free will and can decide what way they want to take. If humanity was free then you will all have the chance to stand at the crossroads and clearly see the different paths and where they lead to.

At the moment you are locked in a low vibrational state and you are convinced that this is the only reality and cosmos does not exist. Illusion is a tool to reinforce this belief. It is an artificial reality, a mind game, a manipulation and a disease that affects everybody on Earth. Nobody is free, but some of you are trying to wake up and restore clarity in them. There is a plan that goes against awakening.

Many of you may never wake up to receive the light of the cosmos and fulfil your purpose. It may be your choice that the darkness will never be replaced by the light. A mechanical way of life, repeated by many, feels safe and comfortable. Have you ever observed yourself? If you are able to observe yourself with purity and honesty you have already started a war against illusion. When you speak, is it your true-self which is connecting to you or the persona? When illusion is reaching you and tries to form your thoughts, actions and expression, are you able to observe it? Are you able to stop it?

The light of the Gods is everywhere in every being that is created by the high light of our source. The whole cosmos is our source his expression of high light and naturally we are all longing to each other and our source. Our growth is our unity with our source. Strengthening our light and going through a transformation are the steps we take to achieve unity. See yourself at the crossroad, look at your path, look at your different paths and with truth and freedom move on and achieve unity.

Questions

1. "When you receive the light of the Gods, you should stay open and try to unblock all passages for the light to go through." What is your experience?
2. How can you change your life and experience the flow of growth?
3. Are you at the crossroads? How can you find your path?
4. How can you grow with others?

Introduction

Colour and sound can be experienced by all human beings on Earth. Humans are surrounded by colours of numerous subtleties in myriad shades, becoming an integral part of their world. In the highest planes colour and sound do not exist; all sounds, colours, shapes and everything else that is being seen as a separate entity or characteristic in lower spheres, it is unified with the whole and exists as one.

Wisdom of Thoth: Colours

In the lower planes there is fragmentation; you experience the light in the form of different colours and then try to imitate it and give it a certain attribute. Religions and spiritual teachers have used colours and sounds to symbolise polarity. Some people believe that colours have power and can help you on your path to growth. There are colours used in ceremonial objects and fabrics that symbolise certain attributes. These beliefs have existed for many years and are part of the human consciousness. This is what makes them powerful; colours can become an effective tool for passing information and create beliefs. People use the colour gold to symbolise wealth, power and divinity and blue is the colour of tranquillity, serenity and transformation. Colours used as a tool of communication, are part of the symbolism created by humans and were used to fragment truth and go against unity which is the main goal of the cosmic creation.

Questions:

1. What is colour?
2. How do people use colour as a communication tool?
3. What is your understanding of colour healing?
4. What do you know about colour symbolism?

Introduction

Now I want to speak to you about communication. All beings are created to communicate energetically and with this I mean receiving as well as creating and generating energy. Even when you use language to express yourselves you also exchange energy at the same time. Why people are not aware of it and how can one develops the ability to communicate energetically?

Wisdom of Thoth: Communication

Beings are in constant communication; a foetus is able to receive and transmit energy. In your early years when language is not is not yet your way of expression, you naturally communicate by receiving and transmitting light. You can communicate by looking at someone or focusing on the essence of a being. Energetic communication cannot be false or deceiving and when others communicate with you this way they can connect to your true-self. As part of your awakening, you have to experience energetic communication; your knowing will expand and clarity will become reality.

A simple way to practise is to experience silence. When you no longer rely on language, you will be able to exchange energy as a way of communication. You can do this when you are on your own but you can also practise it with others. You can be in a company observing yourself and others without using the barrier of language. You can also practise transmitting high energies to people who are weak without talking to them. Another example of exchanging energy will be to create a picture, a piece of music, an object or anything else you wish to create without following certain instructions. Allow the energies around you and in you to create with you. Do not try to explain, justify or analyse your actions also do not blame or feel superior for what you have achieved. Accept all doings as a natural process to help you grow.

Questions

1. What is your understanding of energetic communication?
2. "Energetic communication cannot be false or deceiving and when others communicate with you this way they can connect to your true-self." What is your experience?
3. Can you use your mind to transmit and receive energy?
4. What is your understanding of the following message: "Accept all doings as a natural process to help you grow."

Introduction

There are many people on Earth who try to understand their purpose but they do not succeed because they cannot connect to truth and practise acceptance. When we cannot accept our purpose, we create many false representations often related to social ideals and survival mechanisms such as the ego. The fight between truth and social acceptance can cause blockages and imbalances which can harm all beings. When truth and freedom is with you then you can restore yourself to what you truly are.

Wisdom of Thoth: Beings with a Mental Disability

There are beings in your society that are not able to communicate the way most people do. It is believed that they have a disability and they cannot cope being part of the society.

When these beings are forced and punished in order to be part of a society which is very limited and uniform then they are going to be very confused and perhaps they will have a hard time trying to be "normal". I do not see your society being normal because most people have a limited understanding of existence. Most people are not connected to themselves, the astral growth or even the Earth's energies.

When society wants people to be normal this means that they want you to be limited. Those beings that are not able to use language to express themselves do not rely on it; they are able to communicate using a natural process which is the energetic exchange. If those people were allowed to grow and accepted as beings with great abilities beyond the human understanding then the planet would have many great lightbringers. Unfortunately they are stigmatised and often forced to suppress their abilities. The fight between truth and social acceptance can cause blockages and imbalances which can harm all beings. When truth and freedom is with you then you can restore yourself to what you truly are.

Questions

1. What is your experience connecting to people with disability?
2. How can you communicate truth and connection?
3. Are you being misunderstood?
4. What is your understanding of the following message: "When truth and freedom is with you then you can restore yourself to what you truly are."

Introduction

Most human beings are familiar with the body's functions explained by your science. This is only one of the many layers of wisdom that your body has to offer. Your body is a much more complex, multidimensional organism whose main function is to receive light and create life within. Your body goes through constant rebirth and transformation and this is related to its ability to receive light. There is a motion inside you that keeps you alive and anchors you to the physical plane; you understand that this corresponds to the vibration of your astral body and it is also linked to planetary motion.

Wisdom of Thoth: Life Patterns, Imbalances and Growth

We are working together to help the people of Earth. We are all connected and our light will reach you if you become a true channel. You may ask, how can I achieve that? It has to do with your intention to clear blockages and restore balance. This is the ultimate wisdom you should follow in order to grow. It is important that you start from your body and connect to its energies. Observe your physical imbalances, your stagnation points and your points of growth in your body.

Most human beings are familiar with the body's functions explained by your science. This is only one of the many layers of wisdom that your body has to offer. It is a much more complex, multidimensional organism whose main function is to receive light and create life within. Your body goes through constant rebirth and transformation and this is related to its ability to receive light.

Illness is not a natural phenomenon but is caused by imbalances. When you focus on your imbalances and accept them as being part of your natural state, you lose your connection to the cosmic light which is life itself. Fragmentation becomes deeper in you and creates schisms. A symptom of this is suffering from negativity fear, disappointment, anger and dissatisfaction. If you are in this state you have to observe yourself and look at your blockages and imbalances in your body. Purification is your next step: this is an intense observation of your life patterns, imbalances and growth. The light of the gods is reaching Earth and you have to purify yourselves in order to receive it.

You experience a hierarchy and a system of duality. High quality food and shelter is often related to high income or a high status. Everybody needs nutrients that come directly from the Earth but this becomes a privilege of a small group of people at the top of the financial pyramid. It seems that people with low incomes do not have the change to nurture themselves but this is not true. It is an illusion, it is a way to manipulate the masses and keep people in a low vibrational state.

Bring yourself closer to Earth, be aware of her light and open yourself to receive her grace. Trust your connection with her and let her nourish you. Allow the creator-planet to share her light and create in you and then you produce light and create in your life and others. Cultivate your own plants, help others and share your production. If you open your eyes and are able to listen to your true-self you will find many solutions and ways to connect to Earth. You can be free from illusion only if this is your intention.

We are here to help you open your eyes and experience new possibilities of growth. Your body has a physical aspect but its true purpose is to act as a multidimensional being that connects you to the astral body. Therefore the possibilities of rebirth and transformation of your body as a whole are limitless. You have to focus on clarity and this will help you receive healing and bring balance. The more you are connected to your essence and understand your body as multidimensional the more peace you will receive. The mind should be quietening in order to receive enlightenment. Receiving the light you heal yourself.

DIALOGUE WITH THOTH

We received several questions from order members and students and below we present a dialogue between Thoth and humanity.

Question
Can you give us some information about unknown creatures on Earth?

Answer
Human beings who live in the cities, they think that what they experience is the norm everywhere on Earth. They think that their routines and every day duties are much more important than connecting to Earth. This is a sign of distortion and shows that most people are affected by illusion. Some of you want to know, if there are creatures that are not known to human beings living on the planet how do they survive? There are many areas on Earth that are unspoiled and uninhabited by humans; this means that the problem of overpopulation is another illusion. These areas have not been populated by humans because they are the home of beings that can only exist in the wild. There are some beings that live underground and carry energies that are very similar to the ones that exist in the inner parts of the Earth. These beings cannot enter the inner parts but they have to exist in high vibrational areas away from the pollution that humans create. For them humans are unclean and polluted and are unable to connect to the high energies on the planet. They have abilities that are beyond your understanding and this makes them a mystery to you. Instead of trying to trap these creatures for your own egotistical satisfaction you should focus on purifying yourself. Your next step will be to abandon your distorted life style and seek to unite to Earth's high energies.

Question

Is The Law of Attraction a real universal law or is it another form of illusion?

Answer

Many people are keeping their minds busy with something like the law of attraction and the riches that can bring them. If you believe that by visualising goods and repeating affirmations will help you possess wealth, you have a distorted understanding of yourself and your purpose. If you are looking for a cosmic law, I would like you to focus on the law of truth. People who are in a distorted state they cannot live a life of truth and purpose. Furthermore, desiring certain goods, connections or states to come to you this does not guarantee that you know yourself and experience your purpose. The law of attraction connects you to artificiality and illusion; it is not helping you understand why you are here on Earth, what are your abilities and unique tools and what is your purpose according to your divine plan.

Question

I want to ask Thoth about variation in the universe. Is the human template a common form in the universe?

Answer

If you want an answer to this question you should look at all different trees and their leaves. For beings that exist in low vibrational planets having a growth that is similar to Earth's growth, you will find beings that look very similar to human beings: perhaps different colour, different height or it may be a difference in the formation of some body parts. There are also planets that have the same vibration as Earth but the beings that exist there look different from the Earthlings because they live underground or they were exposed to some major disaster. In higher realms beings consist of energy and have no physicality. There are also realms were beings can be recognised by the aura that surrounds their limited physicality. As you can see there are many variations but there are also similarities: their ability to grow, their connection to the cosmic light and the source and their ability to support cosmic growth.

Question

I want to ask: Did Allister Crowley channeled Thoth?

Answer

I, Thoth, want to connect to all human beings on Earth and support their growth in connection to Earth's growth. There are human beings on Earth that have connected to my light in present time and in previous reincarnations. There are also beings that were able to connect to my light momentarily and then they either connected to their guides or other beings of low or high vibration or were able to communicate with them. Beings on Earth who connect to Thoth of Egypt are not connecting to the creator of Earth. There is a possibility that in previous reincarnations they were priests in temples and focused on connecting to non-physical beings or to high creator gods and perhaps this connection brings to them memories and lessons of the past. My teaching to you is about truth and growth in all planes.

Question

Is it true that all reptilians are bad?

Answer

In recent times, human beings have been bombarded with a variety of explanations and suggestions regarding alien species and their connection to Earth. Most of this information is an embellishment of the truth, to create fear or to convince you that you are opening up to a great truth. There is a variety of humanoid beings that exist in different planets; some of them still exist in the inner parts of Earth. The beings that exist in the inner parts of the planet are the ones with the longest linage. During the golden era and many Earth cycles after that, there were living beings that had forms that cannot be seen on Earth in the present moment. There were beings that had a mixture of characteristics: for example birds that had the form of a snake or fish that could walk and fly or beings that had human characteristics as well as animal features such as reptilian. There were humanoid races that existed on Earth and were able to exist under water but also walk on Earth and sometimes fly. Some of these races left the planet and others exist now in the inner parts of the Earth. These beings have no interest in connecting to human beings on the surface on the planet because it is not attractive to them. They see the surface as a low vibrational part of the Earth, having less resources and more distortion than the inner parts.

Question

How does Thoth currently feel about Earth and humans?

Answer

Earth and humanity are going through a transformation. When people start looking for truth, the manipulators will produce many false truths to take them on a diversion. But there are people who are connecting to the light, there are people who want to escape illusion and find their path and their increasing number supports Earth's transformation. When one receives the light then the light can travel to many others and plant the seed of renewal. Transformation is already happening on Earth so the next step will be growth and unity. For this to happen you all have to connect to your own truth and spread it to humanity and Earth. You are participating in this transformation so it is your responsibility to support the collective growth by sharing the light.

Question

What was the first creation project for Thoth or could he share what it was like for him the first time he created a planet?

Answer

I was involved in the creation of Earth's astral body. The astral plane is the home of all creation and all beings have an astral existence which is the seed that goes through many transformations. Creating Earth's physicality was a transformation what took place very long time ago. There was another seed that needed to be created and this is the seed of physicality. This is how the core of the Earth was created. The core of the Earth was not fully physical. A number of transformations had to take place for the body of the Earth to be created. It was almost like what you understand as a growth in the physical body and it was affected by the Earth's position and connection to other planets.

Question

What are the best methods or choices for disabling the plans of the elite's agenda? What can be done in order to support truth and light being spread, the awakening of Earth, and dissolving the distortion and illusion?

Answer

There are a number of actions you can take in order to empower yourselves. You should not exist in fear and separation; see the distortion on the planet, accept that there is illusion used by manipulators in order to control your growth, you also accept that people can affect some of your life choices only if you yourself connect to illusion. Nobody can control your essence, your truth, divine plan, purpose and your unique abilities given to you in the beginning of your reincarnation. When you focus on these high gifts and you see your life through them, then illusion cannot affect you. The manipulators are also affected by illusion and in their quest to own everything that exists, they also suffer from distortion. Enjoy every moment of truth that you are able to create and this will lead you to your purpose.

Question

I know that originally all creation lived in harmony and that humans did not eat animals. Does Thoth have any guidance on eating meat, fish and dairy in modern times?

Answer

During the golden era, all Earth's creation consisted of light beings with very little physicality and they were nourished by the energies of the cosmos and Earth's energies. From the time Earth became a low vibrational planet and lost its connection to the high light, her creation went into a transformation, developing physicality and new ways to stay alive. In ancient times, people who go and hunt for their food; they will hunt animals and eat them. In those times there were certain communities who did not eat meat because they wanted to connect to the light and disconnect from the low vibrational existence. Now there are people who eat poisonous substances that are made to be addictive. There are also people who choose not to eat meat but they are still consuming chemical substances which are included in the everyday food products. The worst disease that a human being is facing is eating polluted food and not being aware of it. Your industries are going to create polluted food products for meat eaters, vegetarians and vegans so nobody can escape a physical imbalance. What is more important right now is to avoid eating all artificial, chemical and contaminated food that comes in all shapes and sizes; you can also find them in your health shop being branded healthy and nutritious. Then going into a vegetarian or vegan diet will be your next step.

Question

My question has to do with the golden era: are there any parts of the Earth that are experiencing the golden era already; What will be the transformation and growth process for Earth in order to return to the golden era; how this will affect her creation including humanity; how can human beings support Earth's growth and transformation?

Answer

Golden Era has not left Earth. Close to the core of the planet, Earth's essence, the golden era is still affecting Earth's light and tries to move to the surface and reunite the planet's whole being. In the areas close to the core, the golden era is transforming the life that exists there. The light of the golden era can reach the surface of the Earth in places where there are certain entrances that were used in the past as tunnels of communication between all parts of Earth. These are high vibrational areas and most of them are unknown to humanity. If you want to support Earth's transformation and the return of the golden era to the whole planet, you have to purify yourselves, receive light, become a pure receiver and transmitter of the cosmic light and allow it to spread on the surface of Earth. The light of the golden era that exists in the core of the Earth, it is the cosmic light and the source's creative force.

Question

Are crystals a good way to connect with some of these energies from inner Earth?

Answer

I know that human beings are attracted to crystals because they remind them of the golden era where giant crystals were created on Earth to receive the light and transmit it to the planet. During the golden era there were mountains of crystals scattered around the planet, crystals were everywhere in all different shapes and sizes and what you have right now is just rocks and stones. Those crystal formations were not made by human beings but they were created by Earth and the cosmic light to support her growth. There were her receivers and transmitters of light. Later on, these crystals were destroyed or looted by the alien races that came to Earth. The energy of the stones that people can have on Earth right now it is only a fraction of the ones that existed in the golden era. Also crystals are receiving the low energies, the distortion and the limitation that human being carry and they transmit that. If you want to have stones and you want to use them to help you connect to Earth's growth and golden era, they have to be stored underground and when they are used you need to have a clear and pure intention regarding their use. Crystals and stones that are placed constantly in a room, they have no healing qualities and it is also possible that they may transmit distortion.

Question

Are there any teachings relating to the god Horus?

Answer

There are many layers of understanding that human beings can have about this. On one hand, people understand gods the way they are described in the mythology books and traditions and often when they connect to a mythological god, they connect to a person with certain attributes, physical characteristics, special powers and the way they were worshiped and ruled Earth. Mythological gods have been invoked for thousands of years by many religious centres, secret societies and mystery schools. Because of this they have become powerful symbols that can connect to human beings and take them on a diversion in a state that has nothing to do with their own truth and purpose. People on Earth are encouraged to look for hidden knowledge, sacred wisdom that can make them powerful, give them the elixir of eternal life and youth and hidden tricks and shortcuts to get to the top layers of pyramid of social success. The truth in you is much more powerful than any connection to mythological supreme beings. Feeling connected to them it may mean that the energies given to the symbol that you identify as a certain god is affecting you or there is a strong connection with a symbol from a past life.

Question:

While there seems to be a life cycle to solar systems, and we have evidence of stars dying out and planets drifting away, or being consumed by supernovas, or being smashed by asteroids, how can it be that the Earth is eternal?

Answer:

Human beings have physical bodies; planets have physical bodies too. A physical body of a human being has a short life cycle and at the end of this cycle, the being will return to the astral plane and continue to grow and evolve. The astral growth is eternal and limitless. Planets have much longer life cycles and go through many transformations. Human beings are not able to know all Earth's transformations because they have not experienced them; they did not grow with Earth. If Earth loses her physical body will not affect human beings directly.

If this happens human beings will stop reincarnating on Earth. It may be that planets have to lose their physicality similarly to human beings, enter a non-physical vibrational state and start existing as an astral body. We talk about Earth being eternal; this is related to her ability to create life and give opportunities to astral beings to reincarnate and experience physicality. Earth produces life, creates receivers and transmitters of cosmic light and allows energies to create bridges with other cosmic life. She is offering a gift of growth and this makes her a creator.

Question:

Can you give information on having a transcendence, opening up to past lives, messages from ancestors and signs from the gods. Finding out your higher purpose and then having it shut down by very effective medication.

Answer:

Human beings can connect to past lives when there is something they need to learn in order to support their growth and fulfil their purpose in their current life time. Your ancestors or beings that were with you in previous lifetimes can often become your guides in this life time. So opening up to their guidance is very beneficial to help you clear the distortion, understand your purpose and make the right connections to help you fulfil your purpose. It is important for human beings to accept these communications but also stay in a state of peace and avoid going on a diversion.

Many of the guides' messages sent to human beings can be misunderstood. Sometimes human beings try to understand them by using their mind and this triggers limitation and fear. There are many people that use different types of medication. Medication can be harmful as well as helpful, depending on the imbalance and duration of this imbalance. It is true that most medication is designed to shut down parts of your physical body and mind. This is how your science of medicine understands healing. If you have to take medication then you need to find ways to connect to the cosmos and Earth and receive communication that is important for your growth. When you are able to connect to your whole being and exist in a space of peace then you will realize that you will always have the ability to connect to everything that you are, being part of the cosmic creation.

Question

Let me know if inappropriate but I just have to share the experience I had in my sleep last night and would like to know if anyone has experienced the same.

I dreamt a man who was pale and thin knocked on my front door and said follow me. So I did. He had the back end of a mini-van opened and it looked like a lot of equipment with metal drawers. He said stand right there and put his hand on my left shoulder and he put something in my back. It was painful and paralyzing down to my right leg. This feeling only lasted a few seconds I was hunched over trying to stand while he did this then he stood me up tall and showed me that he had repaired my spine! He said rest for 30 days to complete the healing. I woke up this morning to no pain. I have been working on keeping my back in alignment all day too. Has anyone ever had this happen to them?

Answer:

The healing that you received was a lesson that will lead you to growth. You have the ability to heal others the way you were healed in your dream. This experience is a calling for you to open up to your abilities without fear, self judgement or limitation. You can heal others and pass to them wisdom and knowing about the body and the energies that surround it. You do not have to use a certain method to offer healing. You just have to connect to the cosmic light, have a pure intention and allow your body to become a receiver and transmitter of healing energy.

Question:

I want to ask about dark attachments.

Answer:

People, who exist in a confused state, allow beings to control their mind and feed from their energy. Often beings with great light attract non-physical entities that exist in Earth's atmospheres. Similarly to illusion, these beings try to distract you causing different sensations such as sounds, visions, unusual smells, and more. They use fear to manipulate your mind and lock you in a state of limitation. They also affect your ego by making you feel superior, they only one that can communicate with non-physical life.

They get your attention in different ways and without realizing, you allow them to enter your being. People that have long attachments suffer from many imbalances in their whole being and they transmit their imbalances to people around them. If you want to be free then you have to connect to your true-self and go through an intense purification process. You can be free from them when your pure intention focusses on healing yourself and others and experience this in your everyday life.

Question:

Is prayer a worthwhile practice? Are people's prayers and rituals of value to the other realms with which they are meant to connect to?

Answer:

Prayer can be beneficial as a form of meditation, connecting to your true-self and understanding your purpose. If you use prayer to help you communicate with God in order to give you what you believe you need then you have already put a blindfold over your eyes and you are going on a diversion.

Question:

Is there any flora and fauna that are not native to Earth that exists on the planet?

Answer:

Everything that exists on Planet Earth is created by Earth. And this can be explained by looking at each planet's ability to create life. It will be useless trying to plant seeds that are designed to connect to Earth's energies, in Mars. Similarly you will not want to go for a walk in the moon's atmospheres without protection and necessary equipment that will re-connect you to Earth's ability to create.

Question:

How do we leave truth if we do not know what it is or what the illusion is?

Answer:

People are very concerned about the illusion and artificiality that exists around them. They want to live in a world of purity, truth, growth and transformation but it seems impossible to transform every single person on Earth and create new social systems. People who wish to transform everything they see, they are also affected by illusion. There are many who fantasize about growth but there are very few who are able to experience growth. The only way to transform humanity is to transform yourself first. Dealing with your own imbalances, accepting the patters that have blocked your way to connect to your true-self, connecting to your true-self and allow healing to take place in you; these are the first steps to help you purify from illusion and experience growth. Only when you experience growth, you give the opportunity to others to transform.

Question:

I have a question concerning humans being implanted with RFID microchips. 10 years ago I read a book about near death experiences.

Someone got struck by lightning and they received visions of the future before returning to their body. They were also crippled for life upon return having to live in a wheel chair and wear welding goggles because light hurt his eyes afterwards. All his visions came to pass and the final one spoke of someone trying to rule the world forcing humanity to get microchips implanted in them so they could manipulate them further. Now recently I have seen material surfacing much more frequently about people getting implanted with these microchips. Can you share some information about this micro chipping agenda and also what is there to be known about near death experiences? Thankyou

Answer:

Human beings are very interested in technology and they are surrounded by technological "miracles" such as their phone, computers and many other appliances. Technology seems to be very exciting, constantly growing and producing new machines that can make people's life better and easier. So, you are all waiting for the new wonderful machine that is going to be invented in the near future and you are walking the path of technology, the path of illusion, the path of entrapment. Where are these paths leading to? They are leading to absolute control and ownership of your being by the people who are using technology to keep you in a maze of illusion. The time that all human beings will have to be microchipped is not far. The machines that you are using right now are also controlling devices the only difference is that they are not in your body. There is only one suggestion I can share with you: disconnect from artificiality and connect to your beings unlimited growth. This is how you can remain free

Question:

Is fasting good for your body? I have practiced it a little here and there. When I fast for 1-2 days I feel very clear minded and it feels like my body is experiencing something good. I have read how it regenerates cells among other things and how the medical industry will not conduct proper research on fasting.

Answer:

Human's way to consume food that is available to them is very problematic. People who are able to grow the food they eat, they truly nourish their being with food that is alive. This is a way to connect to Earth and receive her energy. When you start consuming fresh fruit and vegetables you are eating patterns will change. The combination of what you eat is also important as well as when you eat it. Most human beings are eating often but they feel constantly hungry.

They do not realize that their food makes them tired and unsatisfied. Eating is a great way to connect to your being and understand its function and ways of growth. When you eat polluted food, you bring imbalance to your body that often leads to disease. Human beings should grow their own food and eat what they produce, connecting to Earth and bringing balance to their body.

If you are not able to produce your own food at this moment, a step forward will be to pick the fruit and vegetables that are grown locally and have what you call "fasting". Limiting your food intake, preparing raw meals and juices should be your everyday diet. This will help you purify your body and also disconnect you from the need of consumption, the fear of survival and the greed that brings destruction to the planet. If you are able to fast for a few days you will experience a feeling of peace and you will be able to disconnect from artificiality and illusions. Your connection to your being will be stronger and the energies of Earth will be flowing in you and nourish you.

Question:

I am wondering if you have any specifics to help us humans to receive the light and transmit it effectively for example cleansing our bodies, grounding, walking barefoot, having a specific diet or practices that enhances the process?

Answer:

There is a lot of advice out there as to how people can experience wellbeing, cleansing their bodies, staying grounded and other important practices that bring balance to your being. Most of these practices are coming to people through their minds not through their whole being.

People are creating a maze with all different choices/advice and they are still confused and in imbalanced state. Do not focus on your mind if you want to connect to your truth in you. Connect and communicate directly with your physical body if you want to experience healing. Connect to Earth's energies and make it a permanent state if you wish to be grounded. Understand the importance of this connection through your growth. Create bridges from within and let them expand. This will show you that you are not following an advice but you are following your truth and purpose.

Question:

Are the governments trying to start WWIII? I feel like Earth is waking up more all the time and the ones trying to rule Earth I think are trying to cause wars to erupt so they can interrupt her transformation. Recently the country I live in fired missiles at another country claiming they had chemically attacked humans. I am almost certain this was a false flag used as an excuse to fire the missiles. It would seem other countries are prepared to go to war with this country if any other lines are crossed from this point forward.

Answer:

The elite are trying to control the masses and Earth's resources but they are also suffering from distortion and illusion. It may seem that the rulers of certain countries are playing a chess game, waiting for the opponent's next move, looking for the right strategy to create tension, instability and fear. This chess game is going to take long to end because there are many players who are taking part and pull the strings. Your global government prefers to create a society of consumers, addicts and confused people that can form civilizations of self-destruction; this is what they trying to achieve. When there is war it means that there is opposition to this plan so this country has to be occupied and after a while will have to accept a global identity. You should not be afraid of the possibility of war; take the time to observe and know yourself instead of observing an illusionary game of chess that has no purpose. Humanity should focus on growth; this way you can avoid destruction.

Question:

As we walk the path and approach a new phase of enlightenment our atomic and cellular structures change. Can you tell us your viewpoint on this?

Answer:

What you experience as your body, it is related to Earth's ability to create. This means that the enlightenment of a human being does not bring a change in its physical structure.

If you consider yourself being enlightened and you are in a process of constant growth, you should share your light with Earth. You are an extension of Earth but you are not the one who creates life on this planet. We want to give humanity the fruit of knowledge and experience of high wisdom in order to open themselves to the cosmic light which is the creating force of our source and through them to reach Earth. We want to see her returning to the Golden Era and becoming a creator of high dimensional beings. Truly, your task is to achieve Earth's recovery to her Golden Era by allowing the cosmic light to purify all imbalances and bring a new force of creation as it is designed by our Source. The light of the Gods is connecting to all of you and showing you the way to achieve this high task. If you consider yourself enlightened you should open yourself to the cosmic light and allow Earth to feed from you in order to transform you into a high being.

Question:

So basically if we all ensure we are connecting to our true-self and maintaining a high vibration filled with a state of peace, love and light, then we are automatically subconsciously all creating the "new world" correct? Does the vibration of the gods on the planet matter more than others? For instance, if a God is in a low vibration and stressed then it will impact all of humanity more?

Answer:

We all are united and our purpose is to maintain life in the cosmos. All beings in higher planes exist in a space of peace and this is why they experience profound growth that leads to the evolution of themselves and the cosmos. Earth has become a low vibrational planet and being in a state of peace is challenging. This is because distortion, fragmentation and illusion takes over and parts of the Earth maintain these and become life patterns.

When you are in a state of peace and you are able to maintain this, you have disconnected from illusion. In a state of peace you have clarity because the cosmic light can reach you and create in you. If you are able to connect to the cosmic light then you are able to heal, grow and help others to do the same. There are beings on Earth that exist in higher vibration than others. On the other hand the cosmic purpose of all beings is the same and this is to grow and maintain growth in themselves and others. All beings were created to fulfil their purpose and they can all help others to grow. Earth beings have a great duty to connect the planet with the cosmic light and heal humanity.

Question

There are so many innocent children and others that are ill and hungry and that die daily. Are those people that are living without basic needs all unenlightened and not worthy of enlightenment or life?

Answer

In the time of the Golden Era Earth's creation was able to feed from the light of the cosmos and the nutrients that were stored on the planet. Having long life cycles without disease, fragmentation, pain and negativity, constant growth was a natural process. This was supported by Earth, the planet creator, her guides the Gods of the Pleroma and the beings that lived on her. All these different aspects of life on Earth supported evolution and they were the receivers and transmitters of light. Looking at the present time we see on Earth fragmentation, distortion and schism; they affect Earth's growth and the growth of her creation. Earth is not always able to safeguard her resources. She is not always able to give shelter and nourishment to her creation because she is suffering from distortion. A reflection of the Earth's state can be seen on the life patterns of human beings.

You experience a hierarchy and a system of duality. High quality food and shelter is often related to high income or a high status. Everybody needs nutrients that come directly from the Earth but this becomes an advantage of a small group of people on the top of the financial pyramid.

It seems that people with low income do not have the chance to nurture themselves but this is not true.

It is an illusion, it is a way to manipulate the masses and keep people to a low vibrational state. Bring yourself closer to Earth, be aware of her light and open yourself to receive her grace. Trust your connection with her and let her nourish you. Allow the creator-planet to share her light and create in you and then you produce light and create in your life and others. Cultivate your own plants, help others and share your production. If you open your eyes and be able to listen to your true-self you will find many solutions and ways to connect to Earth. You can be free from illusion only if this is your intention.

Question:

But what if you don't eat "prepackaged food" or other poor quality food? What if you are trying within your every ability to take care of this physical body? And there simply is no way to care for it any longer? Then one needs to just allow physical death to happen? I ask because of a specific reason. I am not trying to be argumentative.

Answer:

We are here to help you open your eyes and experience new possibilities of growth. Your body has a physical aspect but its true purpose is to act as a multidimensional being that connects you to the astral body. Therefore the possibilities of rebirth and transformation of your body as a whole are limitless. You have to focus on clarity and this will help you receive healing and bring balance. The more you are connected to your essence and understand your body as a multidimensional tool the more peace you will receive. The mind should be quietening in order to receive enlightenment. Receiving the light you heal yourself.

Question

What is Enki and Enlil current state and are they connected to Thoth?

Answer

I know that human beings cannot separate mythology from energy. Enki and Enlil are characters of your mythology but they are also cosmic energy. All energy exists to transform and grow and the essence of all beings can also transform grow, reincarnate and also exist in the astral plane. There are beings on Earth who think that Enki and Enlil were creators on Earth. The names that you are using are not what they were called when they visited Earth. The names of all mythological characters are just descriptions of the way they looked or what they were able to create in a life time. I know that people on Earth have a false idea of these beings and they try to connect to them and see them as creators of Earth. What they were able to achieve is to visit Earth in a period of transformation, where Earth was becoming a low vibrational planet. These events happened very long time ago and the energy of these beings was able to transform and grow. These energies are not connected to the low vibrational parts of the cosmos and do not need to reincarnate.

Question
Who is Ra?

Answer
Ra was a leader and a warrior of a civilisation on Earth. People in ancient times even do they suffered from distortion, they were aware of the cosmic light, the Earth's energies and the astral plane. They were aware that a life cycle on Earth is just a lesson that needs to be experienced in order to support their growth and the growth of the planet. At the end of this person's life time on Earth, the priests stayed connected to the essence of this being and when the essence returned to the astral plane they were able to connect through the essence to astral growth. This wisdom passed on to a number of civilisations but it became distorted over the years.

Question
Why we do not stay grounded all of the time without having to plan, or practice or think about it?

Answer
You are describing human nature when it is affected by distortion having a blindfold and believing they are truly blind. If people were able to connect to their truth, see their divine plan and purpose on Earth accept

their duty as a receiver and transmitter of light and connect to the cosmos and Earth then they will be able to see again.

Human beings do not only have one blindfold; they are as many as the layers of distortion in their being. Some people have to purify from fear by allowing the cosmic light to enter their being. You may have to observe the repeated patterns in you that have blocked you from connecting to the Earth and the cosmos. Do not see yourself as a limitation but as a seed that is growing to become a tree. Experience inner joy, truth and freedom and let them take you on a journey to growth.

Question

I have a question for Thoth and felt it was something that others should benefit from as well so I am sharing it here.

I have had someone close to me recently feeling concerns over technology and specific issues that they have heard are related to technology. Specifically speaking forms of technology such as home wireless systems, and expanding from that the 4G and 5G networks being installed nationwide. I am not sure if these wireless technologies are called something else in other parts of the world, but they are all the same basically.

Some studies have apparently shown these wireless technologies and the fields they produce to be carcinogenic and disruptive to natural human abilities.

I do see certain benefits around these tools. Even in this group we use technology to connect to each other from around the world. But I am curious what the truths of these matters are. Is part of our purification process possibly limiting exposure to excess wireless technology? Is wireless technology toxic to humans? Or is it just another layer of distortion and confusion that keeps people in a fear cycle?

Answer

There are many different sources of pollution on Earth that are produced not only because of greed and distortion but also to shut down parts of human connection with their true-self, the Earth and the cosmos. All different types of pollution including artificial food, polluted water, polluted air, living disconnected from Earth surrounded by different waves, transmissions internet and phone technology have the ability to suppress your growth if you allow it. All these forms of pollution can affect your body to some degree, but you have resources that can help you purify and be in constant growth. Connecting to the cosmic light, receiving Earth's nourishment can purify you from all pollution that exists on Earth. This depends on your intention to stay in a purified and healing space within your being and becoming a receiver and transmitter of the gift of growth. When people suffer from illnesses this has to do with many factors; the main one is not accepting that can experience growth and have a fulfilled life. Create your own life without fear; truth is your essence and it is limitless.

Question

There are many theories on Earth around the concept of words and how they manifest reality. Can Thoth please share some insight into how we might learn to communicate more truthfully. Are there different outcomes to reality based on the words we choose? For instance, many believe they must refrain from speaking in "foul" language as they believe this is somehow negative in some sense or creates negative outcomes in their life. I am curious about these things.

Answer

Manipulators have created a science called public speaking, advertising, and teaching using repetitions of words creating certain structures. The way you speak and the terms you use can create an illusionary space of fear, satisfaction, truth or freedom in people's minds and then they are ready to accept manipulation as a true aspect of their being. If human beings want to speak to others, expressing their true-self and passing the light of the cosmos and Earth than they have to use an authentic expression and allow their truth to become a bridge to help you exist in unity with others. For this to happen you have to connect to your truth in your everyday experience, you have to communicate with a pure intention and allow the cosmic light to be the main source of communication. You can also communicate with what you are creating, with your learning. Or just being in peace connecting to your whole being. Do not rely on words for communication but when you have to speak then do it without restrictions, limitation or fragmentation. Communicate your truth in a way that is unique to you and your ability to grow.

Question:

My intuitive understanding is that Thoth is actually a collective, not one being. If this is the case, can you please clarify this term, "gods?"

Answer:

I know that human beings will always try to understand the life experience and also the cosmic growth being a polarity or a duality. Gods are a not "a being" or many beings coming together to perform an act of creation. The gods are energy that supports and directs creation in the cosmos. We exist in unity with the source and the cosmic light that can be seen as the source's pure intention to expand and regenerate itself. We exist in unity with the source's act of creation. This does not mean that we are not able to act and create through our own electromagnetic field. A better way to explain this is by looking at your hand. Your fingers are part of your hand but they also have individual qualities. The gods have different qualities too but there is something important that they share: their ability to be a part of the source's intention for creation.

Question:

Did humanity elevate them to this position or was it an assignment?

Answer:

The gods are the tools for the source to create. By receiving the cosmic light and the intention of the source, the gods were able to create the different planes of the cosmos including the astral plane. The astral plane is the home of all beings in the cosmos. This is where beings exist before and after their reincarnations. In the astral plane they experience cosmic growth and they support life in the cosmos. Earth has an astral body that was created before the physical body. Human beings have also an astral body and when they reincarnate on Earth, they are given a physical body to support them to fulfil their purpose in this reincarnation. Earth has created their physical bodies. Their astral bodies were created by the gods and the light of the source. Earth was also created by the gods and human beings in ancient times understood this. They wanted to connect to the creators of Earth and for this is why they humanised them and wrote stories about them known as mythology. Humans cannot elevate gods; gods want to elevate humans to help them connect to their truth and purpose.

Question:
If we are all part of Source, then how can one group be elevated to this status (with potential "worshippers") as we perceive it to be, or is this status actually an illusion as well? Thank you.

Answer:
If you worship a god, a human being or an idea then you are disconnected from the light that you carry and you exist in a maze of distortion. All beings are connected to the source, all beings have an astral body and all beings have a light in them that can lead them to their purpose. If you choose to see this truth and make it your guide then you are transforming to a human being that every moment of his life is opportunity of growth and therefore life is effortless. In this state you will be able to support and be supported by other beings that are also on their path. This is how you can create a community of light and truth. These human beings are not superior; they are the ones who are supporting the light of the cosmos to enter humanity and Earth. They have a special gift and a high duty.

Question:
There is much information about chakras becoming blocked and ways to unblock them. Is this illusion?

Answer:
It is illusionary to focus on your chakras and ignore your whole being. Your chakras are gates within your being that allow the energy to flow and heal the imbalances that you may carry; guide you to your purpose; connect you to Earth. Most of the imbalances do not affect the chakras but they exist in the mind, your aura or parts of your being that are in separation from the truth that you carry. You receive the light in order to heal all imbalances and transform your being. Your whole being should experience transformation and this will allow it to be guided to your purpose. This way you fight distortion and fragmentation and you experience unity with the cosmos and Earth.

Question:

Is it possible to integrate the Essence of our Original Creation Or Birth Essence into our current Vessel to heal at the purest level and return to our Original Soul Blueprint and DNA and share this Light, Love, Energy, and Essence with Mother Earth and All Souls from All Kingdoms?

Answer:

Everything exists in unity. You are connected to Earth; you are part of Earth's creation. Human beings are not a superior race; they are just a pebble co-existing with the rest of the creation. Earth has given you a physical body to experience life and fulfil your purpose in this reincarnation. So your body is an extension of the Earth and you can become her tool, when you accept your purpose, being a transmitter and receiver of light. Your body carry the light of your astral body. The astral plane is your home and your astral body exists in unity with your physicality. So light and energy can be received and transmitted. You have a physical body which is part of your being of Earth; this includes your energy, light and physicality. This is helping you experience unity not only with Earth but also with the cosmos, becoming the bridge for growth, knowing and high creation to take place in you, humanity and Earth. It is part of your purpose to experience high growth and unity and this will help you fulfil your purpose and become a perfect transmitter and receiver of light. Excepting your path, allowing healing to take place, connecting to truth will help you fulfil your purpose.

Question:

What happens in my dreams? They are very ethereal and astral for me and I rarely get to have recall but feel subconscious activity going on all day afterwards usually.

Answer:

In your dreams, you able to connect to either the astral plane and connect to your astral body for healing and growth or you may be connecting to your guides that exist in higher planes for guidance and healing. There are some human beings that have the ability to fully disconnect from imbalances and distortion when they enter their sleeping state and this is a great opportunity to connect to your astral body or your guides and receive the high light of creation. You guides want to remind you about the divine plan of this reincarnation, to help you disconnect from distortion and going on diversions. They also want you to bring the cosmic light to Earth and humanity, nourishing the people around you and support their growth. The light that you are receiving is trying to find its way to your mind and being and become your everyday reality. So instead of standing at the crossroads, you should follow the path of your purpose and focus on your growth and the growth of others.

Question:

What would help or benefit me to find inner stillness and peace again?

Answer:

There are parts of you that have remained hidden and you can experience absolute peace when you connect to your whole being. See your being as a house of many rooms. Only when you are able to open all the doors, observe and experience all parts of your house then you will be able to use it effectively for a comfortable living and wellbeing. Do not be afraid to enter all the rooms and discover your special abilities, the truth and growth that you carry, the light that can help you transform becoming a perfect receiver and transmitter of cosmic light on Earth. When you know yourself you will enter a state of peace and you will start to grow.

Question:

I have been having dreams lots of them and wondered if they are messages around my physicality. I had an injury a while ago and have had lots of physical problems for years now. Last few days it's been getting worse all through my body. Just wondered if dreams are trying to guide me. Is my physicality trying to talk to me and I do not understand its message?

Answer:

You are in a phase of transformation so your whole being is supporting you to go through this phase without interruptions. Sometimes physical pain is understood as limitation but very often is helping you to disconnect from distortion, connecting to your truth and start creating your own life. You have abused your physical body in the past and now you are connecting to it in a space of truth. You are going to build a communication with your body and you are going to honour it because it is a gate way to growth. A way to honour your body is to strengthen your connection with Earth. Make this connection your priority and this way you will expand to a space of peace and growth.

Question:

Did Thoth have contact with incarnated masters in past times?

Answer:

There were people like you in the past that reincarnated to build bridges between the Earth and the cosmos. If I am the creator of Earth I should support these bridges and also the people who are building them. My light is the light of the cosmos and there were people who connect to it and tried to bring it to Earth in order to heal her schisms. There were people who wanted to connect to the light but instead they connected to their own limitation. There were others who tried to connect to the cosmic energy but this did not stop them from going on a diversion. The way you connect to me is unique and versatile. You are connected to the light with your energy, your physical body and mind and now you are learning to experience unity within your being; this will help you absorb the light in its purest form. You have the ability to teach others because the light is transforming your whole being right now.

Question:

Can Thoth help us discover this? I have ideas about my archetype. Are there only so many? I suspect I am a teacher, perhaps in some helping field...like counsellor, but don't know if that fits with the types.

Answer:

The Archetypes exist in transformation; this has to do with vibration, the ability of energy to transform, consciousness and many other factors that determine your understanding of yourself. If you are interested in finding you archetype you will have to look at what you really enjoy doing in this life time. I have a question for you: Are you doing right now what makes you happy or you are thinking about doing it? What is stopping you from doing this? In some cases, distortion can pull you away from your purpose and force you to go on a diversion. Other times, what you have in mind as your archetype, it is not what you want to do but what you need to receive. I can see your purpose from previous life times; you have the same purpose and abilities and you are called to navigate your life and your being out of the maze. You are a navigator, the person that will connect to others, to share with them a project or a truth and create the necessary conditions for this to grow.

Question:

Our higher-self is a unique expression of the cosmos. Has our higher self already realized that full expression, which then disseminates the code, or archetype, to express what has already been expressed?

Answer:

All parts of a being such as the astral body, higher-self, creation code and the physical body, are connected similarly to all living beings in the cosmos. At the same time they have their own growth and ways to connect to the source that makes them unique. What makes them different is the ability of a being or its different parts to connect to the source. The higher-self is not busy with archetypes but may support growth that is related to archetypes in other planes. You know that your life on Earth is an experience of growth and the life on the astral plane it is also an opportunity of growth. The higher-self is almost formless and beings that are only the higher-self and the creation code do not reincarnate but they are the ones who support creation in the cosmos.

Question:

The star gates which were created by beings they can be found in secret locations in the physical plane as well as in different planes which mirror the physical Earth.

The different planes that Thoth speaks of, what are these?

Answer:

The cosmos exists in unity and the cosmic light that brings life to all, connects all different planes. The astral plane is a cosmic laboratory of creation. It is the home of all beings was you can all grow according to cosmic laws and see your connection with the source as your purpose. There are many planes and sub-planes; some of them support beings to have a unique lesson or a preparation, moving towards the astral plane and other planes that have a higher vibration than the astral plane. They are created to support the light of the source creating in the cosmos. Earth exists in a low vibrational plane that has a number of layers. At the end of this reincarnation the essence of a human being will go through a purification in order to go through the different layers and finally to reconnect to the astral body and the astral plane.

Question:

Many people use any variety of herbs and woods and grasses as a medium for burning and making smoke for the purpose of "cleansing".

I know these materials and other forms of incense have been used for a long time in many cultures throughout time. Many healers still use these natural materials in their rituals and ceremonies and claim they have abilities of purification. Some say burning sage can clear a house of bad spirits.

I would like to learn more about the truth regarding such practices.

Answer:

Many people use smudging to purify a space but what they achieve is to stay connected with the low energies. It is not the space that needs purification but it is the being that has to disconnect from low energies. A being can pollute a space when is connected to them and this way can affect other people. Smudging has no power to purify the space. In the past, this type of activity was used to attract low energies. When people breathe in the smoke they can be in a less conscious state. They believed that the physical body is a limitation and if they truly want to connect to the energies they have to be in a sleeping state or unconscious state. The use of hallucinogenic plants served the same idea. If you want to purify a space you should purify the people who live there.

Question:

Why do we lose contact with guides, communications?

Answer:

Your guides are constantly connected to you but they do not need to send you messages regularly. Guides connect to you to offer their support when you are standing at the crossroads looking but not being able to see your path; they warn you when you about to take a diversion; they are supporting you when you open to the cosmic energies. Often people ignore these communications or they focus on the sensation rather than the message. The communication between you and your guides is an alignment with your truth, purpose and divine plan.

Question:

Can Thoth tell us what progress is being made to restore Earth's correct mental outlook?

Answer:

Earth is going through a long transformation and if it is not interrupted, she is going to experience a new cycle of growth. Distortion is affecting many people on Earth. Global economy, politics and culture are created to disconnect human beings from Earth, their purpose and the connection to the cosmos. There are human beings who are becoming aware of this truth but they still exist in the bubble of illusion. There is no true energetic balance between different parts of the planet or even within the human being. On the other hand an increasing number of human beings understand the importance of connecting to Earth and looking for truth within their being. If you want to help Earth go through her transformation you have to heal yourself and connect to the cosmic light. If you transform to your true-self, you are supporting Earth, becoming a receiver and transmitter of light.

Question:

I would like to know what Pantheon thinks about the chakra system, whether it is synthetic or organic.

Answer:

Human beings consist of countless cells as well as countless energy points. You are aware of the main organs in your physical body such as the brain, kidney and the heart. These main organs regulate, balance and store information to help the whole being function according to natural laws. What you know as chakras are the main energy points in your being that regulate energy; balance energy and physicality and connect you to other energies that exist on Earth and the cosmos. Your physicality and energy structure work together to support life in your being. They support your connection to everything that exists and your expansion beyond physicality. The only thing you have to know is that they are part of your being and they are connected to your physical body.

Question:

There are many theories on Earth around the concept of words and how they manifest reality. Can Thoth please share some insight into how we might learn to communicate more truthfully. Are there different outcomes to reality based on the words we choose? For instance, many believe they must refrain from speaking in "foul" language as they believe this is somehow negative in some sense or creates negative outcomes in their life. I am curious about these things.

I will admit I sometimes find myself trying to share my own truth and feeling very misunderstood or poorly received. So in some ways I do see how carefully chosen words can help with the inherent problems many have in communicating. But how important are words and the vibrations they carry?

Answer:

Manipulators have created a science called public speaking, advertising, and teaching using repetitions of words creating certain structures. The way you speak and the terms you use can create an illusionary space of fear, satisfaction, truth or freedom in people's minds and then they are ready to accept manipulation as a true aspect of their being. If human beings want to speak to others, expressing their true-self and passing the light of the cosmos and Earth than they have to use an authentic expression and allow their truth to become a bridge to help you exist in unity with others. For this to happen you have to connect to your truth in your everyday experience, you have to communicate with a pure intention and allow the cosmic light to be the main source of communication. You can also communicate with what you are creating, with your learning. Or just being in peace connecting to your whole being. Do not rely on words for communication but when you have to speak then do it without restrictions, limitation or fragmentation. Communicate your truth in a way that is unique to you and your ability to grow.

Question:

The source's intentions are beyond our perception? Do we even get a glimpse? Are we just supposed to play our part? Do we connect to the source through the Gods?

Answer:

Human beings or any other being in the cosmos are not designed to understand the intention of our source but they are designed to experience it. This can be achieved by connecting to your truth and become creator of your life, following the path of growth. Human beings have to focus on their own path if they wish to connect to the cosmos that is the creation of our source. Do not let the river of confusion and limitation to take you away from connecting to your truth and become a perfect transmitter and receiver of cosmic light. People's minds are full of thoughts that are not supporting their purification, growth and creation. When you disconnect from illusionary thinking and acting then you will be able to find the path of your purpose and experience cosmic creation on Earth.

Question:

I have a question about the aura as it relates to consciousness. Can one tune into different 'layers' of the aura to gain access to a deeper consciousness of the Self?

Answer:

You aura is part of your being and supporting your connection with the energies of the Earth and the cosmos. Your aura can suffer from imbalances that can affect your physical body and it can also be purified, transformed able to support your growth and purpose on Earth. Your aura is a tool to connect you to high energies and support your growth and transformation.

Question:
Is it only the ego that feels painful emotions?

Answer:
When you try to understand your light with your ego, you experience illusion that leads to separation. Your ego will tell you that the light in you does not exist; the fear that you are experiencing is making you carry the burden of superiority or inferiority. When you disconnect from your light and you are placed in a place of illusionary polarity what is created in you, it is a sign of separation, schisms or trauma. The fear that you are experiencing is making you carry the burden of a false superiority/inferiority.

In this state you will experience sadness which is just a reaction to separation. Painful emotions are an indication that your mind, body and energy exist in separation therefore in an imbalanced state.

Question:
I have been wondering about the effects of radiation on our planet and our health. What does this interference, 3g, 4g, 5g smart meters etc. that we are surrounded by do to our frequencies and does this create distortion in our energy field?

Answer:
Human beings are not created to be affected by distortion of any kind. If they are able to connect to Earth's energies and the cosmic light, understand their purpose and create a life of truth then distortion cannot reach them. People who try to manipulate humanity and lock them into a space of limitation, they have a powerful weapon and this is fear. Being afraid of possible disasters and how pollution and artificiality can affect your growth is much more harmful than the pollution itself. Focusing on your truth and light you can bring your divine plan into your life and raise your vibration living behind distortion.

Energy flows through all beings throughout the cosmos. Energy is information and the purest way of communication. Everything in the universe is in constant transformation and movement. Nothing stays the same and there no need to concentrate on the specific form but in the process of transformation. When there is transformation, the universe is alive and produces high energy able to sustain life.

VOCABULARY

Astral body is an extension of your physical body and occupies a great area of energetic fields called astral plane. The astral body is in constant growth, connecting to the high light of the cosmos and following the cosmic laws in order to receive and transmit the high light of the cosmos. Having a physical form does not restrict you from connecting to your astral body and becoming part of growth and evolution that takes place there. Connecting to your truth and purpose and go through the process of purification, transformation and growth, you are allowing constant connection and communication between your physical and astral body.

Astral plane is the true home of all beings. In the astral plane all physical beings lose their physicality and exist in their pure form which is their light.

The astral plane is a place of transformation and growth. It is the home of all beings; it is the home of all creation. Beings have their own purpose and their own plan for growth and this is why the astral plane is divided into many sub planes which have different frequency levels. Beings are not left on their own to seek truth and growth but they are connected to many other beings that have the same frequency as them; they connect to higher beings who are their guides and lower beings that are supported by them. In the astral plane there is no destruction, all beings have clarity and therefore they experience their plan of growth.

In this state you receive guidance from your higher-self and divine intervention from your creation code. Your astral body is aware of your purpose and growth cycles; cosmic truth and wisdom goes through the astral body in the form of energy and this is why it is in a process of constant purification and transformation.

Aura is an electromagnetic field that surrounds all physical bodies and allows them to receive and transmit energy. Your aura helps you communicate energetically, supports the body to function and stay balanced, staying grounded and connect to the cosmos and astral body. Distortion and fragmentation can affect the aura as well as the physical body.

Code of Creation (creation code) is a "geometric" code which is used to create and maintain life. Our source is always within us; we all carry the creation code which is a living being and is affected by our consciousness, the light that we possess and the way we use it. The unity that exists in the cosmos is contained in the light of our creator and is spread to the creation through our creation code. The creation code can be understood as the intention of the source to create life. All beings are connected to the source because every part of their being in all planes is connected to the creation code. All beings that exist in all planes are created in the astral plane and therefore they have an astral body which is in constant transformation and growth. The guide of the astral body is the higher self. The higher self is aware of all transformation and growth, all connections, duties and paths that the astral body can experience. The higher self supports the astral body to follow the cosmic laws, experience unity with the cosmos, receive and transmit light and move closer to the source by supporting growth in all planes. The creation code is the high seed of all beings and it exists with the source. All beings are able connect to the source to their creation code. The gods do not have access to the creation code but they do connect to the higher self. The creation code cannot be altered; the source creates through the gods using the cosmic light and then the gods become the source's creative tool.

Consciousness contains the "highlights" of one's growth and has two main uses: one is to record, maintain and stabilise one's growth and second is to be used as a guide for other entities who wish to work with this person in the astral or physical plane. There is also a collective consciousness which some people confuse with the beliefs of certain social groups. Collective is the consciousness of Earth and its reflection to all beings that live on the planet. This is when a unit of growth connects with other units of growth who are affected by the same electromagnetic fields.

Cosmic laws are a reflection of the natural laws which exist on Earth. All planes are regulated by cosmic laws. When these cosmic laws are not followed we have high levels of distortion and imbalances similarly to what Earth is experiencing right now. Enlightenment is the result of our connection and understanding of the cosmic laws. Everything we seek is waiting for us if we connect to the cosmos and act accordingly. Another cosmic law is the unity of all creation brings energy, balance, strength to receivers and transmitters and more opportunity for further growth.

Cosmic light is the light of our source which spreads to all creation. Its purpose is to offer life, growth and guidance and connect all creation. High creator gods have the ability to connect to the light of the creator to create life. Gods are not in control of this high creative force, they do not fully understand how it works and furthermore, they cannot reproduce it. Instead, the light creates through them. When the High Light passes information from the creation code, the form of a being first develops in the astral plane. In the physical plane, beings learn to experience life through the five senses or the limitations of a physical body. Beings that experience an astral existence simultaneously with their physical reality are able to acquire knowledge leading to a new cycle of growth.

Clarity is the clear understanding of one's purpose. Having clarity you are able see your path and create all the necessary circumstances to help you achieve your goal. Clarity is a divine tool given to all beings to enable them to communicate with their astral body and connect them to their purpose. Clarity can be achieved if we simply look deep inside ourselves, connect to our purity, and make it our guide.

Distortion is an energetic imbalance that has affected Earth and her creation on and is caused by the trauma of Earth, the end of her golden era and her disability to cope as a high creator. The third dimensional reality, with its lower vibration, is the ideal space for distortion to grow and expand. As a result people live in a constant hypnotic state of illusion and stagnation disconnected from the purpose and divine plan.

Duality is the separation of self from all that exists. When children start to become aware of society structures, they start to lose their ability to experience unity. The focus in their lives will be indoctrination, focusing on the mind-logic-limitation and be part of a life of duality, fragmentation and non-growth. There is always a fight of the opposites which is the cause of fragmentation and illusion. If you wish to evolve beyond duality, you have to disconnect from the idea of opposites. In nature there is no fight against two elements there is only a union of the elements, bringing new life.

Enlightenment is not our final destination in our quest for growth but is just a single step towards gnosis. Masters have to take many steps of enlightenment in order to comprehend just a small piece of the vastness of cosmos. Becoming receivers and transmitters of light, you allow the cosmic flow to enter humanity and Earth.

Essence is the presence of the High Source which nobody can destroy or alter. Our growth depends on our ability to create and for this to happen we have to recognize and understand our essence and our creation code. The essence of Earth, in the physical plane, can be described as the golden era, a time of high creation.

Fragmentation is an imbalance on Earth that can be understood as a separation of self from all that exists. On Earth, beings experience fragmentation that affects inner unity, clarity and disability to connect to your purpose and truth. Fragmentation can affect the connection between humanity and Earth and allow the cosmic light to be received and transmitted to all life.

Gnosis is wisdom.

Golden Era was a time of high creation. In the golden era, all beings had a different cycle. Their light was eternal and they were able to reborn. The colours and the shapes on Earth gave her a high vibration and all creation was connected to this. The cosmic laws ruled Earth's existence and purity was clearly seen and experienced in all beings. Everything that existed on Earth had to produce light and energy to support the planet's growth. The whole planet was united and went through purification and transformation as a whole being. They received light form the high realms and they transmitted light to support the cosmos. In the golden era, there were many beings that were able to nourish themselves with the light. The animal kingdom received nourishment directly from the Earth and other beings on the planet were connected to the light of cosmos. What you are experiencing in your time, animals eating each other, started to take place when the vibration of Earth became lower. During the golden era, Earth resembled what you now call exotic and tropical nature. Earth was created to have enough resources to feed and nourish all her creation. Plants and animals were fed with the minerals and other nutrients which could be found on Earth as well as the light from the electromagnetic fields of the planet.

Higher-self is the true essence of a being and exists in a much higher vibration than the astral body. The higher-self directs evolution and connects to the astral body when certain light and information is needed for its growth. Everything that exists is really a reflection of a lower or a higher related body. In other words all bodies are reflections of each other.

High Creator has no form, character or attributes. Our High Creator is the perfect representation of life where everything is effortless, whole and limitless. High Gods can only dream to be in this state of absolute perfection, where there is nothing to see and yet everything exists simultaneously. Our High Creator is not a human being; it is a state of the highest growth and the highest consciousness. Our Creator is limitless: its whole creation, everything that exists, it is only a fragment of our source's existence.

Illusion appears as multiple layers of distorted reality that people accept as true. It is highly versatile and being formless can take any temporary form. When human beings receive this temporary form of illusion and accept it as real, they give it life and form which is able to grow and implanted on different people. Illusion does not have a form or growth and has the tendency to connect to low-self; it becomes part of this person's experience and then quickly needs to spread to others in order to acquire power.

Logos is a vibrational creation tool, pure reflection of our source, which is given to high gods to create life. Logos is a communication between source and the living being high god and through this connection the creative intention of the source goes through the lower being who is the creator god and through him/her the source creates.

Pleroma is a separate plane which exists in direct connection with the source. The Pleroma is the highest plane and consists of different energetic layers and sub divisions. It is inhabited by gods and god creators.

Purification is a process of cleansing all imbalances, blockages, fears, limitation, and restrictions illusionary patterns/beliefs/state in order to experience your true abilities, weaknesses, strengths, talents and skills. The process of purification includes observation, practice of self-love and acceptance, creating a space of peace, connecting to Earth and the cosmos and allows truth to guide you to your path.

Purity is this part of you that cannot be affected by any sort of manipulation, fragmentation and distortion. All beings carry purity in them. It is their light, which was given to them when they were created. It is the link between the being, the god and the source. When you follow purity, you are truly happy and satisfied; able to make your greatest contribution in your life and in the life of others; transform yourself and others; have no doubt as to what your purpose is and you will be able to fulfil it.

Purpose of a being is related to the divine plan and the true expression of life. Third dimensional beings can fulfil their purpose and can experience growth if they are able to clear blockages and imbalances.

Reincarnation offers the opportunity to a being to receive and offer teachings. People reincarnate wherever and whenever there is a need for this to happen. They are beings who have reincarnated many times on Earth and they are other beings who have reincarnated on many others planets, galaxies and universes. For every being there is a divine plan, a plan of evolution, and this is stored in its creation code and is manifested on its higher-self. According to this plan, beings will go through a certain learning process that is tailored specifically for them.

Schism is a severe form of fragmentation that can create strong polarities, imbalances and destruction. Earth's inability to heal herself and her creation led to complete detachment from gods' intervention. When human beings create great schisms in them, they can lose their humanity; they become a different species.

Soul is a great educator and guides beings to their true purpose. It is an aid, helping beings to open up to their astral existence and what lies beyond that. In the beginning of a reincarnation, a link is created between the physical and the astral body and when the body dies this link, which is the soul, disconnects from the physical body and goes back to the astral. Soul does not evolve and it is not the purest part of a being as many think.

Transformation is a process of rebirth. When you are in transformation you are able to produce, transmit and receive different energies and use your light to achieve great growth.

True-self help us understand our purpose and our tools. It is important that you safeguard your truth and do not let others to pull you into the illusion with their criticism and negativity. Let your light guide you and others; enjoy a balanced life unknown to many and bring this gift to others. People who follow truth have an effortless life because they are balanced and exist to fulfil their purpose. People who are aware of their true-self have nothing to hide and their evolution and growth are guaranteed.

Wormholes and star gates are entrance points on Earth. There are different types of star gates, some of them are divine creation and others were built by beings from other planets who wish to visit Earth. The star gates created by the gods are placed on important points of the Earth's grid and this corresponds on the star gates on different planets and galaxies. These entrances form an energetic shape which works as a magnet for constant energy flow and balance. The star gates which were created by beings they can be found in secret locations in the physical plane as well as in different planes which mirror the physical Earth. These star gates connect different geographical points on Earth as well as places on other planets and other dimensions.

Lightning Source UK Ltd.
Milton Keynes UK
UKHW012334260219
338081UK00001B/18/P